beirut 39

C.1

NEW WRITING FROM THE ARAB WORLD

EDITED BY SAMUEL SHIMON
WITH A PREFACE BY HANAN AL-SHAYKH

BLOOMSBURY

NEW YORK · BERLIN · LONDON

Published by Bloomsbury USA, New York

All papers used by Bloomsbury USA are natural, recyclable products made from wood grown in well-managed forests. The manufacturing processes conform to the environmental regulations of the country of origin.

LIBRARY OF CONGRESS CATALOGING–IN–PUBLICATION DATA

Beirut 39 : new writing from the Arab world /
edited by Samuel Shimon ; preface by Hanan al-Shaykh. — 1st U.S. ed.
p. cm.
Chiefly translated from Arabic.
Collection of new writing from the Arab world, by thirty-nine writers under thirty-nine.
Includes bibliographical references and index.
ISBN 978-1-60819-202-1 (alk. paper)
1. Arabic literature—20th century—Translations into English. 2. Arabic literature—21st century—Translations into English. I. Shimon, Samuel, 1956-
II. Title: Beirut thirty-nine.
PJ7694.E1B45 2010
892'.70808953—dc22
2009052486

First U.S. edition 2010

1 3 5 7 9 10 8 6 4 2

Typeset by Hewer Text UK Ltd, Edinburgh
Printed in the United States of America by Worldcolor Fairfield

Preface

These thirty-nine Arab writers are all under the age of forty. They have flung open the doors on Arabic culture, inviting the reader to transcend cultural boundaries and land in a region known as the 'Arab World'.

The reader touches, feels, hears, tastes and sees the Middle East and North Africa as it really is: cosmopolitan cities, villages, towns, desolate mountains and deserts. And soon these complex places in a foreign culture become recognisable and familiar as they are revealed in poems, short stories and extracts from novels. We experience the aches and pains of imprisoned freedom like birds in a cage; stifling societies, sexual frustration, corrupt regimes, poverty and illiteracy. And mapping the soil in which the seeds of fanaticism flourish, good women are driven to madness by injustice and oppression. The subject of war, of course, is never far away: between East and West, civil war and the occupation of the West Bank. This writing offers a fresh, often ingenious perspective – a world away from headlines and news stories. Finally, there is the bliss of love and passion, the wisdom of ancient culture, the piety of true believers, the sheer beauty of life on earth to experience, regardless of race and class.

Hanan al-Shaykh
London, January 2010

Acknowledgements

The publishers would like to thank the judges, the thirty-nine authors, the translators, the editor and all those, including Abdelouadoud El Omrani, Cristina Fuentes La Roche and Raquel Vicedo Artero of the Hay Festival, Emily Sweet, Jehan Marei and Rebecca O'Connor, who have contributed to making an ambitious vision a concrete reality. They also gratefully acknowledge the following original publishers of the pieces listed below (pieces not listed have been taken from as yet unpublished works): Department of Culture and Information, Sharja, UAE for the extract from the novel *Bado ala al-Hafa* (2006) by Abdelaziz Errachidi; Dar al-Harf, Rabat, for poems from *Indhur wa-Aktafi bil-Nadhar* (2008) by Abderrahim Elkhassar; Manshoorat Alfa, Algiers, for the extract from the novel *Jildat al-Dhil* (2009) by Abderrazak Boukebba; Dar al-Mada, Damascus, for extracts from the novel *Al-Irhabi 20* (2006) by Abdullah Thabit; Dar al-Dab, Beirut, for extracts from the novel *Kuluna Baied bethat al-Miqdar an al-Hub* (2004) by Adania Shibli; Dar Merit, Cairo, for poems from *Amakin Khatia'a* (2008) and poems from *Shawai'a al-Abyadh wal Aswad* (private edition, Cairo, 2005) by Ahmad Yamani; Dar Al-Ain, Cairo, for the story 'Coexistence' from *al-Ab wal Ibn walrouh al-Taiha* (2008) by Ala Hlehel; Dar Al-Adab, Beirut, for the extracts from the novel *Saq al-Ghurab* (2008) by Yahya Amqassim; Dar al-Mada, Damascus, for two stories from *Tafassil* (2007) by Dima Wannous; *Laha* magazine, Beirut, for the two short stories by Hala Kawtharani; Dar al-Intishar al-Arabi, Beirut, for extracts from the novel *Al-Muaalaqa al-Akhira* (2006) by Hussein al Abri; Al-Muassassa al-Arabiyya lil-Dirassat wal Nasher, Beirut, for the poems from *Kama Yakhssar al-Anbya'a* (2007) by Hussein Jelaad; Dar al-Janoub lil-Nashr, Tunis, for extracts from the novel *Al-Mishrat* (2007) by Kamel Riahi; Manshoorat Maktabat al-Sharif, Sudan, for the extract from the novel *Tukhoom el-Ramad* (2001) by Mansour El Souwaim; *Al-Hayat* newspaper, Beirut, for the short story 'The Path to Madness' by Mansoura Ez Eldin; www. kikah.com for the story 'The Pools and the Piano' by Najwa Binshatwan; Dar Riyad el-Rayess, Beirut, for poems from *Manzil al-Ukhut al-Sughra* (2009) by Nazem El Sayed; Dar al-Adab, Beirut, for the extracts from the novel *America* (2009) by Rabee Jaber; Dar Merit, Cairo, for 'Tharthara bil-Abyadh faqat' from the collection *Man Yussaddiq al-Rasayel* (2001), and University publication, Casablanca, for 'Hatib Hub', from the collection *Tuffah al-Dhi* (2006), both by Yassin Adnan; Dar Riyad al-Rayess, Beirut, for the extract from the novel *Hurras al-Hawa'a* (2009) by Rosa Yassin Hassan; Dar al-Intishar al-Arabi Jundi, Beirut, for poems taken from *Aied min harb el-Bakaloria* (2001) and Dar al-Nahda, Beirut, for poems taken from *Mala'ib min al-waqt al-Dhae'a* (2007), both by Zaki Baydoun.

Contents

Judges' Announcement

The abundance of young entrants in the competition is especially noteworthy: more than 450 young authors from across the Arab world, and from the Arab Diaspora in Europe and America, submitted work.

The members of the committee, headed by Egyptian critic Gaber Asfour, and which includes the Lebanese novelist Alawiya Sobh, Omani poet Saif al-Rahbi and Lebanese poet and critic Abdo Wazen, pored over the multitude of work sent in by authors and publishers in order to make their selection. The committee worked by elimination: it first picked 100 names, then brought the list down to 60, then, after long discussions and much debate, to the 39 finalists. On more than one occasion, the debates stretched for hours at a time, since there were so many wonderful books that deserved to win. Arriving at the final selection was a difficult, demanding and meticulous process.

The 39 names that have been chosen were selected for the superior quality of their work, whether as novels, short stories or poems. They represent an ideal mixture of tradition and modernity, and display high literary and critical standards. These are the voices of young ingénues who have managed to form their personalities and impose their experiences and views, in addition to sharing an exemplary use of language, technique and vision.

The final choice of the 39 names does not detract from the worthiness of many other, important, contributors. Many entrants were eligible to be shortlisted in the competition, but the Hay Festival's commitment to the 39-name rule proved to be unlucky for some.

In conclusion, we would like to pay tribute to young Arab writing, which is emerging as an idiosyncratic and unique literary genre. Perhaps this generation of young writers will forge the future for Arabic literature.

The winners, followed by their country of origin and year of birth, are: Abdelaziz Errachidi (Morocco, 1978), Abdelkader Benali (Morocco/ The Netherlands, 1975), Abdellah Taia (Morocco, 1973), Abderrahim Elkhassar (Morocco, 1975), Abderrazak Boukebba (Algeria, 1977), Abdullah Thabit (Saudi Arabia, 1973), Adania Shibli (Palestine, 1974), Ahmad Saadawi (Iraq, 1973), Ahmad Yamani (Egypt, 1970), Ala Hlehel (Palestine, 1974), Bassim al Ansar (Iraq, 1970), Dima Wannous (Syria, 1982), Faïza Guène (Algeria/France, 1985), Hala Kawtharani (Lebanon, 1977), Hamdy el Gazzar (Egypt, 1970), Hussain al Abri (Oman, 1972), Hussein Jelaad (Jordan, 1970), Hyam Yared (Lebanon, 1975), Islam Samhan (Jordan, 1982), Joumana Haddad (Lebanon, 1970), Kamel Riahi (Tunisia, 1974), Mansour El Souwaim (Sudan, 1970), Mansoura Ez Eldin (Egypt, 1976), Mohammad Hassan Alwan (Saudi Arabia, 1979), Mohamad Salah al Azab (Egypt, 1981), Nagat Ali (Egypt, 1975), Najwa Binshatwan (Lybia, 1975), Najwan Darwish (Palestine, 1978), Nazem El Sayed (Lebanon, 1975), Rabee Jaber (Lebanon, 1972), Randa Jarrar (Palestine/Egypt/USA, 1978), Rosa Yassin Hassan (Syria, 1974), Samar Yezbek (Syria, 1970), Samer Abou Hawwash (Palestine, 1972), Wajdi al Ahdal (Yemen, 1973), Yahya Amqassim (Saudi Arabia, 1971), Yassin Adnan (Morocco, 1970), Youssef Rakha (Egypt, 1976) and Zaki Baydoun (Lebanon, 1981).

Introduction

'Beirut39' is a unique initiative that aims to identify and highlight contemporary literary movements among Arab youth, and to gather young faces and names and provide them with an opportunity to meet, exchange expertise and ideas, and work together in literary workshops.

Young Arab writers have transcended geography and local identity in their creative work, aligning themselves with – and inspired by – global literary currents and movements. It is obvious, for example, that many novelists from all over the Arab world, Mashriq and Maghreb, belong to the same literary current across regional barriers. Through their work, they communicate and bond with each other despite geographical distance, such that one can easily speak of the youthful realist novel, or neo-realist novel, or fantastic novel or post-modern novel that young writers from all the Arab countries have contributed to. The literature of young Arab writers has invaded the Arab literary market, making it difficult to speak of the young Lebanese novel, or the young Egyptian novel, or Syrian, or Saudi, etc. A youthful pan-Arab literary movement currently dominates, bringing together novelists from all the Arab countries, and aiming to break down regional boundaries. This definition also applies to poetry: there is no longer a youthful Lebanese poetry that is different from a youthful Egyptian poetry, or a Saudi, Iraqi or Palestinian one. Poets are collaborating to establish new styles and a new poetic language, in addition to their unique visions. The internet age has certainly helped them to overcome the obstacles posed by the difficulty of meeting and communicating in person.

What brings together most young Arab writers is their tone of protest, and their rebellion against traditional literary culture. They have announced their disobedience against the ideological bent that exhausted Arabic literature during the 1960s and 1970s. They have also risen above the idea of commitment so prominent a few decades ago, which was imposed by a political-party and communal way of thinking. Instead, they strive towards individualism, focusing on the individual, the human being living and struggling and dreaming and aiming for absolute freedom. Many young writers have declared their disdain for what they describe as contrived, 'proper' language. Often, they aim to express their personal concerns as they see fit, freely and spontaneously. And it is important that they protest and reject and announce their frustration with language itself, this language that differs between writing and speech. They want to write as they speak, absolutely spontaneously, unbounded by the censorship imposed upon them firstly by the language itself, and then by religious or moral apparatuses.

These writers believe that the new era, the information age, the computer and internet age does not leave them with enough time to decipher the mysteries of grammar and rhetoric. They seek the language of life. These writers are not afraid to make grammatical errors. Some purposefully don't finish their sentences, others are fond of slang and street talk and dialect.

This book contains selections from novels, short stories and poems by 39 young Arab writers, and presents the reader with a panoramic glimpse of Arab youth literature. It aims to engage the reader in a conversation, and to help illuminate this scene.

Abdo Wazen
Beirut, February 2010

Editor's Note

Once the judges had made their selection, I was able to contact the 39 authors who live in twenty cities in the Middle East and North Africa, as well as in Europe and the USA. As the reader may imagine, I blessed the internet and email frequently, because, despite the short time available, it meant that I could work closely with each author to select the pieces that would best represent their work. It was relief to know that they were happy with my choices.

A word or two about the arrangement of the book: after the Preface, Judges' Announcement and Introduction, the pieces are published in alphabetical order by author, and the translator is acknowledged at the end of each piece. I have only noted the language from which a piece has been translated when it is not Arabic. At the back of the book are Notes on the Text, as an aid to the reader who may be unfamiliar with various aspects of life in the Arab world, and Notes on the Authors and the Translators.

Beirut39 is, of course, only a first step to discovering the extraordinary talents of Arab writers, and it is hoped that readers who enjoy the work in this book will explore further and so encourage the all-important work of translation.

Samuel Shimon
Bleibtrau Hotel, Berlin, February 2010

from the novel

Bedouins on the Edge

Abdelaziz Errachidi

Policemen, arriving from the nearby precinct and annoyed by the cold and insignificance of the place, recorded the details of an accident that night: an elegant white car without a licence plate had hit a wooden electric pole. A snarl of wires from the pole lay beside it. No passengers were to be found at the site despite the fact that the car was new. The damage was minimal, and there didn't appear to be any victims.

The policeman ordered the onlookers from the town to leave. Leaving nothing unturned, the police recorded their observations: the number of miles on the car; how much it had sunk into the thin layer of mud; the estimated power of the impact that had caused a petrol leak, preventing them from continuing; the approximate time of the crash; and other details no one but the obsessed would bother with. And despite the weight of their tired eyes, they didn't forget to question witnesses, although no one had actually seen the accident at the time.

Everything was there in front of them: the new car whose hefty tyres had woken them up in the dark of night. Yet there were no passengers. Where had they gone, leaving their car and their belongings behind? Leaving behind warm comfortable seats on an autumn night cold enough to make people shiver under their covers?

Opening up the boot, they found a seed bag, an axe and an odd-shaped hoe. There was also some food and ripped pieces of paper.

A long time had passed and not one person from the town could claim they knew what had happened. But there were those who would narrate the event endlessly, their faces expressing surprise and their eyes ablaze as they scrutinised the details with the mastery of someone with too much time on his hands. With each new telling, their passion was rekindled anew, proof that desert dwellers compose the music of lies. They mulled over it with profound conviction: Was it the fog that caused the accident? Was it the darkness or booze? Or maybe it was speed? Finally they agreed – after all other possibilities had been exhausted – on the power of the impact, since they had sensed its tremble in their sleep, its echo resonating in their dreams.

The storytellers found the incident entertaining, a pastime to fill their empty, repetitive days. They had become virtuosos in their retellings. One would say, 'Some tourists from Europe came here, they were injured in the accident, but then went back home to their country. They will, no doubt, come back to pick up the car.' And someone would interrupt him, claiming confidently that 'Europeans don't pay attention to money and material goods; it's silly to think they'll come back.' He'd explain it this way: 'They're thieves who came here at peak harvest time for dates. They didn't find the secret spot and they failed to get the people's consent, so they must have been cursed by trying to hide from the law.'

People went on and on talking and asking questions: Where did the strangers come from? What did they want and what was their story? Were they overwhelmed by the serenity of the area as they passed through? And was the accident the price they paid for their stupor? Why did they run away, leaving behind such an expensive car? What were they afraid of? Were they thieves? Who was their leader? Did they treat their own injuries or did someone help them get away? Or was the accident part of their plan, a ruse to divert attention? Maybe they wanted to hide something?

The townspeople speculated endlessly, spending their empty days chatting and arguing about it wherever they happened to be: in fields that had been parched for a long time, taking the opportunity to tie their donkeys to small date palms and sit about, either squatting or stretched out while arguments heated up between them; or dangling their feet above the mud irrigation ditch, moving carelessly from one topic to another, from the lack of water, the effect of which was making them so crazy they would stare out into space absentmindedly, to temptations – like leaving this place, or women; or close to the mud-brick mosque, in front of the clashing tall cement minaret, where they would sit at the end of every prayer. At other times, at nightfall, some of them – the real night owls – would hurry to the lone grocer to carry on talking and arguing. They'd explain the accident according to their own reasoning, conflating details of it with their own anxieties, some of them garnering encouragement and interest the more they got into it, though this could be interpreted as having a dubious relationship with the strangers. In kitchens, women spiced the pot with possibilities, their eyes huge with excitement, the timbre of their arguments ringing out as the wind carried their words away.

Explaining the accident had become a competitive game among the people. Then *al-mahjub*, 'the covered one', spoke. He had only recently arrived in the town from the desert and hadn't quite integrated into the rhythm of their lives. An outcast, he triggered the most extreme dismay in them. They themselves were surprised by how they could have overlooked the most likely possibility; but now that they were alerted to the danger, they carefully hid their children, now that they were alerted to the danger. When the kids got wind of this, they trembled together and quickly began comparing their hands, reading their palms like fortune-tellers do. Some of the townspeople gloated that the strangers had failed in their efforts. The hash smokers, though, didn't buy into the man's story, and held fast to the one that the strangers had brought the stuff with them. They had got used to them taking a shortcut, walking from north to south and bringing what they needed to ease the journey, which they and their friends could get from most of those living in that well-to-do oasis. So they searched tirelessly for chunks of hash near the car and in the trunk, and some found a bit, the talk having given them confidence. Meanwhile others were only interested in the seed sack, the old, odd-shaped hoe and the axe.

In the end, though, all this talk got the better of them and they gave in to temptation: they stripped the car, stealing the seat covers, the good wires for one thing or another and parts of the engine. They stole the hoe and the axe, and left the car exposed to isolation and cold. During their cozy gatherings at the top of the nearby mountain, they cursed the unfortunate circumstances that made them lose their love for *al-sibsi*, their long-stemmed kif-smoking pipe, the pleasures of burning hash and crumbling it into small pieces in their palms.

Al-mahjub, charmed by his own story, didn't stop. He was a gypsy from the desert who had settled in the decrepit old clay castle, which was on the verge of falling down after being abandoned by its inhabitants. They had settled outside on the welcoming expanse of land because without a war they no longer had need of the castle's protective walls, though other transgressions still flared up from time to time. With his thick white beard, resolute eyes and endless tales, he told his own story and explained the accident as he saw fit.

Was anyone interested in all this prattle? Certainly the powerful of the town, that is the 'judicious', were. They are those of land and of rank whose ancestors were the first to colonise the town and who bravely set off to fight in the wars of their time, some of them had taken on the Europeans during colonisation, while others made truces with them, more interested in their money and heirs. They made up the council of notables. They represented the norm, a tradition upheld in complete happiness or sadness. They knew all the thousands of stories, and what was circulated and what ought to be.

For the kids of the area, *al-mahjub* became a game; they would pelt him with stones and swear at him, and no one would stop them. He shaved heads in front of the mosque, split kindling for fires, repaired sandals, got paid, and chattered away . . . His certitude was effective: as far as he knew, there were four passengers in the car. He explained this by the warmth of the seats that cold autumn night and the four banana skins on the road that everyone else had failed to notice. For sure, the driver was the cause: the strangers were on their way, but the driver couldn't resist temptation. He asked them if they could stop so he could take a hit, but they didn't hear him, so he decided to make an adventure of it. He let the car drive them after making sure of a smooth path in the conniving emptiness of the southern road. He took out a small chunk of hash from his pocket and lit it. The hash and the light of the fuel wafted in front of him, creating images. Worlds and dreams clashed in front of his eyes. The car started to play with the wind.

They weren't thieves, and neither did they have rheumatism which the sands of the oasis cure. Nor were they treasure hunters, as was most popularly presumed. Could there be anything other than drought hiding in this oasis? They knew what they wanted. They

were wise and composed, and took orders from an older man, assidu-
ous and well-to-do, and someone who didn't mince words.

Meanwhile, they had stopped off, according to *al-mahjub's* story,
many times before arriving at the town. They talked quietly among
themselves, checking the maps which they could read very well, and
knowing well, thanks to their nous, how hard it would be to get
what they wanted. He thought that they were probably travelling by
memory to the edge of another time, to an old summit for a saint's
innumerable blessings, or to a festival, or a *zawiyya* – a saint's tomb –
or to a popular marketplace where people scramble about, whispering
among themselves about what they want. To where oaths to ancestors and sacrifices are made; to ancient books where one may learn
to be a thief, convincing even arms salesmen and leather vendors.
They paid a lot to ensure victory. They spoke faintly, no doubt, like
fortune-tellers and scared women, and burnt with a desire to possess
maps that would lead them to where they want to go. Patience nour-
ished them as their longing burnt within. How sweet their toil – they
made a mockery of distance in the dark of night, in the heat or chill
of the day, as they searched for those salvaged maps. Strangers, they
were practised in talking to everyone with a false intimacy, in such a
way that they could misrepresent what they wanted and mislead the
curious. Meanwhile they knew all too well the details of where and
how they would take their next step.

He described everything about them, from the colour of their
clothes to their preferred food. They loved money. They loved old
pots and kettles, craving the vintage aroma of their pallor, its swag
making hearts flutter. *Al-mahjub* said that the strangers, without a
doubt, made fun of the sleeping townspeople as they passed through,
often pitying – this time with a light connivance – the simplicity of
desert town buildings. Yet how they loved the gentle tranquillity of
the night and the purity of the air. They came determined to win
their battle. A desire for money brought them together, only braving
the dangers because they could be crushed by their armour: the hoe,
the axe and seed which they would scatter, leading them to the site.
The map was their only provision; they would solve the puzzles and
carry home the prize. Time or place were of no consequence.

All those stories about the strangers that the Bedouin told started to have an effect on him. As if he was with them. As if it was his thing. People were well aware of the levity he brought to reciting those beautiful poems, embellishing them with ambiguity about women and friendships that radiated an aroma of fresh green grass and herbs, and of a scorching heat that had been swallowed up by the sand. They knew he dipped deep into the sea of metaphor, almost to the brink of tears. He was a poet. They knew his stories about the desert, how he mixed seriousness with silliness, and so they weren't very interested. But rumours spread – and there's no smoke without fire – and no one could stop asking questions, even the head of the police force, who spent his time playing cards with the two other night officers of the oasis, drinking strong tea and waiting to leave one day. All the towns around the river were quiet, and the people who lived in them preferred to settle their problems among themselves. They were afraid of the government and didn't have any faith in it. But the story enticed him, and so, according to rumour, he dispatched a storyteller.

Suns set and others were extinguished. Days and nights passed. Between the beginning and the end time stretched, and the policemen never towed the car away. It remained lifeless, like a canvas for those who passed it to contemplate. It had become an everyday sight in the southern part of town, springing up out of the emptiness between the sand and the mountains. Then the children, distracting themselves from the monotony, had adopted it and turned it into a game. They would practise driving, some riding while others pushed, taking turns, but also fighting about whose turn it was each time.

Then the men, after realising how serious it was, started to hide their children as a precaution, because of all that was being said. They gathered in front of the mosque and legislated: there would be no going out after evening prayers. If someone did, then they would be accorded justice; that is, they must feed six members of the tribe in their house according to ancestral law. A surveillance patrol would begin.

Of course, for children, every story takes on a life of its own. For them, the owners of the car were much more interested in children's blood. Blood was their means for discovering what they were looking for. And the elders' warnings and punishments were of no consequence. So the children continued to play, though they became a bit afraid of any stranger who appeared to be travelling, some of them trembling after sunset as they remembered the words of the barber. They would circle every visitor or stranger, but especially the musk and saffron sellers and those light-skinned passers-by who would complain about the staring and questions.

Every chance he had the man would talk about the strangers who came by car. He would be shaving heads, repairing sandals, all the while rhapsodising: what they drank, what they ate, what they did. No one would stop to ask him where they were hiding because they didn't want to stop the pleasant stream of stories. His status in the town grew, until he eventually became its spokesperson. People would laugh at his seasoned chatter, while others were jealous of the extent of his imagination.

And again, days led people who woke up to create another one. For some of these people the story nested in their minds; the more they told it, the bigger it got. For others, time dragged them along and led them each day to some far-off corner. It is said that a groom took the mirror from the abandoned car and gave it to his bride as a present. The lamppost was repaired and electricity was restored, though with its usual repetitive interruptions. And time erased everything. Yet did *al-mahjub* stop his endless prattle? Of course not. Often, standing in front of the mosque and near the grocer, with a seriousness that diminished anyone who stood eye-to-eye with him, he reiterated that the strangers were treasure hunters and had come to dig nearby, and for a child's blood, the lines of his hand proving that he was the one: they would sacrifice him and spread seeds on the blood which would coagulate at the site of the treasure, which they would then dig up. He added that the driver, high on hash and the youngest of the strangers, caused the accident. Then he would say – to himself, this time – that life, days will soon reveal to the 'castrated' élite of the town, those who didn't recognise the value of men, what they had been ignoring all along.

Translated by Alexa Firat

from the novel

The Trip to the Slaughterhouse

Abdelkader Benali

Life would have been different if he hadn't gone to the slaughter-house with his father. He would have gone on living with his parents and been married off to his cousin, who – his sister later informed him – had once had a bowel resection, a fact that the girl's family hushed up out of fear that no one would marry a girl with a blemish.

His father had come to Europe in the 1960s. First Spain, then France, then Holland. He no longer remembered the exact year of his arrival. The main thing was that you'd made it, not when you got here. The names of the cities he'd lived in had likewise faded into oblivion. They lived *here* now, and not *there*, and by *there* he meant the Moroccan village by the sea where his ancestors had been born.

He had been conceived during one of his father's trips back home. His father recalled very little of those years. They had gone by in a flash, like a season without even a rainstorm to remember it by.

His father had no hobbies, except for repairing transistor radios. He didn't like music. He didn't like going out. He didn't like other people. He didn't like sleeping late. No alarm clocks ever went off in their house. His father woke him when it was time to get up. He'd stumble out of bed to find him tinkering with his radios. His father had learned how to fix them by taking them apart and putting them back together again until he could do it blindfold. Once he'd got the hang of it, he started repairing other people's radios, for free. People would bring him one they'd given up on, giving the radio – and his father – one last chance. He'd throw himself wholeheartedly into the project, as if he was repairing some defect in himself.

He continued to fix radios for free until it occurred to him that he could buy up broken radios, repair them and resell them. So he started cruising flea markets, where he would hang around until closing time and then approach the vendors. They were usually so glad to get rid of their broken-down radios that they *gave* them to him. He was doing a brisk business, selling four or five a month, when digital radios hit the market. 'There's nothing left to repair,' he moaned. 'They don't have any replaceable parts.' After that he began fixing up radios that had been lying around for ages and would never be sold.

Once a month a strange excitement seemed to take hold of his father, and he'd pace around, hardly able to contain himself until he went out. Then he'd come home and collapse on the couch, exhausted. He never said where he'd been, but would be all wound up, as if he'd been arguing the ins and outs of some complicated issue.

'Take me with you,' he said to his father one night at the dinner table. His father pretended he hadn't heard him and went on chewing.

'Take me with you,' he said again, louder.

'Take you where?' his mother asked.

'To wherever it is he goes.' His father said nothing, just kept chewing, so he repeated his request, even louder: 'Take me with you.'

'What's got into you?' his father said, and whacked him with a spoon, right on the cheek. A perfect aim. He reared back, his cheek still stinging from the impact, but he didn't give up.

'Take me with you,' he repeated. His father whacked him again, even harder this time and with greater precision: the spoon landed on the exact same spot. It hurt. Then his father used the spoon – his favourite eating utensil – to dig back into his dinner.

Rubbing his cheek, he yelled, 'Take me with you!' This time his father whacked him with a spoon full of food.

'That was unnecessary,' his mother remarked. 'You splattered food all over the table. Couldn't you have hit him somewhere else?' The last blow had been aimed at the other cheek and had left a smear.

Having made his point, his father stood up. 'I don't have to sit here and listen to this.'

Why had he asked to go with his father? Because he was intrigued by his blissful smile? Because his father was nice to him for days afterwards until the magic of that mysterious visit had faded and he'd sunk back into his usual lethargy? Or because he sensed that by going with him he would learn something about himself?

'Why won't Father take me with him?' he asked his mother.

'Take you where?'

'To wherever he goes once a month.'

'I don't know what you're talking about.' His mother didn't say this because she wanted to lie or pull the wool over her son's eyes. She said it to make it clear that there were more important things in life than finding out what makes your father happy. What he hadn't realised at the time was that, with their curt refusal to satisfy his curiosity, his parents had known what they were doing. They had slammed the door because they knew he wouldn't have been able to deal with what went on behind that door. Even his sister, Soraya, who refused to help him when he asked, seemed to be in on the conspiracy, for that's how he thought of it, as a conspiracy to deny him something he was entitled to.

'Why don't you tell them that I ought to be allowed to go? You're older than I am, they'll listen to you.'

'Why should I? Maybe it's none of your business.' She knew where their father went, she just didn't feel like telling him. 'Anyway, you're going about it the wrong way. You can't force them to do something they don't want to do.'

'Why not?'

'Because you're you: their *son*. They can't let their son boss them around. The rest of the world can push them around as much as it likes, but not their own son. They'd rather jump off a cliff.'

Their unequivocal 'no' filled him with a desire for revenge. Only much later did it dawn on him that every fibre of his being had been focused on revenge, and yet all of those pent-up feelings, no matter how powerful, would never have been strong enough to break that taboo.

'Do you really think he won't take me with him?'

'Why do you assume that he doesn't have a good reason? Why do you think that what *you* want is more important?'

'How come he won't tell me? How come nobody will?'

'You're smart. Figure it out for yourself.'

'Shouldn't I be allowed to see whatever it is that gives him so much pleasure? If Mama's in on the secret, and you're in on it too, why can't I be?'

Soraya got up suddenly from her chair and went into the kitchen to get something to drink. 'What really bugs you,' she said as she took a glass out of the rack, 'is that everyone except you knows what's going on. Even people outside the family, people he bumps into at the place where he goes, who ask him when he's going to bring his son.'

What could he say? Soraya had hit the nail on the head as usual. She came back with a glass of apple juice.

'OK,' he said, 'but then tell me why nobody will talk about it. It seems like the whole world is against me!' He was so mad his ears had turned red.

She took a sip and sat down. 'I don't know why you haven't been told. You might as well be, since nobody knows why it's such a big secret.'

'Then tell me! If it's so bad that you're not supposed to talk about it, I have a right to know.'

'It isn't all that big a deal,' she said, lapsing into a reverie. She stared out the window, brushing her hair. 'If I were to tell you, it *would* turn into a big deal, and that's a risk we can't take. Does that sound logical?'

'No.'

'Good, it's not supposed to.'

For a girl her age, she had extremely long hair. Actually, for a girl her age, everything about her was extreme. According to one of her teachers, who had dropped by to discuss her future, Soraya was extremely bright. 'Arithmetic, maths, history, science, P.E. – your daughter excels at everything. You should send her to a good school.'

'Do we want to do that?' his father said after the teacher had left.

'Do what?' his wife asked.

'Send her to a good school.'

'Oh, I'd already forgotten the teacher's advice. Are you really asking me for my opinion, don't you already know what it is?'

'I think you'd like her to drop out of school and stay at home.'

'Nobody wants to marry a woman who's had too much education. Educated girls have loud mouths and opinions of their own. They put off getting married, and we can't have that.'

In eavesdropping on his parents' conversation, he noticed that his father, unlike his mother, was ambivalent about his daughter's future. He wanted what was best for her – up to a certain point – but his mother wanted what was best for tradition. In their household Tradition was spelled with a capital 'T'. His mother, in particular, who had missed out on the wave of modernisation in Morocco, was a powerhouse of tradition. She was a strong woman, in both word and gesture. If she didn't like something, she said so. She was not one to lavish compliments on her children. She hated the country she lived in. You could tell by the way she spoke about the outside world, as if it was an intruder that had forced itself upon her. The outside world was an enemy of her tradition. She knew it, his sister knew it and he knew it.

Everyone always noticed Soraya's long hair. Even perfect strangers complimented her on it. She didn't have to put much effort into keeping it glossy and smooth, since she was at the age in which beauty clings to a young woman like the smell of booze to a drunk. She gave her hair a hundred brushstrokes every night, and that was that. The brush, a gift from her mother, had been a source of strife: the little girl had wanted to brush her own hair. Later, when, according to their mother, Soraya had developed 'a loud mouth and opinions of her own', she claimed that all her woes had begun with that brush. 'I wish I'd never given it to her.'

Their mother had taken her hair-brushing duties seriously. Her daughter meant everything to her. Sometimes, after coming home from visiting friends and listening to their alarming stories about their daughters, she would give Soraya a big hug. 'Thank goodness you're not like *them*,' she would shriek. 'They've been led astray. Girls aren't girls any more. They cut their hair short, walk in and out of the house as if it was a supermarket, speak a language their mothers don't understand and sip on straws. One of the girls,' she nearly choked on her words, 'has bleached her hair!'

He asked his sister if she was going to bleach her hair, but she said she wasn't sure.

'I'm not the trendy type. People who follow the latest trends suffer from low self-esteem, and the only way to raise your self-esteem is to follow the latest trends. It's a cruel trap everyone is bound to fall into sooner or later,' she said. At such moments he understood why his sister's grades were always better than his:

Hers	*His*
Dutch: A	Dutch: B
Arithmetic: A	Arithmetic: C
Geography: A	Geography: C
Physical Education: A	Physical Education: F

And so on down the line. He was lousy at everything. It was his father who noticed that his grades were much lower than his sister's. His mother shrugged. 'Boys are boys,' she said. 'They always have been and always will be.'

One time he was cuddled up to his mother while she was doing some mending when the subject of Soraya's outstanding achievements came up again.

'Her teacher's happy with her,' his father said.

'That doesn't mean anything,' the girl's mother replied.

'So what do you suggest?'

'Her schooling has to stop at some point. And college is out of the question.' At such times even his father, who occasionally agreed with his wife, felt compelled to speak up.

'Education is a good thing.'

'Not for girls. They bleach their hair. They stop speaking our language. They forget tradition. Do you call that "good"?'

'So what options does she have?'

'She can go to a domestic science school.' He didn't realise that his mother was speaking her mind so freely because she'd forgotten he was there. The combination of anxiety, jealousy and outright anger at her daughter, fuelled by her husband's recognition of his daughter's ambitions, had blinded her to his presence. Had she been aware of it, she might have softened her tone, feeling that it might be better for her son's mental health not to have witnessed her machinations, because even though she was convinced that tradition would rescue her daughter only when all other avenues had been blocked, she couldn't help feeling there was something a tad inhuman – not that she would have phrased it that way – about her methods. Nor would she have been able to determine, if she'd given the matter any thought, whether her desire to keep a tight rein on her daughter stemmed from a tendency to be overly protective or was the product of a twisted mind at the mercy of circumstances beyond its control. She acted purely out of instinct. Her instincts had now got the better of her, and that's why she'd forgotten he was there. Getting her husband to agree to her wicked plan was more important than keeping her son from overhearing it.

'We'll send her to a domestic science school, where she'll learn how to cook and clean and sew. There's one nearby. It's an all-girls' school, which is the way things should be. Don't worry, I'll make sure she finds a suitable husband. Leave her to me. Stop complimenting her. Stop praising her good grades. Help me, your wife, to focus her interests on what's going on here at home. We have to protect our daughter. She's the only one we've got.'

His mother's plan was so far-reaching and diabolical that he could hardly believe his ears. He sat up with a jerk so that she suddenly noticed him.

'What are you doing here? Go to bed, young man. Right this minute.' She gave him a push and laughed when she saw the expression on his face. 'Fortunately, we don't have the same problem with you,' she said. Actually, it made him feel good to hear her say this.

His father had sent him to judo lessons so he could learn to defend himself. 'It'll toughen you up.' He was crap at judo. When the class was over, the boys were always sent off to take a shower. They stared at him while he showered; then, when he was through, they hit him. He had no idea why. Maybe because he never hit them back. He was afraid that if he put up a fight they'd pound him even harder. He didn't dare tell his father, for fear that he'd smack him for being such a weakling.

One day in the shower room, when he couldn't stand it any more, he yelled, 'Why are you hitting me?'

'Because you're a dumb Moroccan,' said one of the boys. 'And dumb Moroccans like you don't have foreskins.' They hit him because he didn't have a minuscule piece of skin on his dick? It was the first time he realised that circumcision made such a difference. He was furious with his parents and his religion for circumcising him. 'All these problems because of a little piece of skin!' If he was in Morocco, nobody would have hit him, though they might have hit some guy who did have a foreskin. If war broke out between Muslims and non-Muslims, a quick look at someone's dick would be enough to determine whether or not he should be killed. The idea made him shudder, the way he shuddered at spinach with mustard (his sister's favourite dish), the colour orange and fingernails grating on a blackboard. It would have been better to send his sister to judo class: at least they couldn't pick on her.

'What's wrong?' his sister asked. He felt he could confide in her, even though it wasn't easy to admit to being a human punchbag.

'I always get beaten up after judo.'

'Why?'

'Because of a little nick in my skin.'

'A little nick here and there – nobody's perfect,' she said with her usual shrewdness. Her words were oddly comforting. She seemed to know what she was talking about. He should listen to her: she was the only person he could confess such things to. 'Who beats you up?'

Their father was in the other room, bent over a transistor radio. He worked in silence, since that was the only way his fingers could do their meticulous work in harmony with his mind.

'The guys in my judo class.'

'It's an ancient sport,' his sister said. 'Too bad it attracts so many morons.'

'I've noticed,' he said.

'So where's the nick?'

He pointed to his crotch.

She giggled, then giggled harder, as if she was being tickled. 'This is the first time I've ever heard that there's a disadvantage to being a boy! I'll spare you the details of what we girls have to go through. The less said the better. May that knowledge be forever denied you. May it be a fortress you'll never have to enter, a fortress that looks out over a magnificent hillside but is a cold, damp place in which to live. Especially for a girl from a family like ours, with all its restrictions and unrealistic expectations. That fortress is an ordeal that girls have to undergo. Even when we step through the gates, we can never forget that it's there and that we'll eventually have to go back to it.'

He didn't have the vaguest idea what she was talking about, and certainly didn't realise that she had summed up both their futures in a nutshell. She smiled and put her arms around him to keep him from crying.

'It'll all blow over. You're a boy. A little nick here or there – at some point it'll work in your favour. After all, boys are always given a second chance. The next time those guys hit you, maybe you ought to give them a nice surprise.'

'What do you mean?'

'Hit them back! Hard! With your fist.' She showed him how to make a fist.

'I wouldn't dare.'

'Yes you would. And you want to know why? Because you're going to think of me. You'll picture me, and I'll be urging you to hit them back. With your fist. That's not judo, but boxing. OK?'

He nodded. He'd do it. They hugged, and his troubles seemed to melt away. He forgot the judo lessons, the humiliating blows and his father's mysterious visits to a place that turned out to be a slaughterhouse. And the next time he went to his judo class and the boys started hitting him, he pictured his sister and hit the bastards back.

Translated by Susan Massotty

The Wounded Man

Abdellah Taia

We had broken fast about two hours earlier. It was dark now. And Hay Salam was abnormally quiet. It was as though the whole population of this working-class district of Salé except our family had suddenly moved to the far side of the river Bou Regreg, close to Rabat Beach. It felt as though something extraordinary was about to happen, something that might engulf the country, the earth and all those still here below. A squall bringing with it hope, rain and a new year. Or perhaps the apocalypse: the end, right now.

My mother, M'Barka, was sleeping soundly.

Ramadan was hard on her. But despite the exhaustion of fasting, every day she insisted on preparing sweet treats, crêpes, *harira* of course, a soup she preferred sour, with lots of tomatoes and lemon juice. There was a time when my sisters would have helped her to make every day of the sacred month a spiritual and gastronomic feast, an endless ritual. Now, the house was deserted. Three floors empty of people. Everyone had left, moved to some other place, some other town, some other country, another world, living among strangers, people I would never know, people I would never truly accept. Now there was only my mother, my little brother Mustapha, whom we saw very little of, and me at home. Now M'Barka was constantly afraid that she would be left alone. 'Loneliness,' she told me over and over, 'is a slow and agonising poison'. This made me terribly sad. Though I couldn't quite understand her pain, when I heard her say such things, it made me want to cry. Every day she begged me not to hang around in the city after my lectures at Rabat University, begged me to get home early, before it got dark, to take the bus and come back and occupy the house, keep her company, do everyday things with her, brighten her day by my simple presence, amuse her, cheer her, warm her, re-fashion our family before nightfall.

Late at night, when we were about to be separated again, she would beg me not to go up to my room, beg me to stay by her side until she fell asleep. Sleep was death. Ever since my father's sudden death a year earlier, my mother suffered from terrible fears, from crippling panic. And so she clung to me. M'Barka slept on a bed in the living room, dominated by the imposing television. She who had always hated 'that contraption', as she called it, had finally found in it a friend to keep her company through the day, a machine that produced sounds that would comfort her a little, though not always.

Recently, thanks to the satellite dish – now that they had finally become affordable – we could get French channels, which particularly interested me. I watched *Arte* whenever I could. It made me feel like someone, like some hip intellectual student interested in things other people found boring or challenging. I felt proud. Alone in the living room, I gave myself airs.

This was the role I was playing that night, having wolfed down the delicious Ramadan treats mother had prepared. I turned on the television. There was a film on *Arte*. A film that had started without me. Locked in the toilets of a train station, Jean-Hugues Anglade was crying his heart out. He, too, obviously felt abandoned. He was, also, obviously struggling with something, with loneliness maybe. I felt an immediate empathy for him (for the actor and the role he was playing). Through my extensive knowledge of cinema, I managed in less than a minute to identify this film I had never seen before. It was Patrice Chéreau's *The Wounded Man*. A French film made in 1984. A cult film. Banned.

My mother was sound asleep. This film was showing and there was nothing anyone in Morocco could do to stop it or interrupt it to deliver some religious or moral homily to the young hero, an outcast, his hair a little too long, who loved men, who loved a man.

I was confronted by a dilemma. Confronted by my desires. I was determined to watch this film to the end, even as fear gripped my guts. Constantly on the alert. My mother, sleeping in the bed just behind me, might wake at any moment and catch me in the act. Then she would know my secret, my only secret, the other part of me, the object of my affection. She would have hysterics. There would be a scandal. I would be ashamed, I wouldn't know what to do or what to say.

My stomach hurt. I had eaten too much when I broke my fast and the meal sat heavily on my stomach. I was aroused by the passion that suffused the film, that haunted Jean-Hugues Anglade and the other characters. They lived only for this, for sex, for love, for danger. You feel attracted to a man, flirt with him, pick him up, cajole him, buy him, you play with him, rape him, dump him, little by little tear him to pieces. I was fascinated, hypnotised by these images. And I wanted to do what these characters did, I wanted to be one of them. An outcast. I wanted to love as they did. Love another man. Alone. Savage. I wanted to touch myself. Caress myself. Lick myself. Bite myself. Let myself be drawn to a strong man and give myself to him.

My stomach grew bloated. My penis grew hard. And I did not know what to do because I was still terrified, in spite of this desire that streamed from the screen, bathing me, turning my world upside down, driving me insane.

My mother was snoring, her breathing regular, her snoring sometimes loud, sometimes soft. Now and then it stopped. When it did, I immediately changed channels. I couldn't help but interpret each silence as a sign that she was about to wake up, come round, discover me watching this forbidden film. After an interminable minute waiting, watching her intently to make sure her eyes were really closed, that she was still far from me and the images I was watching, I would feel somewhat reassured and would turn back to *The Wounded Man* and his story. And immediately I would feel the same passion, the same primal fear.

Jean-Hugues Anglade was in love with a tall, handsome, dark-haired man, I think. A bit like Gérard Depardieu in the early '80s. A masculine, sensitive, tough, ruthless man. A king. A dictator. A pimp.

Anglade had fallen for this man the moment he first set eyes on him. His world henceforth would revolve around this man; he would forget everyone else. No one else could matter to him as much as this man. Almost immediately, he abandons everything to follow him

— his former life, his family. He finds himself following the man, stalking him through streets, train stations, car parks, trying clumsily to seduce him so he might spend a moment with this, with his body. So that he might be loved by him. But in vain. Anglade's passion is absolute. It could not but be heartbreaking and tragic.

Patrice Chéreau's film, tumultuous and brutal as it overwhelmed me that night and as I remember it still, is extreme in its presentation of love, extreme in the power sex exerts over all bodies. The film is a litany of punches, arguments, chases, trafficking of all sorts, tears, orgies, blood, sperm, sordidness, obsessions and death. It is the tale of a bleeding young man, doomed in advance, hurtling inexorably towards a crime of love.

I've forgotten his first name. I was him. Loving and frustrated as he was. Ready, like him, to abandon everything for a dream, for a strong man, for this rare feeling, this exceptional creature. And yet still petrified. In a desperate search for the unique object of desire. The beloved. What Americans call 'The One'.

One man and no other. A man older than I was so I could learn from him, relive a certain past with him as part of an unacknowledged couple. A *faqih*, a master, a baker, a man of God who prays five times a day, a visionary, a parent, an uncle, a cousin . . .

The film played on, its power, its despair, its religion burning themselves on to my eyes, into my mind. Without realising it, I was already a convert, a master, an adept of this way of living, of seeing, of straying, the jostling bodies, the surge of pleasure before you go insane, more insane. Here before me was the forbidden, touching my scrawny now suddenly courageous body. Behind me, too, was the forbidden.

My penis grew harder. My heart grew darker. My eyes grew redder. I was happy and sad. Thrilled yet frozen as though whipped by a wind from the north, from Tangiers. There were moments when I wanted to shake my mother awake, have her see these images, connect her to this film which so moved, so overwhelmed her well-brought-up son. And I wanted to go to her, press myself to her, climb on to her lap, place my hand on her belly, feel her breath on my back, on my neck, smell her scent in my nostrils, on my skin. Go back to the source, the first door, to my first opening on to the world, on to life, on to light. And there, in that place where it all began, that first threshold, carve out a space, a seat, a hole, and weep, all the while watching this wounded man, this young man, this brother bewildered by the searing intensity of love, weep, cry for him, go with him in my tears. Gently take his eyes into my mouth, lick them slowly one by one then finally drink the faintly salted water that streamed from them, trickled over his cheeks, his skin.

I identified with him. I was dreaming. I was fantasising. I wasn't thinking. Not any more. I was in pain. Pain in my eyes, my thighs, my knees, my penis.

When I came to myself again, the wounded man was still on the *via crucis* of love. This man's fate – *mektoub* – was being played out here, in our home, this house without a father, in our almost empty living room, in our privacy, our silence, our darkness.

I had thought I was sophisticated. Now, watching Patrice Chéreau's film for the first time, I realised I was still a naïve film fan watching films, all films, the way I had before. Before: when, at childhood's end, programmed by others, the religion of Indian movies and kung-fu films entered me for ever. I rediscovered myself. In dark, crowded cinemas surrounded by prostitutes and wicked boys, I drank in these images, and these films delivered me from the bounds of my country and connected me to an art which was gradually to become my reason for living, for looking beyond, looking above. Soaring up above the world, seeing myself naked and coming back down to earth prepared to do battle.

Now I was at war. In revolt. A few days before the sacred night of Laylat al-Qadr.

My mother's music stopped suddenly. No sound came from her mouth, no wheeze, no snore, no breath. Was she holding her breath? Was she dead, had she gone, fearless and unafraid, to join my father? Was she awake? Was she, like me, watching *The Wounded Man*? Did she understand the meaning of these strange images from another world, from hell? Would she suddenly get to her feet, scream, shout at me with the voice she used on her bad days, pull my hair, punish me, pinch me, curse me? Castrate me there and then?

My heart hammered in my chest, I turned to look at her. Her eyes were open but she was staring at the ceiling. She was still dreaming, still caught up in the images of a dream that was hers alone. A little reassured, I switched channels and, in a small voice filled with respect, asked her if she needed anything. Her reply came immediately, as though she had prepared it long ago, while still asleep. 'A glass of water, *habibi*!' I rushed to the kitchen to get her one. She was very thirsty, she had come back from a long journey. She asked for a second glass. 'Another glass, *habibi*, or I'll die . . . May God ble—' I didn't need to be told twice. I all but ran back into the kitchen, overjoyed at the blessings she was heaping on me, as always, blessings that were always the same, that spoke of paradise as something certain, not imagined.

Her thirst quenched, M'Barka returned to her sleep, her dreams. But just before she closed her eyes again, she gave me a blessing that stunned me even more: 'Watch, my son . . . watch television if you want . . . You're not bothering me . . . watch whatever you like . . .'

I turned down the volume and waited for the sound of my mother snoring before turning back to *The Wounded Man* and its bruised hero. By now, he had come to the end of his tether, he was tired of this unrequited love, of the humiliations, tired of wandering, yet still hopelessly in love. The road to his crime – to the first and last time he would possess the body of the beloved – was almost at an end. Only death, only murder could give this young man's tragic story, his sublime love, a meaning, a goal, a structure.

Naked, pressed against the man he loved, he was suffocating him with his bare hands, suffocating him even as he made love to him. He was giving himself completely to this man, his body, his heart, his mind, his skin, his blood, his breath. He was giving his life in taking the life of the man who, to the end, had refused to commune with him in this embrace, in this religion of emotion.

It was a tragedy.

Love, like life, which in miraculous moments brings light and passion, is a tragedy. I knew this intuitively. I was twenty years old. *The Wounded Man* reminded me of the fact once more, once and for all. I had been warned. It was up to me to decide. Give up? Never.

The credits rolled. Hervé Guibert's name, the writer who co-written the screenplay with Patrice Chéreau, appeared. I had forgotten Guibert: this film, this story, they are his, too. His life.

His way of life. A life I had discovered and loved in his books. He had been dead four or five years now. Tears streamed from my eyes. Finally. For what? For whom? I did not know precisely how to answer, how to answer myself. For Hervé Guibert, whom I knew intimately through his books? For the hero of the film who had become a murderer, a brother, a friend, myself? For my father, who had passed away too soon, before he could see me become a book, a written record? For my mother, who was slipping back into child-hood fears? For life, which, deep down, in spite of the pleasures of Ramadan, was sad and terribly lonely?

Even now I do not know. Even now, I weep when I think about that moment, the end of the film, Hervé Guibert, me . . . and my mother screaming in silence. I weep for all of us.

The following morning I woke up late. I had only one thought. To go and see my favourite cousin Chouaïb, who I was a little in love with, seduce him, corrupt him, press myself against him, persuade him to break fast with me before dark, break fast together, both of us thinking sexual thoughts. Then climb the hill in Bettana, his neigh-bourhood, from where, next to the old cemetery, we could see the far bank of the river Bou Regreg, Rabat, the Tour Hassan, the Kasbah of the Udayas, the public beach where poor people went. Smoke some kif together. Lay my head in his lap. Close my eyes. Then, calmly and reverently, tell him about the film I had seen the night before and gently, openly, tempt him into sin, into transgression.

Sin deliberately.

God would be watching us.

We would go on. To the end. To the sea. To the heavens.

Cursed. One day I would be cursed in love like *The Wounded Man*. But while I wait, with Chouaïb in my heart, my cousin with his faint moustache, a wicked boy, his sturdy body holding me, I go almost every day towards the lights of the cinema, eyes tight shut.

Translated from the French by Frank Wynne

Amazigh

Abderrahim Elkhassar

I am the grandson of the Amazigh king of old
who died betrayed by a stab from a Roman hand.
My hobby is to light fire in the ice
and build traps for birds that never reach the ground.
I sometimes think to draw a fish from the river then send it back,
   and I stand against the current, waiting, deluding myself that I'll
   catch it some day.
I sometimes think to open cages on the roof
and set free the birds on whose care I've wasted years away.

I am the grandson of the Amazigh king of old.
I know no sentence of my language, remember nothing of my line.
Except that my grandfather was a shepherd in the Atlas mountains
   chasing flocks of Barbary sheep,
across the almond slopes he ran night and day
setting his nets and snares for the forest and valley game,
and like the other displaced famine was to propel him to the plains
to fix the Arabs' pots and court a woman who was to become my
   grandmother.

I am the grandson of the Amazigh king of old.
No book speaks of that for which I wait.
All the books always tell the opposite story.
Except that when I look at my grandmother's face
It is as though I'm looking at the face of a Red Indian woman

she told me once: You're a grandchild of the mountains
so I headed south like an archaeologist towards uncharted desert
I asked the elders, the fortune-tellers, the shepherds and the sages
I asked the night bandits and the tomb-raiders and the
    well-diggers
I followed the tracks of our ancestors in the foothills and along the
    fissures
in the twisting village lanes and their common land, in the caves
    and the caverns
I heard nothing but the echo of my voice like the roar of an
    avalanche.
An old woman, leaning on a stick and more than a hundred years
    told me
that my grandfather was a woodcutter, so he picked up his axe
    before he departed
and in the heat of anger felled the family tree.

I am the grandson of the Amazigh king of old
herds of wild buffalo chase inside me till they tire
eagles battle and their feathers scatter between the mountains
wolves howl in their hills
but their harsh sound does not transcend the lair.
Inside, many thoughts die by friendly fire
my father looks at the picture of his father hanging over the
    wardrobe
the words drop from his lips heavy in the hollow of the night
why do you knit your brow and carry gun and dagger
when no one hunts us today?
Why did you leave the others and roll from the south
like a rock that rolls from the mountain tops
and crumbles on the slopes?

I am the grandson of the Amazigh king of old.
I've inherited nothing from my ancestors except my doubting eyes.
And my constant feeling that I walk a teetering plank
and lean on a wall soon to fall.

I stretch out my hand into endless darkness and swim in treacherous
    waters
oh world, whatever shall I do with you, when all I own is a paper
    and pen?
I stay awake at night refining words,
I entreat pictures in the album to dance with me,
I open my window in the depths of winter on to windows firmly
    shut.
People run anxiously towards Life while the current pulls me
    towards a different life
people shout out each other's names as if they are saints
for me it's better to live in silence than to shout out anyone's name
better blind than to witness the idiotic cavalcades that pass vainly
    before my house
better deaf, Life, than to hear your dissonance
my forbears were probably used to sitting on the mountain tops,
fearing the foothills' deceit.
That's why I live in a room on the roof,
reading a book on the Mayan people
and listening to the songs of the sons of Assyria.
I stare at the sky, gathering one by one the sprinkled stars.
I sit like an owl on the world's shoulder,
fearing that I'll fall and its extremities will crush me,
fearing that a hand will snatch me up and hurl me on to the plains
    far below.

I am the grandson of the Amazigh king of old
who ruled this earth two thousand years before
and whose picture does not hang on my bedroom wall
I can only imagine him to resemble the men of legends
with a sceptre of ivory and a crown of feathers and gold
I saw him once in a dream, in a turban like a Kurdish man
perhaps many things link me to the Kurds,
although I breathe the air of a land as it pleases me
and I creep like every other creature on the slopes.
Yet it's the desire of water to know its source

before the waterfall drags it away.
It's my desire to turn and look behind
so as to reveal my face
that it may be clear, like my reflection in the mirror.

Translated by Tristan Cranfield

from the novel

Skin of Shadow

Abderrazak Boukebba

She wondered, as she stopped singing and began weaving a burnous for her only child, have I no purpose in life other than to marry off Dhiab? Then she glanced over at Al-Amry's grave up there on the hill and immediately answered herself: no, I have no purpose other than to marry him off. This is what I promised you on the morning I first visited your grave, and this is what I will do. As for me, I have forgotten myself, and I only remember it in our son. You know, I hated you when I received news of your death in the battle with the village of Aala Al-Jabal. I did not cry, but said, 'He had no right not to come back when he promised me he would, or to go where he couldn't return or take me with him.' But when my sister – who had just given birth to Al-Jazeya – pointed out that you had indeed returned through your son, I forgave you from my heart and fell into a long and silent weeping that has not ceased to this day.

I

Time: the summer of 1847.

Place: the high carob tree, where the sages of Awlad Jahish assemble and where the youngsters memorise the Great Quran.

The older sage Halafana asked, after he had directed the others to bless the Prophet, 'Would this rosary have any significance if it lost one of its beads?'

Sage Faleh, advanced in years and wisdom, replied, 'These beads are our heritage, and it would be treason to lose any one of them.'

As a reward for his assistance in the introduction of the matter, Sage Halafana fixed his eyes on Faleh as he said, 'So is the village, Faleh. It lasts as long as its people last, and perishes with their breaking away from it, like the beads of this rosary. Accordingly, I suggest that we bring together all the youth and prompt them to swear on the holy book of their great-grandfather Hassan Ben Jahish not to leave the village until they are buried in it.'

Sage Faleh, taking his cue from Halafana, continued, 'We shouldn't forget that the people of Aala Al-Jabal village grew up believing that the grave of their great-grandmother Washiya Bent Maeya lies in Awlad Jahish, and if the village loses its sons, this would give them a chance to seize it.'

Sage Othman cleared his throat, 'Say this to the youth, as for us . . .' and without finishing his sentence, he rose, tripping on his burnous.

2

Not a single one of the Awlad Jahish youths missed the meeting of the sages under the high carob tree. However, they were unaware that they had been summoned in order to take an oath not to leave the village until their death. So, when the Sage Halafana confronted them with his intention, murmurs rose among them, and some of them decided among themselves to upset neither the shepherd nor the wolf – to take the oath without the intention of honouring it. But when they found out that the oath would be sworn on their great-grandfather Hassan Ben Jahish's holy book, they were taken aback and quickly changed their minds. They had been brought up not to respect the holy book of the dear sheikh.

However, the sages' joy at this accomplishment was shortlived: Dhiab, intentionally the last in line, placed his hand on the holy book, then withdrew it, refusing to take the oath.

3

His father died on a frosty night, in one of the attacks launched by the Aala Al-Jabal tribe on Awlad Jahish. He was born on the same day his father was buried.

In a dream, his mother saw a sheikh with white hair, a white beard and a white horse approaching her. Frightened for her infant and herself, she ran away from the strange sheikh, who spurred his horse to catch up with her as she ran while Dhiab cried and shook in her arms.

'Stop, oh creature. Stop, Umm Dhiab.'

Her fear and astonishment heightened when this sheikh whom she did not know recognised her and her infant, who had been born on the eve of that very day. She thought he was Death come to take him from her; she had heard that Death was the colour of the shroud. When she didn't stop as he requested, he ordered his horse to fly into the sky, outrun her, then alight in front of her. The sheikh extended his hand to her bosom and snatched the boy, flying with him high in the sky, as she wailed and hit her head against the trunk of the carob tree. The tree then spoke to her: 'Do not be afraid, Umm Dhiab. This sheikh is your master, Hassan Ben Jahish. He has taken your son because he felt he was the grandson who most resembled him. He will bring him back to you after he opens up his head and puts his own brain in it, so that the child will have two.'

When she woke in the morning, she checked on her son and found that his head was bigger. She prayed to God to protect them and called the teacher of the Great Quran, Si Salem – God bless him – from under the carob tree. She told him about her dream and he recited the *fatiha* on a date that he sucked then squeezed into the infant's mouth. He then asked her not to repeat her account of the dream to anyone, not even to herself, otherwise Dhiab would be harmed.

The older sage, filled with anger, yelled, 'How could you refuse to swear on the holy book of your master Ben Jahish, like all the other youths did, not to leave the village?'

Dhiab sank into a long silence caused by a conflict in his head between his two brains, as each tried to answer the question.

The Big Brain told the Small Brain: 'The Earth belongs to Allah, and we are His servants. We have a right to what He owns; in fact, that is the reason we were born. Then why should we deprive ourselves of other places where we are allowed to live? The homeland is not the dust we are born on, but the memory of that dust that accompanies us. Wherever we go, we see new faces, new souls, new minds and new mountains. And when we yearn for home, we sit at night in a corner and weep in delicious silence.'

The older sage yelled in great anger, 'Answer us, Dhiab! You have insulted us by refusing to swear. Do not insult us with your silence.'

The Small Brain said to the Big Brain: 'Then why do we leave the homeland if we will cry over it in the end?'

The Big Brain replied: 'So we can say to it, "We have not forgotten you. We remain loyal to your memory, although we have discovered new things that you do not have."'

Sage Faleh yelled, 'If you do not answer us, we will tie you to the carob tree and deprive you of food and drink. Why will you not swear as everyone else did?'

The Small Brain almost screamed with fear: 'Forgive me, sirs, I have made a mistake. And here I swear never to leave the mountain until the day I am buried.'

Except that the Big Brain covered his mouth with his hand, stopping him from talking: 'This is surrender! Do not swear to what you cannot honour. How do you know that you will not leave? Your destiny is in the hands of Allah.'

The Small Brain replied, shaking with fear: 'But they will tie me to the tree, and the wolves will eat me! Have you forgotten that huge wolf that was caught by the guard? It was terrifying, even after it was dead! What if the wolf came to me, alive, when I was tied up? Before, when I saw it, I dreamt that I was among a pack of wolves under a tree. They were all around me and kept making frightening noises. I moved closer to the tree and they drew nearer. The closer I came to the tree, the nearer they drew. They were about to bite me when I realised that I could climb the tree, which I did. They paced around it, and their howling grew louder. Since they wouldn't go away, I stayed up in the tree until I became a sheikh.'

The Big Brain laughed: 'See? You rose above them.'

Sage Othman yelled, 'Tie him up.'

Halafana added, annoyed at Othman having beaten him to the decision, 'And don't let anyone come near him.'

4

Dhiab tried to untie himself but realised that it was impossible. He felt a dryness in his throat, and let out a scream the entire mountain could hear. He began to feel that he was losing consciousness. He saw a clear sky shrouded with clouds, and an earth that was celebrating spring, covered by nothing but tree stumps. He heard thunder fuelled with rage and rain fill the earth. He let out an echoing shriek and tried to open his eyes. As he wiped the water away, he saw a sheikh with white hair and a white beard galloping towards him. His white horse engulfed the land with its hoofs and was accompanied with the anger of thunder and lightning. It arrived before him, letting out a resounding neigh. The sheikh dismounted and wiped the rain from Dhiab's forehead with the tip of his burnous.

'Are you hungry? Look what I brought you: grapes and pomegranate.'

He fed Dhiab until he was no longer hungry or thirsty.

Dhiab screamed, 'Free me!'

The sheikh looked at him quietly and sadly.

'Anything but that. That I cannot do.'

Dhiab wondered, stifling his tears, 'Why not?'

'So you can learn to free yourself. Others can help you in all matters except freedom.'

The Big Brain told the Small Brain in Dhiab's head: 'What an idiot! What are you afraid of?'

'The wolves.'

'The tree is in the middle of the village and its dogs will not let a wolf in.'

'Then the dogs.'

'They all know you. They would not deceive you. Have you ever heard of a dog deceiving someone they know?'

'And who will keep my mother company?'

'She will get used to sleeping alone in a few days, as will you.'

Lightning struck the mountain and Dhiab regained consciousness.

Translated by Asmaa Abdallah

from the novel

The Twentieth Terrorist

Abdullah Thabit

I wrote this piece between 1999 and 2005. It is writing that I tried hard not to classify. It was my intention that the reader get to know Zahi al-Jibali, the man who was probably, almost certainly, the complement to the nineteen killers in America's 9/11. He was the twentieth terrorist. It is more likely that there were twenty-six on a list, and he was the twenty-seventh in Saudi Arabia. I have hesitated about the way I might present these two propositions. In the end I thought the piece would proceed as in the following way, without any embellishment. I have left it to Zahi to speak for himself.

Maybe these pages will have some significance one day. They start with me and end with me. I will be content to celebrate them in my own way once I've put down my pen after writing the last word of the last line. I will go off by myself and buy a cake, a candle and a fine bottle of some forbidden beverage. I will pile up the bundle of papers on the chair over there. I will turn up the music as loud as is permissible at that time of day or night. I will do a little dance by myself, light a cigarette and knock back a few glasses. I will shout out curses that I know and curses that I do not know. I will declaim all the poetry I have learnt by heart and some I don't know. I will do all this and more. And more. Like the man who celebrated his birthday alone, in a country where he knew no one and of whose language he spoke only a few words.

Everything recorded in these pages happened in one or other of two places, the first in my village and the second in my city, Abha, but they are not really two different places: they are in fact one and the same, for there is nothing between them. They both sit on top of those lofty peaks that tower over land that sparkles with greenery and streams, and is adorned with mist, fog and hail. If rain returns after an absence of a few days it reshapes the features of town and village.

Abha is no more than a village in spite of the street lamps and all those buildings, tarred roads, shops and souks. It is a village dressed up like a city, like a country girl who has put on city clothes: they do not alter her essential physique. In this way I am a mountain lad twice over.

I'm going to talk about the people here, their nature, their culture, how they talk, what life is like for them. The people of Asir are good folk. They don't go off the rails unless there is good reason, unless someone drives them mad with rage. They are impetuous and highly strung, never far from anxiety and confusion. They are proud and even arrogant, sometimes ridiculously so. A man may walk backwards and forwards past something he wants intensely but he will not let his eyes look at it otherwise he would feel belittled and lose his self-esteem! The peaks among which they dwell are like cloaks: they cover a blend of wind and shapes, confusion and questions. The Asiris are part bluster, part question, part confusion. They are as fiery as the sun, as insubstantial as the fog, as ferocious as frost, as menacing as the clouds. If nature flares up, threatening them with rain and thunder and frost, they joke among themselves, 'We believe that the rain of our Lord is an Asiri rain.'

A word affecting the honour of any one of them is sufficient pretext for them to commit murder, for a man in these parts lives by his pride, and is proud about everything. The man who kills for a word is the same man who will be undone by another word. He will weep and withdraw, crushed in spirit and in feeling! In such cases he is not driven to reach for his sword or his gun, as he would if a dear friend betrayed or offended him.

Their feelings about honour are very strong indeed, strong enough for death to be preferred to dishonour. Dishonour embraces an endless list of deeds. Someone touching your face, for example, is an insult that cannot be allowed to pass without the shedding of blood. And if two people are involved in a fight, each will contrive to scratch the

other's face and leave some mark on him as an emblem of his triumph
and the other man's everlasting submission. When that happens death
is inevitable. Either the one who is scratched kills himself, or, if he
can find a way, he kills the one who has humiliated him.

They are tribal, and their feuds, wars and battles are endless. If a
family does not lose a man in battle, then that family loses face in
terms of tribal honour. Touching one individual in the tribe is an
issue for the tribe as a whole, and one has to exact some penalty on
the offender or to wage war against his tribe.

They are great lovers. All love stories start at springs or in pastures,
or as a result of a chance encounter among the mud houses, or behind
some huge rock or wall, or in a garden. Love is something they only
talk about in their poetry, and people will go out of their way to
attend a wedding ceremony in order to listen to the poetry recited
there. They come and recount tales to each other, with their hopes
and disappointments, telling of the lover's suffering. It may be that
they draw attention to those who have come between the lover and
his woman; and as soon as those concerned understand the drift they
reach for their knives or rifles.

The people of Asir love music. They are enchanted by song and
dance. A village without a poet is a poor village, a village with something missing. The poet of the whole tribe is venerated by all. The
men who chant at weddings and celebrations are on everyone's lips
and are in greatest demand. People here can quote from memory
long lines of poetry, especially those dealing with love and war.

Moreover, the people of Asir have deeply-rooted values. They are
all you can imagine when it comes to horsemanship or matters of
honour or manliness. They are generous people, yes, that's what they
are. They are so absurdly generous that a man may be poor and needy
all his life because he has given so much to his guests. The Asiri gives
splendid feasts and is happy to stand over his guests at his table. He
swears by Allah that they should show no restraint in taking whatever
food they want.

My mother always says that I was a calm child, never saying anything.
Here in the south they are apprehensive about a child who does

not talk. They believe in some great secret lurking in the background, obliging him to be silent. Whenever there is concern about a child's silence, they offer up prayers. These may not be in earnest, or it may be that they are really scared of Him. For they say: May Allah give us His bounty and protect us from His evil.

My family left the village and moved to the city, as did others, to seek a living. They built houses in the city although Abha never lost its village-like character, however much money was thrown around its streets. At most, it was in a transitional state, neither completely rural nor completely urban. Our village and the city were only three kilometres apart. And so we lived in a new house, and the rest of the villagers looked at us as if we were among the wealthiest people of the city.

In the south we used to call the village our homeland. By this we did not mean the state or the larger region. All we meant by it was the smaller villages. We used to say, 'I was in the homeland,' 'I came from the homeland,' 'I'm going to the homeland,' 'I met people from the homeland' . . . and so on.

My father was the first to buy a black and white television set. People living in our quarter were amazed; it was as if they were listening to the fabulous tales of a professional storyteller. They came from another world and told them about lives they had never seen before.

You would see men and women all sitting round this television. They would listen very carefully and were dazzled by it. When work finished at sunset they raced to our house to watch this enchanting machine. They ate doughy bread with oil and sugar. They drank red tea and were fascinated by the television series about Bedouin life, *Wadha wa bin Aajlan*. They murmured to the songs of Samira Tawfiq, Umm Kulthum, Faiza Ahmad, Abdul Halim Hafiz, Saadun Jabir, Fairuz and others.

In those days, that is in the late seventies, my eldest brother was very religious, much under the influence of radicals who had come in from neighbouring countries. He was also affected in his work in Quranic schools by a group of extremists. They enrolled him and brought him over to their way of thinking. He became a zealot and disapproved of everything that went on at home. There were huge arguments, especially between him and my other older brothers who were vehemently against him. One extraordinary event that lives on in the family memories is when they went out to switch on the electrical generator to get the television to work. My eldest brother flared up and went out and switched it off. My other brothers then switched it on again. This went on all night. Things often reached the stage of fisticuffs and violent arguments. Father finally intervened and decided then to thrash everybody. When he was angry, my father would not distinguish between who was right and who was wrong.

My big brother became an extremist at a time when the faction launched by the Arabian Peninsula's famous extremist Juhaiman became active. His disciples used to go around preaching to people and garnering support, protesting against what they saw as moral corruption – songs and women appearing on the television and so on and so forth. The climax of their activity was the occupation of the sacred site of Mecca. Their objective in this was to overthrow the Saudi regime, which they considered corrupt. It was their job to purge the state of what they claimed was godless government. However, the authorities managed to suppress them and clear them out of the sacred places. Juhaiman and a number of his followers were arrested and sentenced to death.

My eldest brother was brought to trial by the state at that time and nearly lost his life, for he was accused of being one of them. But he was discharged because there was insufficient evidence to convict him of involvement in any extremist activity. This all happened when they were eliminated in 1979.

My family will never forget the day one of the security forces knocked at the door of our house, arresting my brother. According to my mother, I opened the door and the man immediately asked for my brother. It was a painful night, and we were all convinced we would never see him again.

In 1979 I was six. This meant that it was time for me to go to school, the place that my two immediately older brothers teased me about: 'Today we had play, today we enjoyed ourselves.' 'Today the teacher told us this and that.' 'Tomorrow we will be having fun . . . and drawing.'

Before the summer was over and before the start of the new school year, Father and my eldest brother had a row. Father wanted me to go to the same school as my two brothers, on the principle that sticks are harder to break if they are fastened together. It was an ordinary government school, just like any other. My extremist brother insisted that he take me with him to the Quranic school where he was teaching. He put forward every argument for me to be registered there. ('He'll learn the Quran by heart . . . I'll be with him . . . I'll look after him and keep an eye on his education at close hand . . . Every month they give him an allowance.')

Father was not easily swayed by my brother's arguments, and he became quite weary as a result. He was afraid that his little boy might become a tiresome fanatic like his brother. My eldest brother took me to one side and persuaded me to want to go to this school. ('Zahi, the Quranic school will ensure for you a place in Heaven . . . You will be able to learn the Quran by heart . . . You will become a great sheikh. People will think the world of you and ask you to pray for them . . . There are lots of games and fun and money . . . You'll have cash to buy whatever you want . . . Don't you wonder why your other brothers can't get any money at their schools? . . . I'll get you whatever you want if you ask Father to attend this school.')

It was all very tempting and my mind was filled with dreams of what was in this school. I wept and wailed. I screamed and argued to be enrolled at the Quranic school. Father gave in to my tears and agreed.

The people of Asir are able to overlook everything except the tears of small children. It is said that the Asiri tigers do not trouble women or children. For us, tigers are paragons of courage, strength and nobility. The wolf, on the other hand, does not hesitate to commit any act. He does not care whether his prey is man, woman, child or chicken!

As soon as I got my way with the school, I became fearful and anxious, but also exhilarated. I joined my classmates and at once heard people shouting menacing threats. The teachers were all shouting, scolding the little ones. 'Go to your class.' 'What's keeping you?' 'Stand where you are and, you, bring me the stick.' As soon as my first teacher came in and sat down he began to threaten us with all kinds of punishments if we did not obey him and do what he told us.

At the break, the school principal, a ferocious man, came to the snack bar to see a Syrian pupil who was wearing trousers. He shouted so loudly that the pupils all fell silent.

'Come here,' he said to the boy. The boy almost fainted from fright as he approached him.

'Where is the *thawb*, the smock you should be wearing?' the principal asked. 'Why have you come in these trousers? Men do not wear them!'

The boy tried to explain that he had just arrived from his own country and had not known that he had to wear the *thawb*, and that his father had not been able to go to the shops yet to buy him one.

That day the principal thrashed him all over his body. He was flogged mercilessly. He pulled him around by his hair as he staggered this way and that.

The principal said, 'We'll make you a man in spite of yourself. You will not wear the infidels' clothes here.'

I shall never forget the tears and the terror of the child I was with and his pleas for help. Nor will I forget how, when the principal was out of sight, I raced to my classroom and hid under a desk, terrified lest this man would come our way and do to me what he had done to that Syrian boy. It was a violent shock. All those words of my brother about playing and joking and the road to Paradise and bliss turned into frightful spectres with sharp teeth that stared at me mockingly.

One day I had failed to memorise the allotted portion of the Quran. I was scared that I would be flogged severely, so I pretended to Father that I was suffering from tummy ache and was very ill. Father agreed that I should not go to school that day. But so surprised and delighted was I at his consent that I could not stay in bed. A few minutes later Father summoned me and told me to put on my *thawb* and get my satchel. He would take me to school himself. All pleading was useless.

It was terrible. When we arrived at the school, Father asked the principal to thrash me because I had lied to him, pretending to be ill. The principal asked me why I had done this. From my heart I told the truth; this might help me, for they could see that I was exchanging my lies for truth. I said, 'I lied because I had been unable to learn that part of the Quran and was afraid the teacher would beat me.' At this Father gave a sign to the principal, excused himself and left. It was immediately obvious that a scheme had been plotted and was now out in the open. I was slightly built and not very strong. All I could do was watch and wait, but inside I felt a sense of total collapse as I realised that they were both conspiring against me. Father never asked me again about my having deceived him. There is nothing worse than implosion.

The principal detained me in his room for two hours: two hours of humiliation and psychological agony, especially when he took out the knotted bamboo cane and placed it on the edge of his desk. Every now and again he would throw me a look that would shoot through my body like an electric shock. Finally he said, 'Put out your hand.' Then he caned me on the palm of my right hand, then on the left. I lost control and couldn't stand another blow. I refused to put out my hand and he started to beat me on the rest of my body. He beat me until I was on my knees, then stretched out on the floor. The brutality only stopped when some teachers, moved to compassion, intervened to prevent him from continuing the punishment.

I wore a short *thawb*, as religious people do, letting it hang down from the sides of my forehead. I always had a *sawak*, the stick used for brushing teeth, in my mouth. I learnt the words and special prayers. But deep inside I was someone else. I loved songs and pictures. I liked to draw and play, but I wasn't allowed to do any of that. Indeed, I used to pray with the *sawak* in my mouth. But I was never at the ritual washing. I did pray and sit in the mosque but I hated it.

This is how I used to spend my days: I woke up at dawn frightened at the sound of my father shouting and calling me to the dawn prayer. He used to call us all at once and we all hurried and lined up behind him. I was severely punished when I was late in my prostrations. Sometimes I missed the prayer altogether. During the first moments of daylight I would get ready to go to school. I finished the last of my homework, memorising what I had not already done. I always had in my mind an image of the cruel school principal and the strict teachers.

I had a terrible time at school, lessons about the Quran, frightful lessons about religion, with questions afterwards. The only moment of happiness in the whole day arrived when we left that concentration camp to go home. At home I finished off my homework, memorising the Quran before the afternoon prayer. As soon as the afternoon prayer was over it was my task to go out with the sheep and goats to their pastures.

With these animals, I often passed the lads of the quarter. They would be playing football and riding around on their small bikes. Their laughter would reach me: 'The shepherd boy, the shepherd boy, the shepherd boy!' I ignored them with affected indifference, but inside I was deeply hurt because I wasn't one of them, enjoying their games and amusements. I would go off with my sheep and goats, hitting and cursing them. I blamed them for what I was missing and then wept bitter tears.

Translated by Peter Clark

At the Post Office

Adania Shibli

She quit school today. After she repeated both fourth and seventh grade twice, and almost repeated ninth grade this year as well, her father raised his eyebrows in disapproval. This gesture was exactly what Afaf had been expecting since fourth grade, but his laziness had delayed its appearance for all those years.

Her father was a collaborator, despite the fact that her grandfather was among the revolutionaries who were killed in 1948. The government had put her father in charge of a number of tasks related to various ministries, such as receiving applications for issuing identity cards, travel permits, building authorisations, postal services, approval of new telephone connections, selling diesel fuel and so on. But due to his sluggishness, as a result of the excess fat that had settled on every part of his body, and because of his thick moustache and the large gold ring on his right ring finger, he delegated most of the tasks of spying among his family members and contented himself, of course, with operating the small tape recorder placed in the pocket of his clean white and always ironed shirt. He was an extremely lazy man, rarely budging from his spot under the almond tree. But then there was hardly any need for him to do so, or even to leave his chair to find out what conspiracies people in the neighbourhood were hatching that could threaten state security, since these very people would come to him of their own volition. Indeed, if he could, given his excessive indolence and lethargy, he would have called her to come and press the 'record' button inside the breast-pocket of his shirt.

Afaf crossed the courtyard towards the house, leaving her father sitting in the shade under the tree. She climbed the steps and breathed a sigh of relief upon finding the house clean, evidence that her stepmother had actually finished the housework, then went inside and entered her and her siblings' room.

Sitting down on the edge of the bed, she ran both hands over her face, wiped the sweat from it and then took a deep breath, which meant 'thank God'. Then she began to examine her hands, which were glistening despite the sparse light in the room. Gradually she began to regain consciousness. The sun's heat had made her dizzy. Only then did she realise how heavy the schoolbag on her back was, so she took it off and put it down on the ground for the last time. Goodbye!

She got up to take off her school uniform and then headed to the sewing machine in the living room; from under its cover she fished out a pair of scissors. Of course her stepmother pounced, asking what she needed the scissors for. She didn't answer. This creature didn't seem to understand that she didn't want to talk to her, ever. She proceeded to shear her school trousers, thus severing all her ties with the educational system and confirming the impossibility of a return to it.

She cut them just up to the knees so as to stop people from opening their mouths, even though she knew they would anyway. But what mattered was her father. She ate some of her stepmother's bland food for lunch, then went out. And she heard it; every letter rang in her ears:

'Slut.'

And such a word could only confirm that it was she, her stepmother, who was the slut. But there is no justice in this world. She didn't feel like going back to squabble with her. That would spoil her good mood and happiness at the disappearance of school from her world at last.

She headed across the courtyard towards her father, who was sitting under the almond tree, staring at her legs from a distance. As she reached him, his voice was barely audible from beneath his moustache:

'What are these trousers?'

'They're up to my knees,' she replied indifferently.

And he echoed:

'To your knees, eh?!'

And after maybe a moment or two:

'You really are your mother's daughter!'

She found herself answering:

'And possibly my father's.'

Instantly his slipper flew through the air towards her head and struck it; for a few moments all she could feel was the spot it hit.

'Oh, you slut!' he continued.

She turned back and retraced her steps, with her father's slipper still throbbing in her head. His orders trailed after her:

'Tomorrow you are to wake up early and open the post office. Don't think that just because you've quit school you'll laze in bed till noon.'

One day, God willing, she would shoot him and his wife with that very same gun that he carried behind his back. She would not take off the trousers, even over her dead body. And let *him* handle the mail every day!

She went into the bathroom, then stood in front of the mirror combing her hair and reconsidering her situation: well, the mail, the mail, so be it! The important thing was that she was done with school, and likewise with doing housework.

Her only problem in life now was her frizzy hair.

She brought with her into the bathroom what was formerly a box of chocolates and now held all those things that her mother had left behind. From among these she fished out a dozen black hairpins and pulled them all from the piece of cardboard to which they'd been attached for so many years. She set them down in front of her and, for a moment, a beautiful soft jangling, coming from the collision of the pins with one another and with the edge of the mirror where she had poured them out, merged with the darkness around her.

She resumed brushing her hair after parting it to the left, then began to push the hairpins in, wrapping the hair around her scalp

from left to right, separating each pin from the next by a distance of
three fingers. After finishing, she covered it with a headscarf, then
went back into her and her siblings' bedroom, laid her head on the
pillow and fell asleep.

And as she was sinking into a deep afternoon slumber, the pillow
under her started to moisten slowly but surely due to her wet hair
and the sweat dripping from her face in the heat of the day, which
was only intensified by the horrible dreams induced by her father and
stepmother's hurtful words.

After about two hours she woke up for a few moments, during
which she remained in bed, feeling an intense grogginess and heaviness in her head as the voices of the characters from some television
serial echoed through the emptiness of the house. Then she went
back to sleep until the morning.

In the morning she undid the headscarf and removed the pins
from her hair. To her delight her hair was smooth. She looked pretty
enough. But she fastened the pins back over her hair and wrapped
it with the scarf once again, since she didn't want to ruin her beauty
in vain.

She poured a glass of tea for herself and drank it standing in front
of the kitchen sink while her siblings sat behind her, eating breakfast
next to her stepmother, who was polluting the morning air with her
breath and her words. After she had finished and put the empty glass
in the sink, she picked up the post office keys from the peg and went
downstairs.

The moment she opened the door she was hit by a draft of cold air
that made goose pimples crawl over her arms, while the light seeping
in from behind her through the opening gradually revealed, for the
millionth time, the contents of the office. But since from now on she
would work among these contents and would be beside them every
day, she looked at them differently and deliberately this time. A faded
white fan was affixed to the wall on her right, and below it a large
board that elaborately detailed the postal rates according to weight
and distance. There was no need though to continue reading it down
until the end; the first column on the left was more than enough,

since all that the people of the neighbourhood sent were domestic letters weighing less than 50 grams. Yes indeed, a wave of hobbies of letter-writing, horse-riding and swimming would occasionally arise, but since horses were few and swimming pools non-existent, only letter-writing remained a possibility. So one of them would send a letter or two abroad during his whole lifetime; or, to be precise, in the period between ninth and twelfth grade when he or she was finally able to write a letter in English, after long years of studying the language.

And their hearts were all searching for a rich old woman from Europe or America who would adopt them and rescue them from life in the country, which was considered monotonous to the point of being fatal. They were all fantasies … without which they wouldn't be able to complete even one assignment of English or geography homework. Then everything would collapse and it would become clear through the influence of the family that such dreams were illusory, so the hobby of correspondence would cease and they would move on to the next fantasy: marriage. At which point they would start to practise the hobby of hunting: for a composed young woman who did not laugh and looked neither left nor right. And together, hand in hand, he and his prey would begin the eternal journey of boredom, whose ordained path did not include the need for a means of communication embodied in the postal system. And it was the responsibilities and duties enjoined by the operation of this postal system that, from today, fell on Afaf's shoulders.

Near the wall on the right stood an enormous purple plastic bucket that served as a wastebasket, and above it was a grey public telephone. In the middle of the room there stretched a long, dark, wooden counter that was practically 'the post office'. And on it were placed some of the necessary implements: an ink pen on the end of a long string tied to a nail that was hammered into the inside of the counter and a small box made from a piece of carved wood and filled with water, inside of which was a broad cylindrical seal used for sticking stamps. Afaf wouldn't use it as she preferred to use her own spit.

As for the inner portion of the counter, it concealed another world. On it was a second shelf where there lay a spy's logbook, one for receipts and a folder for stamps, all of which were hidden from the eyes of the senders. And behind the shelf there was a revolving chair.

The atmosphere of the place was completed by a large wall clock. In its centre was a caption indicating that it was a gift from a well-known car insurance company. To the left of the clock hung a dirty, tattered Israeli flag, beneath which was a picture of the head of state that was not as dusty as the flag, since they were forced to change it now and then due to democracy.

Afaf pulled out the chair and sat down to receive customers who did not arrive.

More than three months had passed since she had started working in the post office and her suffering had neither worsened nor lessened, since she had completely surrendered to her fate from the very first day. Her main duty in the post office was to open and read the letters and, after that, to report their contents to her father. So, there was someone from the neighbourhood living in America who would sometimes send letters to his family and address them to 'Palestine'. It was Afaf's duty to cross out that word and write 'Israel' instead. Other than that, none of the letters contained anything at all that could possibly undermine state security, not even interesting news that could amuse Afaf. It was therefore normal for the inhabitants of the neighbourhood to receive their letters opened. Except that with Afaf's arrival, there were some new developments: letters arrived with words crossed out, which provoked a number of disputes between her and the addressees. The prevailing belief was that what was crossed out was a sentence mentioning something enclosed in the letter, such as a gift from the sender that Afaf had decided to confiscate after it caught her fancy.

Likewise, for the first time since the entry of the postal authority into the neighbourhood, something else emerged, only in her tenure: some scrawling on the wooden counter that her hand, seized by boredom, had engraved with the help of the mailroom key. And from among them appeared the following inscriptions: 'Afaf'; a dagger with three drops of blood dripping from it; '9-8-71', her birthday; '9-13-81', her mother's 'date'; '6-31-87', the date she quit school; and a heart penetrated by an arrow coming out of a point that began with the letter 'ayn for Afaf and ended in a question mark.

This question mark could only have one solution and that was that she would never have the good fortune of a love story. She would get married for sure, because her father's arm stretched very far indeed and would surely reach under the earth to bring out a bridegroom for her sooner or later, most likely between now and then – that is, before she became an old maid and after he had exploited her a little more in the postal service.

Afaf tried to picture conjugal life and the housework that she would get saddled with once again – the housework she was currently relieved of. Maybe she could be happy, but it seemed impossible. If her entire life was a pile of shit, then her luck would never change nor could she become happy in the blink of an eye. What would change? The bridegroom, a stranger, would certainly not be more loving or affectionate towards her than her parents! Then she sighed. Her mother used to sigh frequently, generating a melody and rhythm that she liked very much.

Sometimes Afaf found herself missing her mother in spite of all that the latter had done.

She did not know where her mother was now or what she was up to, nor did she know how and why everything had happened. One day in fourth grade, only a few days after the first term had begun, she and her siblings woke up to find that neither the tea nor the breakfast was ready. So she went looking for her mother in her parents' bedroom, but found it empty. She searched the whole house and didn't find her. However long she went on searching and wandering through it, it made no difference. Maybe she was in the backyard? She decided to go and search for her there – sometimes she could be found there. She encountered her aunt on the steps outside, and before she even opened her mouth, her aunt said to her contemptuously:

'Not a word. Make your siblings breakfast and go to school.'

From the afternoon of that day, 13 September 1981, while she and her siblings sat around the table eating lunch, her father proclaimed from under his moustache, as his right hand gripped the gun and his left dangled empty except for a few streaks drawn on it by the light coming from the kitchen window, that it was forbidden for any of them to utter the word 'Mum' or to ask about her. What became clear to Afaf after she had secretly gathered fragments of people's gossip had made that day the longest of her life. Or rather, it stretched out to become her whole life, transforming it into a never-ending scandal and a heap of shit that would never stop growing: her mother had run off with another man.

Suddenly Afaf heard the sound of a dove's wings flapping; it was standing at the post office door. It distracted her from these harsh memories; she wondered what a dove could possibly be doing in a dark, desolate place like this.

Afaf meshed her fingers together and with her palms began to feel out the pins fastened in her hair, casting a fleeting glance at the clock on the wall behind her as she did so. It was approaching ten o'clock. Approximately twenty minutes of utter boredom lay before her, after which time the advent of the letters would return a semblance of life to her.

Translated by Suneela Mubayi

from the novel

Frankenstein in Baghdad

Ahmad Saadawi

Today he added the final piece to the hybrid body lying on the roof. It was missing a nose, that soft-fleshed lump which is the first to succumb in late-night brawls down alleyways. It falls quickly to knives and razors drawn suddenly in each other's faces by drunks. The nose melts as if made only of wax, and beauty fades with every heat wave brought on by a fire or an explosion. This is why it was difficult for him to find an intact nose. He did not want to snatch any of the faces that were offered before him or that he had jumped on during their final moments on the pavement. He wanted a single nose, alone and neglected, that no one else wanted. This is what made his mission so difficult.

The corpse was rotting. And if it wasn't for the nocturnal chill on the rooftop, he would have lost it a long time ago; it was rotting nonetheless, as if with the odour, born out of the wrinkled flesh and skin folds that he had so skilfully sewn together, it was reprimanding him and ordering him to finish what he had started.

Today he found it: a great nose with two wide nostrils. He raced with the firemen, who were washing away the blood and corpses' remains, and snatched the nose off the pavement before the water hose pushed it into the gutter.

We could mock him, or phone the police to inform them of his whereabouts. But he did not steal anything from anyone. He only took what was discarded like garbage, which is what he usually does anyway, gathering others' refuse off pavements and from garbage dumps then selling them on to antique and scrap dealers. What drives him to pick up corpses' remains may just be an extension of his appreciation for human waste. But the essence is the same; he collects trash so that collectively it may be turned into something useful. But what use is there in another corpse? What's the use of that stranger's naked cadaver lying on the rooftop? Why did he not leave him scattered about on the pavements and the streets?

He does not have an answer to this at the moment. He is confused and he is mad, as his mother before her death used to tell Umm Daniel, her Ashurian neighbour. And as Umm Daniel herself, along with all the other neighbours, thought, those neighbours of the ruined alley in the Bataween quarter of Baghdad, that alley that has been awaiting God's wrath for a very long time, according to Umm Daniel. So now he does not fear the pursuit of the police or the discovery of the strange corpse in his house. Because he is mad, and he would like to remain so; he laughs within to think that none of the neighbours would believe he had such great skill in needlework, patchwork, and merging disparate parts. No one would believe – and this was comforting – that he had made, of his own volition, an intact corpse out of the remains of the dead from the 'Aviation Square' and the 'Eastern Gate'.

Now he has an intact corpse on the rooftop lying between canvas bags filled with Pepsi cans; and he carries another half-full bag on his back as he walks back along the pavement from Andalous Square, where he takes the arak bottle from Edward's shop, the boiled *baklaa* from Yasser Elsafiry's cart and his dinner from the liver and kidney vendor whose name he does not know. His thoughts are scattered, watching the cars' lights rush by into the darkness and the cold, as he passes by the hotel Sadir Novotel. He usually walks on the other side of the street to avoid the warnings of the anxious-looking security guards. He does this purposely because he's always carrying a big suspicious-looking bag on his back. Many people have blown up bags similar to his in front of shops and hotels and government buildings. But tonight he is tipsy; he is only concerned with his footsteps as he crosses over water stains and garbage. The guard gets up from his place behind the wooden cabin at the wide entrance to the hotel and comes towards him. He looks at his dirty appearance, and for the very brief moment as he passes slowly by the front of the wide iron gates he notices the boredom on the guard's face.

Then, because of the bad luck that he believes is his lot, a municipal garbage truck drove by and splashed his trousers with rainwater as it quickly headed towards the hotel entrance about fifty metres behind him. This was not the only ghastly occurrence that evening.

The pressure of the sound of the explosion in his head pushed him a few metres into the air and he lost his canvas bag, his dinner and the bottle of drink. He twirled in the air, feeling stoned and dizzy, feeling that he had died and that finally the boredom he felt had passed.

He was contemplating the next step, although he does not usually contemplate much. So this was a strange state to be in. He let the drink weigh heavily on his head as the cold night air slapped his face over the rooftop, which then hurled him into doing something that occurred to him intuitively. He did many things in response to that intuition. Life had progressed in a good way, without having much to contemplate, until that rotten corpse appeared. He was a scrap vendor. He was a collector of empty bottles, plastic containers and wood from the remnants of furniture, among other things. And even though he sold all these at the end of the day, he believed they stayed in his head, never abandoning him. His head was full of this heavy pile of scrap weighing on his senses, but then the alcohol took its effect and the pile dispersed like startled butterflies.

He kicked the corpse with his plastic shoes, as if he now realised that it was impure. He turned it over with a fierce boot so that it bowed over, singly intact, on its face; the result of his six days of work was good, very skilful; all the parts, despite their number, were bound together so that when he turned the corpse over on its back once again, it seemed that the dusty nose rose smugly into the night air that it was unable to inhale.

He tried to think about the next step, but the matter seemed to perplex his confused head, which was weighed down already by the pile of mounting scrap; or maybe the confusion was due to the many small bruises that he had sustained all over his body, including his head, earlier on this evening near the Sadir Novotel. He was warming his hands over the gas fire as the cries of the wind accelerated over the decaying building and the palm leaves swished between the rooftops of the neighbouring houses. As he opened the bottle of bootleg drink in his attic room, the cold worsened, stripping everything outside and then attacking from under the doorsill, mocking the weakening flame of the old fireplace. He drank and cursed Abou Selima, who sells these bootleg drinks at his house at the end of the alley.

He said to himself: 'I will toss the corpse from the rooftop into the alley at night and no one will know that it was at my place and in my possession, and no one will know who did this terrible and mad deed. No one will question the identity of the deceased, because he is the only one here, among the living and the dead of the neighbourhood, who has no identity. They will inform the police, who will come in their squad cars. Two policemen will step out of their car with white plastic bags; they will raise the corpse slowly and wearily and fling it into the back of the car. The corpse will then remain in the morgue for a while. And when no one comes to claim it, it will be buried in the capital cemetery with a small post indicating that it is anonymous.'

He had his last drink of the night and his insides began to rumble, which may have been due to some parasites, or maybe the boiled *bakla'a* was spoiled or the drink ill-brewed. He stood in front of the washbasin by the window and peed before preparing to go to sleep. He looked towards the dirty moonlit rooftop that hadn't been swept since his mother died. The corpse was sitting, gazing over at the far corner of the roof. It seemed as if it was really gazing into the room. Its back clearly straight, like the back of an energetic man who had awoken from a satisfying sleep. But why does this mad monster wake up at three in the morning?

In the morning, he found him kneeling and gathered up in a foetal position, as if he had suffered the consequences of a chilly night. He ignored him as he locked the steel door of the roof and started down the staircase leading directly to the alley. His footsteps were agonised, and his head weighed heavily from the effect of nightmares and the burden of sins, as if the previous night was some kind of punishment for his terrible deed. 'It is best to toss this corpse far away, so that I do not have to have cars blow up in front of me and behind me all the time,' he said to himself as he was confronted by the cold breeze in the public street.

He wanted to go to the other side of the capital, to collect tin pop cans from the dumps of the residential neighbourhoods. But the sky remained frozen with dark clouds foreboding heavy rains at midday, and he felt a terrible hunger and a pain in his joints, so he went into Aziz El Masry's coffee shop located behind the 'Stars' photographer near the Eastern Gate. There he had his breakfast and listened to Helal the Sudanese watch repairman as he laughed at a fellow Sudanese who had gone mad and blown himself up the night before in front of Sadir Novotel. He blew up the garbage truck full of dynamite that he was driving, which resulted in a hole six metres deep.

'If he had taken some arak and drunk it with a whore, would it not have been a more honourable thing?'

Helal the Sudanese man was retelling the climax of the story while attempting not to speak with a Sudanese accent, so that the words that came out of his mouth sounded contrived, the accent unlike any other. There was only one person in the coffee shop not laughing at the tale, or at Helal's strange accent, a person who kept eating his breakfast and did not want to listen to the funny side of the story, had no desire to tell its dark side because he had witnessed it close at hand. He stared at the wide dirty coffee-shop windows and noticed that a heavy downpour had begun suddenly, so that as he left the coffee shop he headed directly towards his attic room at the top of the Meazeyat house with the empty canvas bag folded under his arm. He did not think about work today, he felt he wanted to immerse himself in sleep for the rest of the morning.

When he climbed the metal stairs and opened the door, the rooftop was empty and wet with rain. The corpse wasn't where he had left it, and a multitude of ideas struck him all at once: maybe one of the sons of bitches crossed over from the neighbouring roofs and took the corpse. Maybe the police came at last, in response to a report from the neighbours, and transported the corpse to the forensic office. Maybe Umm Daniel called for help when she saw the corpse while she was hanging out the clothes to dry on the rooftop and thought it may have been me there.

As senile as she was, Umm Daniel wouldn't have hung clothes out to dry on a cloudy, rainy day. All these thoughts entered his head rapidly while he walked in long strides on the wet rooftop towards the door of his room.

Translated by Anne Shaker

eight poems from

The Utopia of Cemeteries

Ahmad Yamani

I

Unpainted walls,
stone-filled ground
fragile bones not even able to stand
and my bones are stuck in the middle
I am thinking of a small demonstration
to protest against the angels
who deprived us of the necessary calcium
God is above the ditch extending His shadow over us
and letting us sleep late
A drop of light falls from His hands
A darkened body enters
The drop dries
and we get to know our new colleague
with an open heart
He gives us cigarettes with extra generosity
We like His voice when He mutters:
'What the hell is happening here?'

4

Nobody heard
the cries we emitted close to sunrise
The sound of dogs outside
makes us feel friendliness
We crawl so that our bones touch
and we love one another even more
Each one speaks of his black childhood
We exchange laughter
We have no clock on the wall
to know when the end of time is

5

Mother
please
do not cry
when you know that I have entered my new home
because I want to save your eyes for coming days
Be calm
and shake your head thrice
Blow a kiss
and I will roar with my friends here
as they congratulate me on my new house
I will leave the door ajar
waiting for your kiss
And when you have a new house like me
please let it be nearby
so I can hear your breaths
breathe almost without pain
and my death has that final image
I worked so hard to make

6

In the room next to us
which is only separated by a curtain
women lie after taking off their shrouds
still very white
After many desperate attempts we managed
to prise a hole in the separation wall
Our bones stood all of a sudden
when we saw the first woman taking off her clothes
and putting them in the corner
On this night
we tried to tear the curtain
but it became more solid
So we resigned ourselves
to gazing at white bones
which are still far away
even now

8

They shut the place well
and threw the keys into the ditch
Why do you leave us at the edges of cities?
We have to be together
when the rains fall
to sing under them
We can talk about carriages
which took us on long roads
and returned without us
But the tears gathered in them
were enough to wet our bones
We did not find matches for heat

and when one of us snuck out to steal matches
we lit the cemetery
and it lit half of the world's cemeteries for three days
Then the gravedigger threw up
and we passed by in an orderly line
all singing about the flies
sleeping in our ears
about our height which excited teenage girls
and repeated masturbation
in a huge barrel they call life

Funeral

Chimo died this morning
Chimo is not my friend, but he died
He used to talk non-stop as if paying an old debt to words
which were about to abandon him
Tomorrow I will put on my black coat and go to the funeral
When I come back home I will smile to myself
Today Chimo, one of my acquaintances, died
and I am no longer a stranger in this country

Five O'Clock

No crow, fly or birds perch on the window. A withering flower, which fell from the upper floor, perches on the window. It will stay on the table all evening. I gaze at it under the light, which makes eyes bleed. There is a Klimt on the wall in which joyous colourful life wilts before the messenger of death who looks pompously at the piled boiling bodies, heads bowed. They are dead even before the angel stabs his spear. I put the flower in the space between the angel's skeleton and the colourful creatures, but the flower is annoyed and fails at being a bridge. Wasn't it withering too? I move it to the empty eye in the angel's head and it sits more comfortably there. But the flower wasn't created to fill empty eyes. The flower was created to fill the upper floor balcony, but it's dead. The truth is that it came down to me because it died. To my window, where no crow, fly or birds perch.

The Red Notebook

I used to pass my long night as a novice factory guard by reading as much as I could for the night to end. A tiny book by Paul Auster, *The Red Notebook*, told of realistic coincidences, and did not view coincidence as being blind at all. I moved from one coincidence to another until I came across this one: as a young man, Paul Auster worked, together with his girlfriend, as a temporary guard for a house in the countryside in southern France, in return for room and board. I hastily looked for a piece of paper to write this note down and consoled myself that working as a guard was not all that bad. I was looking for any discarded paper, and there it was lying on the desk in the control room: the little red notebook.

Translated by Sinan Antoon

Coexistence

Ala Hlehel

I must speak to him. It can't be put off any longer, even if he doesn't know me or has never heard of me. I'll call him and say: 'I'm doing the talking here, and I want X, Y and Z from you!' Just like that, with candour and without equivocation. If he struggles to speak or refuses to, then I'll change tack. I'll say to him: 'Listen, we're Arabs; we understand one another. All I'm asking of you is X, Y and Z; that's all.' I'm sure he'll listen, because he's supposedly a heroic and coura-geous leader who listens to his fellow men. And I'm Palestinian – he'll listen to me for sure. And if he doesn't, then when that happens I'll be within my rights to say: 'So why is that, may I ask?'

Essentially, all I'm asking him to do is to keep away from here. Nothing difficult to understand about that. He can target his lava flows towards Al Khadira, Afula and Netanya. What's wrong with those towns? Get lost, mate. Why does it have to be Haifa? Haifa's full of Arabs. They're everywhere: in the cafés, the bars, the mosques, the churches, the streets, on the buses . . . The buses! The buses are full of Arabs, pal – they're teeming with them, overflowing with them, pullulating with them. And the Arabs are poor and the stal-wart bus passengers are always poor. And the poor are the ones who are forced to eat shit in the Jewish state and, throughout history, the first to feel resentment. Or they eat, and nothing sweet enters their mouths to take the taste away. I'll say that to him, and he'll under-stand me for sure. He's bound to. For I'm a Palestinian like him, and every Palestinian is another's support, strength and stay. We're all in the same boat and we all grow on the same tree.

Yes, we're all Palestinian, in spite of our different tastes, philosophies and geographical connections. We're all like the woman who buys two ties for her husband as a birthday present; the next day he has to pick one of them to wear and she, taken aback, will invariably say to him, 'Why have you got that one on? Didn't you like the other one?', leaving him at a loss as to what to think or, for that matter, to feel or say!

In a way, now that I consider it, maybe it would be more proper to send him a letter than to phone him. It could turn out that the phones are tapped or that his aide will tell me that he doesn't speak on the phone to make it harder for them to work out where he is. But I reckon they know where he lives. It's not hard to find out. Having said that, it could be that he doesn't stay in his house, or constantly moves around from place to place in order to avoid risking detection. I settled on that idea and on what it entailed.

The upshot was that I made the decision to write him a letter. I got out my yellow jotter and the black pen to which I'm most attached, and wrote: 'Most Respected General . . .' by way of salutation and so on.

Re: I HATE THE OPERATIONS IN HAIFA

I have no doubt that you are aware, sir, that there are more than 35,000 Arabs living in Haifa. And I also have no doubt that you know that the young Palestinian men whom you dispatch to blow up the streets in the Jewish State blow themselves up in Haifa on occasion.

Dearest General, I implore you not to question the depth of my national feeling or my fidelity to the cause. I am a committed Palestinian of unparalleled zeal. However, would it be overstepping the mark to request your good self not to send men to Haifa? It is not because I fear for my own life, believe me. It is only that I do not like all the talk that ensues afterwards concerning the 'coexistence' of Jews and Arabs in Haifa. I hate that as much as I hate the sea and its smell. I urge you not to misunderstand me. I wish you all the best and extend my thanks to you . . .'

I read the letter closely. I was surprised at the bit where it said 'of unparalleled zeal' because I'd used the Arabic word *hamas* there, albeit it in a different context, but it must have had an unconscious effect on me because it's also the name of his organisation and his darling. I read the letter for a third time. Carefully. I don't know if I should retain the issue of my hating the sea and its smell. Our general is from Gaza and, unlike me, he may be enamoured of the sea and the coast generally; I'm the yokel who remains aloof, son of the mountains, valleys and hills, deprived of any funds. To be honest, I don't want to get caught up in the whirlpool of eternal infighting between the coastal people and the mountain folk. It's unnecessary nowadays and does nobody any good. No good whatsoever. All that I want here is for him to accord my request its due importance and to regard it with a sympathetic eye. So I'll cross out the matter of the sea.

I read the letter for the fourth time. Carefully. Maybe I could do without the part which says, 'the young Palestinian men whom you dispatch to blow up streets in the Jewish State'. He might see in it a value judgement and a criticism of him and his movement. And that would no doubt create unwanted and uncommendable tension here. What's it got to do with me whether they're the ones sending forth these young men or if it's the young men themselves who are begging to be the next in line to go to Paradise? It's absolutely nothing to do with me. It's true that I'm a Palestinian, but I live in Haifa and don't know about the different standpoints and the inevitable build-up of varying speculations that my brothers in the Occupied Territories have to concern themselves with. Only the wearer knows where the shoe pinches. And I've never walked a mile in their shoes. So I told myself I'd cross out that part, and did so.

Then I read the letter for the fifth time. I was nearly fully satisfied with what I had written, but then I felt it only right to retract the bit which said, 'I urge you not to misunderstand me', because it might be taken as an admonishment that his intellect was incapable of grasping what I was saying, which would be terrible in a first-time correspondence between two Palestinians. So I struck out that part and saw that what I had made was indeed good, and I still wasn't happy. I decided to read the letter for a sixth time. Haste is from the

place on the bus that goes to the university and my brother was on the
bus that goes to the university.

Distraught, I rushed out into the street, and she had only been
proven right: I was indeed an ass. If only I had been won over by her
constantly urging me to purchase a mobile phone, I wouldn't have
been running at that point down the street like an idiot looking for a
stupid public telephone to carry me down the stupid telephone lines
to the warm embrace of my brother's voice. Wearied from the search,
I put my trust in my Maker and decided to go back to the restaurant.
I sat down and the restaurant owner came up and said 'Coffee?' I said:
'The bill.' She said such and such and I complained to her about this
and that to do with my shekels and then I made my way up towards
my house, situated right at the bottom of Mount Carmel. In the house,
I found my brother; no one had laid a finger on him.

'Thank God you didn't get bloodied today', I said.

And he said, 'Thank God you didn't either'.

We relaxed and sat down to watch blood fall, blood on blood.
Then he said, 'The Hebrew newspaper's been in touch with you.
They want to ask you about the effect this operation will have on the
coexistence of Arabs and Jews in Haifa.'

I replied, 'Tell them to beware my hunger . . . and my anger!'

I sighed over my dish of hummus and beans, which I had almost
finished by then, and I recited to that old puddle of green oil the
words of the poet:

You I remembered when lances drank my blood and Indian
    blades dripped therewith,
I longed to kiss those swords because they glittered like the
    sparkle of your tooth when you smile.

Translated by Tristan Cranfield

Three Poems

Bassim al Ansar

An Outing

for Kasper Thomsen

On the path to the sea I saw
boys bearing Ishtar in a wooden litter,
a statue of Rimbaud clasped in her arms.
I saw children chew autumn leaves
and fingertips make fire from the canal waters.
Zeico! Zeico! The sea is there . . .
Listening to the music of the roadside weeds
brought to mind the music of the land that crucified me.
Watching Godot carry his lantern through the woods
I recalled the captain borne back a century by the storm.
The waves send me the words of Ulysses,
for me, the foxes filch the pages of the sea.
Let us go to the lighthouse and ask it for news of the sunken ships,
let us go to the village and ask after the storyteller seared by winter.
Zeico! Zeico! The sea is there . . .
I saw trees send their fragrance to the house alone in the woods
and the hills smile down at wagons trailing after the bodies of
    gazelles.
I saw the monk speak to vultures of the land delivered by God's hand
and the road's weeds applaud the footsteps of Paradise's fugitives.
Here are the radiant souls, leaving their war with virtue,

and here, the bells of the new temple, pealing with joy for their prophet.
I store my phantoms in a lonely house, I can do nothing else,
nothing else save sing in the woods of the wondrous day.
Zeico! Zeico! The sea is there . . .
They say that the rains of autumn have burnt up the anthems,
that the wind toyed with the fallen tree, alone beyond the fields.
I never saw the train departing towards the sun,
nor heard the sound of water falling from a countrywoman's palm!
I saw one of them flip the Joker's picture between his palms as he
    flew through the air,
and another sitting beneath a dead tree weaving a cloak from winter
    leaves.
I saw the rising steam from coffee cups sketch forgotten dreams
and the fingers of café patrons rap out the countryside's melody on
    tabletops.
Who will send us news of the wagon that comes from the sun?
Who will tell us when the circus caravans are here?
Zeico! Zeico! The sea is there . . .
I watched bullets dropping from hearts,
birds circling eyes.
I caught the scent of thoughts sown in emptiness,
inhaled the odour of rains slumbering in prisons.
I remembered the guitar abandoned in the desert,
remembered those journeying towards the caves in search of candles.
Ah!
The sunset starts to seep from the road's pores,
the swamps eat at the skyline.
Zeico! Zeico! My tender hound: let us return; the sea is there no
    more.

A Life Surrounded by Trees

There it is, your time, tumbling down a mountain of ice,
and here am I, watching you forge towards days of faith.
There they are, your desires, honey-hued in caves,
and here am I, watching as you bed down with ancient pain.
You wanted to weep for the past,
to keen for the time to come:
you sought to sweep up autumn and eternity in a single embrace.
You've yet to draw up to the poets' convoy,
you've been chasing after dead stories, nothing more.
I told you to walk with me towards fleeting dreams,
not to set out alone after eternal creeds.
You dreamt of stuffing green grass into bags
yet you filled the room with the colour of the sky.
Remember that you and pleasure are twins;
remember that the sky never sleeps beneath your desires;
remember that your life is surrounded by trees.
I hoped you would wage war on taboos
but you rained down theories on my head.
I hoped you'd stand defiant in the face of eternity
but you scarred my soul with antique melody.
I looked on as you entered the uprising through its red doorway
though you'd sworn you would go in through the white.
The coming dawn: why do you say farewell?
Why do you welcome me, evening?
When I had not seen you for a long while, I knocked cautiously on
    your door; knocked until my heart
hung from a strange nail,
and when I saw the postman pass by without a glance towards your
    life, the trees gently enfolded me.

A Panorama of Wonder

Ah!
Boys peek at widows through holes in the day
and men lick fortune-tellers' palms.
Ah!
The soldiers eat their rifles
and street vendors bear stars above their carts.
Ah!
Into the mirror steps the silver lady and gathers mist into sacks.
Ah!
The devil fashions butterflies from dust
and around the tower the serpent coils, the infant choking in his mouth.
Ah!
I see war frolicking around our houses.
Ah!
I see war, creation of those that war, and the blood of thought.
Ah!
With the watcher I see eternity through the old tavern window.
Ah!
My mother buys a handful of years from the alley bakery.
Ah!
My siblings entomb their souls in identity.
Ah!
With a knife my father cuts off the head of war and, desire spent,
    makes his way towards death.
Ah!
I see five roses on the pavement and in their side a blood-spattered
    dagger.
Ah!
I see a child go out from the graveyard, singing a cryptic song.
Ah!
His song at an end, he vanishes from sight.
Ah!

Translated by Robin Moger

Two Stories

Dima Wannous

Hanan

Whenever her name was mentioned, smiles concealing a secret knowledge appeared on faces, and eyes shone, winking. She was Hanan. Attractive Hanan, with hazel eyes and an upturned Russian nose, red-lipped, tall, full-bodied, with long chestnut hair.

Hanan, who treated everyone with the same warmth and intimacy. She loved bustle and noise. She abhorred rituals and religious rites. Her husband took an entire hour in the morning to drink a cup of coffee and smoke four cigarettes while listening to Fairuz singing behind the walls. Hanan hated that morning ritual. She woke up at ten, drinking coffee and smoking a quick cigarette, tuning the radio dial for a loud song, then humming along with the tune to begin her day, which resembled all the others. Osama worked from home, and rarely went out in the morning. He read the three official papers that arrived at dawn, focusing on their headlines and contemplating the subjects of their editorials before writing his article and sending it to the newspaper. Hanan did not care for global affairs and didn't read the papers, but she always said that she preferred *as-Safir* and *al-Hayat* because the poor quality paper of the Syrian papers scratched the glass, and their cheap ink only made the glass more streaked. Also, the crosswords in Syrian newspapers were uneven and repetitive, and only made her more ignorant.

This day seemed like all the rest. The sun, as usual, had spread its rays and latched on to the horizon from the east, clambering over it slowly before being snatched up by the summer sky and thrown right into the middle of the page.

Yes, this morning was like all the others. All the mornings since the first living being had appeared on earth. The birds flocked out of their nests, announcing the start of the new day. And the retired, well-off men emerged on to the streets in scary numbers to practise morning sports in the hope that they would lose some of the weight that time had carefully implanted on their bodies.

Without a doubt, this morning was like all other Damascene July mornings. The windows of houses exhausted from long nights were not yet open. The cars selling propane and fruit and vegetables and tissues were not yet bored of honking on the lonely early morning streets, oblivious to the women leaning out of windows to flag them down to buy gas or haggle over the price of potatoes, which just kept rising constantly, shamelessly.

Speaking of shame, this morning had begun just like all the other humid Damascus mornings. But from this moment, it was no longer so. Hanan, unusually, had left her bed at 7. She did not even glance at Osama, sleeping like a child beside her. Normally, Osama's body would not even show in their large bed. His small, thin frame would curl so tightly under the quilt that it would merely look like a fold in it. But when a thin frame sleeps so deeply, it turns into a lifeless corpse.

The morning was still normal up until then, because the deeply-sleeping Osama didn't know that Hanan had left their bed so early.

Unusually, Hanan snuck out of bed at precisely 7 a.m. She walked slowly, deliberately refraining from waking Osama. She opened the balcony door. She breathed in the morning air that God prepared in a good mood when he woke up each day. She went into the kitchen and poured some water into the copper coffee pot. She loved the smell of rust. She turned the gas on. The water boiled. She added two teaspoons of bronze coffee ground with cardamom. The foam began to rise on the surface until Hanan could no longer see her face in it. She took down her favourite coffee cup, the first ever detail to have brought out an appreciation for ritual in her. That cup had become part of her coffee ritual. She went out on the balcony facing the Kasyoun Mountain to be close to him. Close to his mornings, which usually began at 7.15.

She sat on the wicker chair and began to think of those details, savouring them one by one. She loved one detail more than the next, so she
would imagine him – and it – again. Her left hand held the coffee cup
while the finger of her right hand circled the rim slowly, as if it were
an integral part of the delicate structure of the glass. She touched its rim
with exquisite pleasure. She thought that she loved him. She would
die if she could no longer see him. She recalled the details of his face,
and the cup in those moments became those details. She caressed its
rim, as if she were caressing the specific con tours of his face. His wide
forehead. Then, a bit lower, touching his frowning, magical eyebrows,
sliding her fingers down a little further until she reached his long, sweet
nose, then dropping her hand in fear and landing on his lips, chapped
from biting her so often. There, right at the space between his lips, she
took a sip of coffee and a deep breath.

      Osama knows everything. But every time he decides to declare
his suffering and put a stop to Hanan's philandering, he remembers
her strong personality, her tiger eyes and confident voice. He's afraid
of confrontation. He's afraid of losing her, of losing the pleasure of
living with her. This way, at least, he lies down next to her each
night. He breathes in her scent and sleeps contentedly. Hanan is
nothing like him at all, but he has become addicted to her. Her bold
personality, striking initiative and ability to sneak into the lives of
others have helped Osama in his work and have protected him. Her
affair with Jaber made Osama the most prominent journalist at his
newspaper. Everyone is at his beck and call at work, and the editor-
in-chief consults him on every new decision or change, sometimes
even seeking his advice on his clothing or his relationship with his
wife (who has become as passive as a table since giving birth to their
sixth child), even on the best techniques for child-rearing.

      Suddenly, Hanan felt his scent wafting into her thin nostrils and fill-
ing her sinuses. It was not just a scent. She remembered that night they
were dancing, surrounded by a crowd of people dripping with sweat
and love. That night her nose was overcome by the aroma of countless
bodies, by the smell of their breath emerging moist and sweet from
their noses and mouths, collecting in the room's corners and inhabiting
them for ever. That night Hanan was able to distinguish his particular

scent, and she felt love bubbling in her veins, felt an intense security, felt for a moment that that was what grounded her spiritually and phys- ically in this strange, sometimes cruel, life. She inhaled, implanting the smell into her memory and the folds of her brain, becoming obsessed with it, revisiting it every morning. She was addicted, and could no longer control her desire to see him continually.

For Jaber was not like old, glutinous Qussay. And he was not like Jaafar Taha, who in time had just become a dirty mop to be used only in emergencies. And he was nothing at all like Issa Khudr, that retiree who wouldn't stop weeping over the ruins of his pride and glory, which had since been depleted. Jaber was something else. A young man, pulsating with vitality. His sand-coloured eyes hadn't lost their lustre. His attractiveness was rare, and idiosyncratic – he wasn't one of those familiar people, whose faces one stares at for hours while trying to remember where one had seen them before. His loud voice wasn't repulsive, and his hearty laugh wasn't fake. His complexion was halfway between dark chocolate and fresh milk, or roasted chest- nut, or maybe cinnamon. His cheeks were planted with a soft down, whose shadow, particularly in the dark, was captivating.

Hanan looked down from her balcony on to the old, narrow alley below, which was now considered to be historical, after Damascus's other streets had been paved over with pink and yellow stones that looked gaudy and cheap. Her alley had retained its black French marble cobblestone, which was revived with every rainfall, and from beneath which the smell of clay mixed with salty rainwater would be released. Hanan poured her body over the white balcony railing. She contem- plated her new car, parked near their building's entrance. The expen- sive new red car was at odds with the old French building, decorated with carvings of animal heads, lions, tigers and cunning foxes.

She remembered that night they were dancing, surrounded by a crowd of people dripping with sweat and love. That night Hanan had whispered in Jaber's ear, dewy with sweat and love. She said that she could no longer tolerate the lewd behaviour of curious cab drivers, or those who wrote daily reports about the opinions of downtrodden citizens, or even those old men who regained their youth in momen- tary bursts when they caught sight of a beautiful young woman. She would die of envy thinking of his spoilt wife. She whispered in his ear that she adored him, that he was different from all the other men she had slept with and that she had failed completely to erase the image of his body and the feel of his delicate fingers from her imagination, and that she wanted a car, just a car! What does a car mean to someone like you, Jaber? It won't affect your budget, won't cost you a thing, won't even dent the stacks of cash piled up in your safe.

That's how things always went, and Jaber was like Hatem al-Tai when compared with old Qussay al-Safi, whose enthusiasm was measured in mere rolls of thousands that Hanan would use to buy clothes, or artificial – sometimes real – jewellery. Jaafar Taha contented himself with giving her the expensive watches that he received as gifts, or golden Mont Blanc pens, and sometimes worry beads made from real pearls and studded with diamonds whose brilliance hurt the eyes. Issa Khudr was another story altogether. He bought Hanan cheap, tacky dresses whose fabric mimicked that of his ugly, vulgar suits, which were cut from thick, scratchy cloth. Only Jaber was astoundingly generous. Hanan and Osama's rent was paid for an entire year. Her closets were choked with the most beautiful, most expensive dresses. Her jewellery box pulsated with bright, shiny colours. Even her body had been spoiled, by the red car parked near the building and lovingly waiting for her.

Abu Alaa had called her last night. His voice was shaky with desire. He asked her to meet him in his office. Hanan didn't normally have a problem with satisfying such requests. Life, after all, consisted of these tiring, yet productive, affairs. Abu Alaa had met her at his friend Qussay al-Safi's house two years earlier, on 5 June. And since that meeting, Abu Alaa had lost his grip on his once-formidable strength and usually dominating power. Hanan began to decide the fate of his friends for him: isolate this one and get closer to that. She made him resent one and love the other. Abu Alaa submitted completely to her desires. But the situation was no longer what it was, because Abu Alaa was Jaber's sworn enemy. And, for the first time, Hanan found herself facing a difficult choice: Abu Alaa, that experienced sexagenarian whose friendship Hanan could use to extend her power and participate in decision-making, or beautiful Jaber, exciting Jaber, who was close and yet far, magical, strong and yet delicate, and a whole slew of other characteristics that she could not remember now. The choice seemed to be extremely difficult. Each of these men had his particular flavour, and each had his particular strength. Hanan mused that, at this early hour in the day, she should be doing nothing but staring at her new car and at that old alley paved with dreams. She should postpone her decision until night-time, when she was cuddled up in bed in the dark. Her kind husband, who curled up beside her like a housecat every night, would look at her face and thank God for bequeathing him this woman, so great and so devoted.

Jihad

The stones of the pavement are aligned, adjoining neatly, unlike those on other streets. An iron gate, its cruel steel covered by plants that had been climbing it for ages, twining themselves around the inner walls until they peeked over the top and on to the lives taking place outside. A thick black door, wide enough to fit any car. Behind the gate, a large garden, whose ancient trees had journeyed from Morocco and France before settling there. Its generous flowers responded to the gentlest touch by releasing their aroma. The verdant lawn was ingeniously watered so that all the grass grew at the same time, and not one blade was allowed to outgrow the rest. The front door to the house was made of a rare, precious wood. It protected their lives from the prying, envious eyes of passers-by. Those passers-by who envied those whom God had blessed with honest fortunes and with wealth that had poured down upon them and accumulated.

Directly behind the door was a large living room that exuded luxury and opulence. Its marble floors supported Italian furniture and gilded antiques. Naked statues stood proudly erect in its corners. Paintings – originals – hung on the wall in deliberate randomness; the painting that had a bit of red in it hung over the red couch, for example, and the yellow sofas sat beneath the painting of sunflowers, and so on. There were four tables, one in each corner of the living room, round oak tables that posed no threat to bumped heads. Plants, whose colours went from dark green to a yellowish green to deep autumnal red, were scattered about the room, and light streamed in from hidden crevices in the ceiling.

In a corner, underneath the araucaria tree where the light sneaked in between its leaves to draw delicate patterns on the white wall, sat Jihad, on his favourite painted wooden chair. His small side table, which he had brought back from India, stood at his feet, an ashtray on top. A thick cigar. Long matches and a cup of coffee. Jihad held a copy of *Beautiful Butush*, by the Turkish author Aziz Nesin in his left hand, leaving his right hand free to hold either the cup of coffee or the cigar between his thick fingers while mechanically tapping the ash into the long, rectangular ashtray made especially for cigars. That damned urge for excellence pushed him to read. It forced him to leaf through recently published books on politics, and novels, and plays and short stories, just so that he could tell his damned friends, who had nothing but cultural capital to brag about, that he, too, loved to read and shared their passion, and that they could not surpass him, not even with any habit or obsession. Maybe it wasn't so much of a desire as it was a complex that pricked his soul constantly and reminded him that he was Jihad Mustafa Agha, son of one of the most important former ministers, who had held his post for thirty years, and had become as famous and as sought-after as a movie star. If such people are in public places, people jump out of their seats to get an autograph or to get their picture taken with them, or merely to see their famous faces up close.

Jihad insists upon removing that image from the minds of all his acquaintances. But he just can't compete against the thirty years' worth of memories accumulated in their bloodstream. Particularly around the coronary area, where they make the heart beat faster with fear and contempt. Mustafa Agha has become like perfume, his name has only to be pronounced for a shudder to run through people's bodies and ruin their days. He is a legend in their minds; years passed, and Mustafa Agha remained sitting at his desk in the Ministry, without an earthly power able to budge him, not even an inch. People fell ill, died, emigrated and returned, and Mustafa Agha still sat at his usual place, waiting.

In that corner, the cigar smoke made a small cloud over Jihad's head like a beatific halo. Jihad continued reading, with enviable pleasure. But there was a problem. Every time Jihad succeeded in removing his wife's image from his mind, it would return again in the form of 'beautiful Butush'. He pictured her, coddling his guests and flirting with them. She spoke to them, humouring their literary, political, economic, astrological and sometimes emotional tastes. He had married her when she was fifteen. She was slim and soft; a child, whose only aim from marriage was to move away from her parents' home in Aleppo to her husband's in Damascus. She lived in his home. Her body opened up. Suddenly, she became a large woman. Her dark body filled out. Her frame was tall and attractive. Her eyes were blue. Her hair was coal-black, thick and soft.

Jihad was of average height. He was slim, but had a pot belly that could sustain him through several months' famine. He was light-skinned, almost red-headed. His soft face was filled with freckles. His hair was brown, thin and slightly wavy. His eyes were rather mean. His nose seemed like a detail, an accidental afterthought of God's, a small bulb that had been placed there in a hurry and might fall off at a moment's notice. His teeth were short and crowded in his mouth, as if he hadn't lost a single tooth since childhood, and his wisdom teeth had just always been there too and weren't going to budge for thirty years, voraciously chewing upon grace, making it digestible.

Jihad owned nothing but a large holding company, which included a textile factory and a meat processing plant, and another factory that made shoes, a fourth that made cardboard and a fifth that made paint. Those were the ones that were publicly declared. The undeclared holdings were a licence to produce a certain brand of Italian clothes, a huge depot for household goods – everything from flour to furniture – a car rental agency and an import agency for a French shoe company. These all made Jihad one of the most important investors in the national economy and a major contributor to raising the standard of living and employing domestic labour, and thus fighting unemployment.

In that corner, where the araucaria tree had begun to wilt from the cigar smoke, Jihad was still sunk into his book, as his wife's shadow danced before him on a stage, just like beautiful Butush. She leaned back provocatively, her breasts swaying and her thick hair brushing

the stage as drops of sweat fell on to the wood and evaporated immediately from the heat of her waist. Her waist moved with such an
incredible agility that it looked like it was separate from her body.

In the garden was a cloud that had rained the sweat of labour,
and that, so far, had produced five cars parked under an iron awning
covered by a neglected grapevine. A big car, with black tinted windows
that exhausted the eye and raised questioning eyebrows. A small one,
whose silver colour made it seem bigger than it was. A large red car.
A blue one, a present from Jihad to Mrs Butush Jihad Agha on her
thirtieth birthday, because it matched her aquamarine, or sky-blue,
eyes. And the last car was for taking the five children to school, and
to birthday parties and on trips. But Jihad kept reminding his friends
and acquaintances that these possessions were not the perks that came
with his father's job, which had grown and grown and showered them
with luxury – God forbid, no – they were the result of his hard work,
his 7 a.m. to 9 p.m. shifts, struggling like any other citizen to feed his
children and put a bit of money aside to keep their dignity intact.

Having contributed constructively to his country and collaborated
in bolstering the national economy, Jihad suddenly realised that culture
also needed his talents and abilities. And people suddenly discovered
that Jihad loved theatre, and had become obsessed with funding a huge
theatrical production. Then his love of cinema emerged, and he rushed
to the most famous film director, whose films were all banned for 'tech-
nical reasons', of course, and asked him to direct his upcoming film
project. He suggested that the movie's theme should be the poverty
and hunger of the average citizen, and the oppression he suffers, and the
hoarseness that silences his oppressed voice. The film would capture the
insult to the citizen who saw his purloined money spent lavishly on one
segment of society and not on others. The film would tell the story of a
man who worked as an employee, a cab driver, a janitor and an electri-
cian merely to feed his large family. A film that spoke of our need to
come together and discuss how we can protect our nation, the nation of
the Syrian people, who have since eternity walked proudly, faces turned
to the sky, with a dignity that not even the devil could tarnish. But the
director did not share Jihad's courage or enthusiasm.

A few days later Jihad discovered a talent for music and became the patron of a patriotic song that exalted strong principles and 'the heart of Arab' youth, while cursing enemies and evil-doers. He produced the song, and personally supervised the filming of the video in Palmyra, Basra and Apamea, as well as the dead cities in Idlib and the fortresses of Aleppo, Mirqib and Saladin. In old Tartous, and in the Umayyad mosque and the Hamidiyya market and the Damascus fort, and all the other sites of interest, which remained impervious to the goings-on throughout.

Then, as he walked through the streets of his beloved Damascus, he heard her crying at the edge of the Barada River, which had dried up from drought and neglect. So he sponsored a clean-up campaign and had the riverbed planted with flowers and jasmine. Damascus began to exude a magical fragrance that seeped into a body's cells and bloomed with love and forgiveness. This was the good life, the clean life, a nation grateful for Jihad's efforts; he who had sacrificed blood and tears for the citizenry.

In that corner, the tale of 'Beautiful Butush' was almost at an end, and the long cigar had lost its former glory to become a mound of cheap ash. The bottom of the coffee cup shone through the sediment of coffee grounds, and the araucaria had collapsed from exhaustion. There, in that corner, Jihad took a whiff of air and decided that all that criticism would not stifle his enthusiasm to 'share in the progress of the nation and fortify national unity, aiding the citizen to regain his right to live and work in dignity and safety.' The Syrian people have since eternity walked proudly, faces turned to the sky, with a dignity that not even the devil could tarnish.

Translated by Ghenwa Hayek

Mimouna

Faïza Guène

1 The Cry

I let out a great cry.

So loud it crashes against the ceiling before shattering on the tiled floor, like a thousand ball-bearings.

A strident, irritating, horrible cry; you can't imagine how piercing. Right up in the heavyweight category; on a par with those 'sound guns' now used by paramilitaries and the police to push back hostile crowds. Capable of triggering an earthquake.

But the old women bustling around me have these satisfied expressions on their faces, in fact they look relieved.

A strong smell of butchery fills the air, the heat is stifling; I'm close to suffocating, and all the hustle and bustle isn't helping.

At last I can see a very young woman lying there, trembling, with a gleaming forehead, pink face; and her eyes brim over with tears as she looks at me for the first time.

It's the 19th August 1947 and I am born.

Being born is only the start of dying.
Théophile Gautier

2 The Start of Dying

If you're wondering why we start screaming as soon as we've poked our noses outside, here's my answer: 'Don't you remember what it felt like, after nine months in the dark?'

For one thing, I thought those nine months would never end. I felt profoundly alone. Forced to experience, ALONE, the countless breath-taking changes happening to me. I was constantly aware of new things sprouting from me in every direction; arms, legs, fingers and new hair. . . It was traumatic. Imagine if, every time you looked at yourself in the mirror of a morning, you saw a new ear or a fresh foot sticking out. I got used to it in the end, as with everything else. It was beautiful to witness and incredibly well done, I have to say. I admired the quality, those precise proportions. I particularly remember the moment I discovered my hands. I think I can safely say, on that day I knew . . .

I slept a lot. I'd be a liar if I said the place was uncomfortable. I enjoyed the best naps of my life in there, especially during the first few months, when there was plenty of space and I could stretch out. After that, things got more difficult. I rapidly put on millimetres, then centimetres, and by the end, frankly, I was cramped.

The outside world . . . Of course, you have an intuition about it, an awareness, there are clues, and some things you're sure about.

Well one, mainly: nobody turns up by chance.

Even when I was an embryo, I expected the future to be gloomy. So I made the most of that comforting world during my stay, floating in its moist atmosphere, knowing the feeling of being safe wouldn't last.

Luckily, I had a few markers; voices which, over time, grew familiar. Sometimes I got exasperated by what I heard, and I'd give a hard kick against one of the surrounding walls. On several occasions, I let my anger slam into the sides of what I called my 'makeshift bedroom'. The trouble was, far from being understood, my gestures of indignation prompted joy. At this early stage, they clearly thought I was vigorous.

So much is beyond our knowing. We can't help wondering why we landed here and not somewhere else. How come we ended up in this village, in the bosom of this family, speaking this language and bearing this history?

If we want an answer to these questions, we're faced with a choice: believing in a Will that set up all these circumstances in a specific order, and with an ultimate objective. Or deciding to trust in what is commonly known as Chance, with the burden that brings: living with the same niggling questions, until the final exit no one can ignore.

So I Believe, and strongly.

As with many of us, I don't like it when my questions go unanswered.

An old woman with a tattoo on her forehead put me down on my mother's burning chest. I could feel her heart pounding. She seemed frail and terribly young. I noticed she was still crying, almost like a child, and the old tattooed woman asked her to be quiet the way you'd talk to a child. Another old woman, this one had no teeth, grabbed the umbilical cord and cut it. She lifted me up and carried me over to a bidet where she washed me with a rough piece of cloth, which she soaked in warm water. It scratched my skin, I didn't like it.

I looked at the old woman's hands; slender, bony and speckled with brownish stains. Every so often, she tucked a strand of her grey hair back inside her coloured headscarf.

There must have been at least a dozen women flurrying around my poor mother. They were like old hens, these aged limping carcasses all skin and bone, and the screeching of their vocal chords was like rough rope being flung across the room.

My young mother was exhausted and surrendered wearily.

They went through the motions of washing her, propping her up again, talking to her in hushed voices, while the toothless old woman carried on cleaning me. She smeared me with black soap, poured warm water over me, covered me in henna, then warm water again. Next, she traced a stick dipped in kohl powder over my eyelids. Last of all, she robed me in a long specially woven sheet, and wedged my hands between the folds of the cloth, to stop me reaching for my face. At this point, the old woman took a small white handkerchief out of her apron pocket: there was a fresh date inside. With those naked gums her only tools, she struggled to chomp on half of it, before popping the other half in my mouth, just for a few seconds. It left a delicious sugary taste. She chanted some invocations for my protection, before returning me, swaddled and mummified, to the arms of my parent. My mother's gaze wandered forlornly in space and she paid me no attention.

Suddenly, a boy burst into the room. He was holding a wooden stick that was taller than him, and his curly hair looked dishevelled and dusty. While he was talking to my toothless old washerwoman, he fiddled at the hem of his blue shorts with one hand, and leant against his walking stick with the other.

'Mother! Well?? Father and everybody wants to know! We didn't hear you!'

She turned, shooting him a look that could kill.

Suddenly, she bent down and picked up a sandal, which she hurled at him. He dodged just in time, and laughed.

'So, if they haven't heard anything. . . Haven't they at least understood? Go back and tell him there's no point slitting the bull's throat, surely he can understand *that*?! Go on, be off with you, and give that walking stick back to your father!'

A gentle breeze lifted the green flowery curtain that served as a door, revealing a small courtyard in which hens roamed and cackled under a leaden sun. As he skipped off, the boy-man chased the chickens and tried to beat them with his wooden stick.

I was tired, and I could feel my eyelids growing heavy.

'What about its name?' enquired the tattooed woman drily of my mother.

Turning towards me at last, my mother gave me a short, hard look before answering: 'Mimouna'. A heavy silence. Three or four of the old ladies took their *hayek* which they wound around them. They became anonymous again, and with gestures that swept the warm air they greeted the rest of the hens before vanishing inside their white costumes.

A fresh dance from the green flowery curtain meant that we glimpsed the procession of old hens crossing paths with the real hens, the ones with feathers.

3 The Return

How I envied Abdelhaq.

The little boy with dishevelled hair and blue shorts, who used to run everywhere, became a studious young man. He went to school nine kilometres away. He would rise earlier than the cockerel, setting out before dawn for the end of the world. His mother Khelthoum, the toothless old carcass, didn't want him to study. She tried to stop him by every means possible. Luckily, she ended up giving in. After the death of her husband, my grandfather Ahmed, she gave in a lot. All that was left of him was his walking stick, hanging from a nail by the bread oven.

Oh, and I almost forgot: fifteen children.

People said that my grandfather sired strong children. He'd built his reputation on it. They even asked him if he ate any special food. I don't understand the Arabs and their superstitions. If all his children survived, it wasn't down to magic, still less to chance or something he ate or drank, but to Allah, who made my two grandparents particularly fertile and gave their fifteen children good health. Fifteen children! Considering, I reckon they're ungrateful taking all the credit for it. My grandfather was an old grouch who complained about everything. He never thanked God, despite being showered with favours. Not only was his wife fertile but so too was his land – sadly, it was his heart that was arid.

Every day, the same ritual would take place. Our house was high up, overlooking our family's land, our fields and in the middle of it all, the path that ran through the olive trees. My mother, who knew what time Grandfather Ahmed generally came back from the souk, would be on the lookout as she hung up the washing to dry in the courtyard. He tended to wear a *razza*, a sort of brightly coloured turban, in yellow or orange, so he was easy to spot. I used to enjoy helping my mother with this chore, the feeling that I was on a very important mission. The laden mule would struggle with the climb, while my grandfather chewed tobacco on the beast's back.

The way was so long and so steep that, between the yellow *razza* first breaking on the horizon and my grandfather Ahmed getting off the mule, my mother could prepare her defence. She had to get the loaves out of the oven, heat up the water, put the olive oil in a small dish, get the tea ready, and spread out the straw carpet in the courtyard, with cushions for his back.

No sooner had he tethered his mule to a tree than my mother would run towards him, relieving him of his baskets and going ahead to unload them in the kitchen. Next she would make my grandfather comfortable, taking off his shoes and soaking his feet in the warm water to which she'd added coarse salt ahead of time. Finally, she served him his tea and the warm bread, which he loved soaking in the olive oil. When it was all done, mother could rest easy. But if any hitch occurred during this well-oiled operation, my grandfather would fly into a temper, sometimes spitting in my mother's face.

He wasn't her father, but her father-in-law, her husband's father. Perhaps that made it worse.

Abdelhaq was the fifteenth and last child of that great family. All the others married and left home. Well, 'left' is overstating it, they lived a few hundred metres away. They built stone houses of their own and imagined they were independent, now that they were scattered around the fields. All except one, who had scattered his soul by going to work much further afield. The eighth child, Mohammed, my father, was in France and I'd never seen him.

It's the winter of 1953 and I'm knitting my father a pair of thick socks using the wool from our sheep and the shafts of two cockerel feathers as needles. He's coming back to Algeria at the beginning of spring. I can't wait.

4 The Last Exile

My mother and I were in a state of excitement about my father's return. At last I was going to get answers to the questions I'd been pestering my mother with all those years. Up until that point, my father had been as unreal to me as the 'mother ogress' cited by adults to scare children into behaving; or that maverick Juha, whose extraordinary adventures are told across the Arab world. He belonged with all the other fictional characters that peopled my imagination. I wouldn't have been able to recognise his face or voice, and his tastes were unfamiliar to me. My grandmother Khelthoum didn't so much reminisce about things as muddle the past. With fifteen children, it's not easy to remember all the different stories. . . My mother had told me a few bits and pieces, but they seemed pretty dull. From what little I could glean, my father wasn't much of a talker.

We were standing in the doorway, on the lookout, just as when grandfather came home from the souk. My father headed towards us in the early morning mist, as if in a dream: it was magical and confusing at the same time. He looked so handsome. My grandmother burst into tears as she ran to him, followed by my mother. I was used to seeing my mother cry, but Grandmother Khelthoum shedding tears – that was a sight to behold; I'd as good as convinced myself there was an old toad inside her chest, crouching where her heart should have been.

The hugs and kisses were short but intense. I stood to one side, feeling intimidated, so he asked me to come closer.

My mother encouraged me with a little pat on my back, saying to my father: 'This is Mimouna! She's a great help to me!'

Yes, he was very handsome. With an elegant slim moustache – you could see his lips and, when he smiled, a good set of teeth too. Unlike all my uncles who had foul teeth from chewing tobacco, as well as enormous brown moustaches that covered their mouths. You'd think they'd gone and stuck a mule's tail on their faces. What a handsome man my father was!

As I said, from the outset you have a choice: believing, or trusting to chance.

My father returned a few months before the war. He realised he had to come home thanks to a letter from his brother Abdelhaziz, written by Abdelhaq (the only person in the family who could read and write), in which he urged: 'Come back as quickly as you can, we're going to Harvest the Barley.' Of course, it was all in code.

And so there was the war. Hunger. The Red Cross. Exile over by Morocco. School. Fear. The soldier who put his gun to the temples of my little brother, Mustafa, when he was only a few months old and asleep on our mother's back. The soldier said: 'We're going to shoot him now, before he grows up and joins the others in the *jbel*.'

And then freedom.

After singing the following song with all my heart –

The Pledge

We swear by the lightning that destroys,
By the streams of generous blood being shed,
By the bright flags that wave,
Flying proudly on the high mountains,
That we are in revolt, whether to live or to die,

We are determined that Algeria should live,
So be our witness – be our witness – be our witness!

We are soldiers in revolt for truth
And we have fought for our independence.
When we spoke, nobody listened to us,
So we have taken the noise of gunpowder as our rhythm
And the sound of machine guns as our melody,

We are determined that Algeria should live,
So be our witness – be our witness – be our witness!

O France! Past is the time of idle talk,
We have closed it as we close a book.
O France! The day to settle the accounts has come!
Prepare yourself! Here is our answer!
The verdict, our Revolution will return it,

We are determined that Algeria should live,
So be our witness – be our witness – be our witness!

– it was my turn to set foot in France. At twenty, I married an unskilled
worker. He was short, tubby, a bit clumsy and a chain smoker, but
he was also very kind. His heart was in the right place. That's what I
liked about him.

The trouble was he worked a lot and I felt cut off. Alone, every
day that God made. The cruelty of exile. Abandoning a large family,
all that space, all that love, your nearest and dearest, your mother
country, to find yourself stuck on the tenth floor of a concrete tower
containing sadness and tenants in equal measure. I didn't understand
their language let alone their leisure interests, and the way the French
made their dogs wear smart coats in winter seemed so alien. When I
was pregnant with my first child, I became very ill, no appetite, I was
getting visibly thinner. A serious depression, the doctors said. They
didn't hold out much hope for me or the baby.

Every day at ten o'clock, two o'clock and six o'clock, the nuns from
the parish of Saint-Germain would pay me a visit. They comforted
me and gave me injections. But I was anaesthetised by sadness, and
their needles didn't have any effect.

As time went by, it got better; I met other women like me. We
found each other through the nostalgia we shared. Our children grew
up and we had to deal with so many changes. I learnt to speak the
language eventually, but it wasn't easy.

We're old now. Our children are married. My eldest daughter has
just given birth to a little girl! Happily, these are different times. We
celebrated it the way a birth should be celebrated. And if there'd

been a bull, I would have slit its throat myself. It's my turn to be a grandmother, for the first time. How strange that feels. I can't help thinking of Grandmother Khelthoum, peace upon her soul.

As I trawl through these memories, I can honestly say that, no, I don't think Chance randomly governs our lives. Or that I'm the fruit of a senseless lottery.

My father died. He was a true believer and he passed on his love and faith to me. Without which, I'd have told you that life has no meaning, just unbearable suffering, along with a few fleeting and futile small pleasures. As I crouch by his grave, I pray for Allah to have mercy on him and, once again, I see him as he was on the day he struggled, in the mist, to climb the path through the olive trees.

Translated from the French by Sarah Ardizzone

Three Stories

Hala Kawtharani

Thirty-three Years

I'm breathing down the back of forty years of failure. Saying that, I change my mind: it's forty years of foolish conviction that I've been on the run; fleeing the lightless ignorance of those in whose company I found myself. Not my mother, of course, rather the relatives I was forced to live with following my father's death. And I mean my friends, too. Not a moment went by that I wasn't aware of the need to alter my destiny.

I lacked for nothing. I always got what I wanted. Our quality of life suffered no great change in the wake of my father's sudden disappearance. But I raised myself. My mother smothered me with tenderness yet never let me know if I had made a mistake or not. I taught myself. It never fails to amaze me that I avoided losing myself to study or the merry-go-round of street battles and turf wars that swept up my friends, neighbours and contemporaries during the years of civil war in Lebanon. Art saved me. My need to engage with colours saved me, my need to fashion something, to draw or sculpt, to use my fingers and hands, to savour the peace of some public library where I came to know faces by sight and not through the sounds they made.

I fled the family, fled the problems of my father's inheritance and the land that my uncles sought to embezzle from my widowed mother and me and my three sisters. I fled, the only boy among four women. I fled to America. My eldest sister, who married before she reached twenty, regards the African country where she went to live with her husband as home. She calls my mother just once a week. Mother waits for Saturday to come around to hear her voice. She used to say she felt guilty about her eldest daughter, who threw herself into the arms of the first man to knock on the door, and preferred to live in Africa than with her mother. I don't know Najla that well. I was still little when she celebrated the wedding at home. The war had just begun, still nothing more than a brief diversion, a game we thought would soon be over.

They accuse me of being sensitive like a woman. Must a man be a block of wood? Are we supposed to feel nothing? I've eaten brain and marrow sandwiches from Abu Ali's with the ones who accuse me of effeminacy (a serious charge in my country). I've starred in football matches between local teams in my district. But I cried with Susu, the neighbours' daughter, when an explosion shook the street and her mother hadn't come home. 'Susu, be still,' I told her. 'You watch plenty of action and horror films. Don't think of the blood. Close your eyes and imagine other colours. Blue's pretty. Blue is the prettiest colour: as calm and deep as the sea, and rich in secrets.'

'Enough philosophy,' said my friend Jad, and we carried on with the game.

Forty years of walking the streets. Thirty-three years, to be more accurate. I walked in Beirut and New York and southern Lebanon. I walked between the graves in my village. I walked behind my childhood sweetheart, the one they're now calling 'the slut'. The idea that I lived by walking – lived through my feet – excited me, but it was a calm excitement. I never lose my cool and my cool never leaves me. I don't get angry, only sad. There's no connection between my calmness and the fact that I was raised by women. My mother loses her mind to anger. It robs her of the ability to think and move; it paralyses her. And so it was, calmly, that I came to terms with my failure as an artist and accepted that I'd never make my mark. I sank into history: the history of art and the history of oppression in my region, that part of the world where the sun gleams darkly.

Lebanon/Switzerland? Beirut/Paris?

My identity card sits in my pocket with the cigarettes. My identity card and my Arab name hide in my pocket with my picture, my eyes and my lips, my brow and my memory. My desire to see you keeps step with me as I stroll along. It's not too late. I could still get you back if I wanted. I return on tomorrow's flight to Paris, and from there, New York. Nothing is impossible.

Tuesday, 17 February: a date printed on another identity card in my pocket. Do you remember that day we spent at the museum? I long to be transported to that city beneath the city: charging from one enchanted gateway to the next. In the metro I lie in wait for surprises and delight in them. I rush to beat time.

In the end I overcame my fear of the cold. I left it to you to try and live alone. I left you time to forget you'd made a pact to spend your life with a man from the south; that you'd borne him a boy. A boy I let call me 'Dad'. No matter. My heart will grow no kinder and I shall not let you steal my fine words on my special bond – my fond regard – for the solitary life, just so you can say that you, too, wish to live alone. I returned from your country to mine. My name today is the same I bore yesterday. I still listen to Asmahan and the melodies of Astor Piazzolla, and horror flicks still frighten me. I am here and there at the same time. I may have claimed to have lost my affection for Beirut and my village in the south of Lebanon, but I have always been here and there.

I review your emails and make a reckoning of the old haunts in Beirut that have vanished since I abandoned it twenty years ago. Their disappearance, I tell myself, is punishment for my memory and my self-loathing: a combined sense of inadequacy, suspicion that I am complete with you and a breathtaking terror of what you might mean for my isolation. I am not me: I'm another person now. I'm the hero of a story I have lived. I was born in Lebanon, I grew up there, and I returned as a man in middle age. The forty years I've lived since my birth on 22 March 1968 may be all the life I get: who knows? I still don't understand Lebanon. I don't understand the relationships between its parties and its politicians. I don't understand the articles in the newspapers. I don't understand who loves who and who hates who. I don't understand why one war started and another came to an end, why young men in the streets carry knives in their pockets, or why they call Lebanon the Switzerland of the East and Beirut the Paris of the Middle East.

The idea that Beirut resembles Paris makes me laugh. When my obsession with reading history books first surfaced, along with my attempt to understand the recent history of the region, I became fascinated with my mother's account of Beirut in the fifties and sixties: a time when the faces of many colours from many lands walked al-Hamra Street and all the languages of the world could be heard. In Beirut, everything was tolerated: 'every idea, every identity', as I read in the conclusion of that wonderful book by the thinker Edward Said – an Arab New Yorker like myself – that shares its title with Mahmoud Darwish's poem 'After the Last Sky'. I quickly saw how idiotic it was to feel affection for a past I had not lived, an era whose events took place before I was born. All the talk of the Switzerland of the East was a mirage. Visiting Switzerland, I realised how great a disservice we had done it by comparing it to Lebanon, where we live beset by the threat of war, constantly on the verge of rounding on each other, our fragile stability turned to hell.

I open my eyes in defiance of a long night played out to a radio's song. The radio belongs to a soldier who guards my neighbour, a political heavyweight and one of the idols of our immortal wars. If I were in New York I'd wait until the first hours of morning to tell you, 'I want us to live together.' But the morning's beauty and my deep attachment to it make me forget my need for you. Somewhere in among the pages and their words and the lines scored beneath the sentences in books I confess that I am forgetting you.

The Sin of Silence

All I did was to do nothing. My indifference brought her round. She slept thirty hours or more and I made no attempt to wake her. I entered the room: how could I not? I checked that she was breathing, but made no attempt to wake her. I did nothing. I felt none of that fear that stabs the heart, nor readied myself for the worst. I left her sleeping. Before falling asleep she'd been in a reverie, dozing in a cave surrounded by the incident of a life now sixty years or more in the past. I did nothing, and it helped, because once woken from her long sleep she returned to the present.

She called out to me. I tried not to hear her but was swept with a sudden longing for her. I am her youngest child, the last of the brood come back to a life I rebelled against. I came back to her, to my mother. I cannot escape her influence over me. I fight the effects of a childhood spent with her, effects that overwhelm my determination to fight them. They rule me. I fight what remains in me of her inquisitive nature while she still has the ability to cling on to it. This curiosity often resurfaces during the bouts of unconsciousness that afflict her. Maybe due to forgetfulness, the question marks pile up in her mind until she can master them no longer, and she falls silent or asleep.

I can't understand why I returned to a life I left. I longed for the old family home in the South, for its sun, for the coffee whose aroma I never knew in twenty years of exile. I fled to America to escape the war and complete my studies. The American University in Beirut had been drawn into the war despite itself. Politics, plots and pay-offs stormed its courtyards and seized its buildings, surrounding the trees and roses that leaned out over the most beautiful sea in the world.

Around the time I officially joined the university's student body, about two years before I travelled, I still firmly believed that I could make my most beautiful dreams come true. The war didn't concern me. I never tried to find out what was going on. I remained untouched by that kind of curiosity, the political inquisitiveness that would lead me to adopt some position or other. I left the country before I was forced to take sides: picked up my drawings and fled. Twenty years later I returned to sketch the sun from the balcony of my family's house in the village. My mother had forgotten the house and lost the key, and conceivably had forgotten me. The day of my return I sang out to her before entering her room. She kissed my eyes and forehead. I kissed her hands as she liked me to do the morning of

Eid. Her absent spells had not yet begun. She would tell us stories I suggested we tape so they wouldn't be lost. I was able to draw these stories; if I'd been a writer I would have written them down, but I never could deal in words and was often accused of being too quiet. At our family gatherings silence was a sin: understood variously and broadly to signify sarcasm, superiority, disgust, boredom, conspiracy and evasion . . . And then my mother was forced to fall silent. Perhaps the best thing about her illness was that it freed her of the obligation to explain my failure to marry, or address inquiries about my approaching fifty, my loneliness and my 'unnerving' silence.

My sister Randa was relieved when I told her I'd take our mother to our house in the village: relieved of our mother. But she feigned concern at, or maybe was genuinely worried by, my inexperience in dealing with her now she was ill, and the idea of the two of us alone together in a·neglected house that would require a Herculean effort to restore to life. I made a present to myself of one room in the house, which I converted into a studio. I cleaned and tidied the place so we would be able to live there. I made a deal with Umm Abdallah that she would bathe mother and take care of her laundry and food. For just a few seconds I felt content, happy even. That was before the nightmares began hammering at the doors of my sleep.

Translated by Robin Moger

from the novel

Secret Pleasures

Hamdy el Gazzar

An Ascetic

I can see him still, in his jubbah, kaftan and turban, tall as a wooden electricity pole of the kind that has now disappeared, his chest and shoulders broad, his body firm, his face dark brown and pockmarked, his eyes unseeing, his moustache as luxuriant as an Upper Egyptian's, and his long beard still black despite his fifty years. His walking stick of yellow cane with its down-curved crook rises in the powerful grasp of his right hand, cleaving the air before him and descending to strike the ground ahead of his steps.

He walks in total darkness, his heart full of light.

I was about ten and Sheikh Hubb el-Din was the imam of the mosque in Bayumiya Square and master of the attached Quran school for children. His delicate, melodious voice was the thing I loved most, as a child and as a boy. At his hands I memorised about half the Noble Quran in two years.

Only Sheikh Hubb el-Din would be invited to recite in the large funeral marquees that in Giza were erected only for the rich and the big families.

The sheikh would set off to recite as though on his way to a wedding or a concert of classical music – in the fullness of his gravity and splendour, his striped satin waistcoat, kaftan and jubbah clean and ironed to perfection.

Morsi the ironer gave the sheikh's clothes the special care of a disciple and lover of God, not of a professional. He would wash them, iron them and perfume them with musk, then help the sheikh into them. Thus the sheikh was never to be seen, in mosque or marquee or on the street, other than elegantly dressed, imposing, the smell of perfume wafting from him and from his clothes.

Sometimes the sheikh was led by a small boy, the grandson of his mortal friend Hagg Issa. That boy was me.

I'd pray the evening prayer behind him at the Bayumiya Square mosque, then, after the prayer, approach him as he uttered the concluding devotions and whisper politely, 'May we pray together in Mecca one day!' and he would smile, continue muttering under his breath, and finally, leaning on his stick and my shoulder, rise with me till he was standing, towering over me like a camel.

As we passed through the large wooden door, I'd help him to step over the raised threshold, then take his stick from him and tuck it under my arm while he placed his heavy left hand on my shoulder, and thus we'd set off together through the heart of Giza. In the sheikh's company, I would lord it over my peers, making as though to stick my tongue out at any of them that I might see. I would tour the alleys, lanes and streets with him, taking the longest way round so that everyone could see me leading 'Our Master'.

He didn't mind, or get annoyed or fidgety. I'd look up at him and all I'd see was a face full of tranquillity that seemed to smile at my slyness and boasting. His lips never moved. In general, his words were few but precious.

When we got to a marquee where a wake was being held, I'd sit him down on the reciters' wooden bench with its decorative blue velvet covering and lift his feet up so that he could sit on it cross-legged, and he'd squat there like a statue of an Ancient Egyptian scribe. I would straighten his white turban and his shawl, pour water into the glass in front of him and keep the bottle of cold water in my hand in case he should ask for a drink; then I'd position the microphone in front of his mouth, tapping on it to test it and breathing into it 'Allah! Allah!' When I was satisfied that the microphone was properly positioned and that the sound quality was good enough, I'd seat myself at his feet, cross-legged like him on the carpet, ears straining to catch his voice.

Sheikh Hubb el-Din recited the verses of the Quran with a veneration that shook men's hearts, a submissiveness that forced men to bow their heads. His voice was omnipresent, manifest yet hidden and internal, mysterious as the sound of the earth turning. It issued from heart and soul, not from mouth, gullet, vocal cords and throat. My every limb strained to hear him, and my tongue would move, repeating after him the verses exactly the way that he recited them, at the same pitch, and with the same rendering, tone and piety. I'd spread my fingers to their limit, place my hands over my ears and sway to the right and left where I sat, exactly like him. My body would shake, and a melody of the utmost sweetness would course through it as my soul filled with his celestial voice, and I'd pass into a state of ecstasy, my eyes closed, my heart seeming to circle as though riding a shooting star, doting.

He would be reciting, his voice plangent as a curlew's, and then he'd recede further and further, till he was no longer with us at all, leaving his listeners with nothing but the body and face of one who was no longer present, who had flown from our world to the highest heavens, entered Paradise, drunk of its rivers, its milk and honey and wine, and beheld its dark-eyed maidens – a pious believer who had had commerce with them and known a heavenly pleasure and ecstasy without equal here on earth.

The sheikh always began his recital of the first quarter section with the chapter called 'The Believers'; in the second, he would recite from 'Forgiver'; in the third from his favourite, 'Yusuf'; and he would conclude his recital with his gem, 'The Compassionate'. This was a rigorous order from which the sheikh never diverged, in which no substitutions were permitted, and with regard to which he would submit to no requests for change, for he cared nothing for his listeners. He recited for himself and chanted for his own sake and no one else's, for his own pleasure and enjoyment. And the strange thing was that people loved him for precisely that reason – for his obliviousness to their presence and indifference to their existence. His blindness bestowed on him complete freedom, causing him to dive deep into his own being, unconcerned by what was around him, unaware of anything but the image of his soul suspended before him from the holy words.

And whether the occasion was a rich man's wake, the fulfilment of a vow or the celebration of a saint's day, our sheikh never compromised his probity or his conscience, or his four beloved sections.

Out of just four sections Sheikh Hubb el-Din created his far-flung fame, in Giza and beyond its borders as far as the villages of Badrashin and el-Ayat to the south and Bashtil and the Barrages to the north. Wherever he went, wherever the sheikh recited his four sections, the exclamations of 'Allah! Allah!' rose all around him to the ceilings of the tents, the sighs and gasps of the connoisseurs followed one after another entranced by that beseeching, submissive voice, and people's tongues repeated, 'God grant you blessings, Sheikh!' after each pause, each silence, each terminal cadence.

Our Master held classes in the memorisation of the Quran in the chamber belonging to the small school on the second floor of the mosque from after the afternoon prayer until the sunset prayer. Following the latter, he would go home to rest until a little before the evening prayer. I would walk him home, this time cutting straight through the market and taking the shortest route to his house, for the lanes and streets of the market area would still be thronged with people.

The market women sitting on the ground in front of their displays of cheese and molasses, limes and vegetables, the women standing in front of the hand-carts, behind the crates of fruit and at the doors of the stores big and small, the women sitting at the doors of their houses would gaze at us, their looks trained upon us, winking at one another, staring at us shamelessly and displaying none of the manners appropriate to the passing of a sheikh. Sometimes even worse would happen. One rosy-cheeked woman would lean towards another and whisper something in her ear, smiling, and the other, after a small show of embarrassment, would allow her lips to soften into a broad grin, as the first continued to whisper circumspectly, as though revealing terrible secrets, and then laugh as she stealthily looked Our Master's towering body over, her eyes settling on his crotch and remaining glued there.

I would look at them with exasperation, resentment and anger as they continued with their staring, their whispering, their nodding and winking. I'd try to rebuke them, silently, with an angry movement of my head and neck, my face red and ears burning, but they'd smile mockingly at me, striking palm on palm, their laughter rising. I'd grow furious and brandish the sheikh's stick in their faces, making their laughter grow louder and lewder still. Though the sheikh heard their obscene laughing, nothing about him showed that he did so, and he would utter not a word. Looking into his face, I'd see nothing there but tranquillity and contentment, and a radiant smile. Gently, he'd squeeze my shoulder to tell me to calm down and that we should keep going, and I'd bid them farewell with an angry look and curses that never left my mouth, but all I'd hear would be their lavish, raucous laughter behind our backs.

I knew that the sheikh's secret reputation as a lover and as the possessor of a huge member was almost as great as his acknowledged reputation for his reverence and piety, the beauty of his voice and the magnificence of his recitation. In fact, the sheikh, who had neither sons nor daughters, was known as 'the three-legged man'. Some said this was because he walked with two legs and a stick, and some said other things. The malicious rabble put it about that he had gained the title after his last wife died of an excess of pleasure during a lovemaking that had lasted ten hours, when the sheikh had convulsed her with a staff the length and thickness of the leg of a man of average height.

All I could see was a man getting on in years, sweet and refined, and alone.

The sheikh had married many women in the bloom of his youth, none of whom bore him children or remained in his house for more than a year. After that it'd be over for her – either because, divorced, she'd leave Giza entirely and disappear or because she'd be borne to her grave. So it was until he married Sabiha, the last of his wives. She bore him no children either, but was everything to him, devoting herself to him and taking care of him with unstaunchable love for a number of years until she died. After her passing, the sheikh had nothing more to do with women and his recitation became heartrending, low and sad, and he took to singing when he

was alone, and sometimes at Buhluq's café, on Priest's Alley, where
they sold hashish.

At his private sessions at the café, the sheikh would dispel his sorrows
in the company of a few friends – my uncle Musa, Hasan Effendi the
songwriter, Morsi the laundryman and two or three other intimates.

He would become merry, and sway and sing. He sang with intoxi-
cating virtuosity the *qasaids* of Sheikh Ali Mahmud, his voice turned
delicate and tender with the *mawwals* and *doors* of Nazim el-Ghazali, and he chanted the *taqatiq* and *qasaid* of Sabah Fakhri. He never
touched beer, the only drink served at the café, but would smoke a
few bowls of hashish on the *goza*.

In the darkness of the night, towards three in the morning, the
sheikh would return to his house, my uncle Musa and Hasan Effendi
leading him by the arm. On the way, he would always tell them the
same story, the story of how, when on his own, he wept incessantly
from grief, grief at the loss of Sabiha, who had died in his arms as she
bent over his hand to kiss it, and of how he yearned to join her.

Hasan Effendi would leave them at the corner and set off in the
direction of Station Street, where he lived, while my uncle led the
sheikh to his green, single-storey house that was next to ours, take
him into his bedroom and leave him. A minute later, I would hear
my uncle's footfall as he climbed our stairs to his apartment.

I had been into Our Master's house so often that I knew, knew
that the sheikh's house and his bedroom were completely dark, with
no lamp to light them and no sun entering from the outside. The
house was desolate. There was no one to share it with him, and no
voice or other sound to be heard.

On his own, the sheikh, in the process of removing his kaftan and
turban, would stumble at length between the bed and the closet.
He would nap for two hours at the most, then wake up of his own
accord and go to the square to give the call to prayer.

The sheikh had foresworn women for the rest of his life ten
minutes after Sabiha had died, and not one, either relative or maid,
had entered his house. I know that he would turn on his tape recorder
and play his tapes of Sheikh Rifaat reciting, over and over again,
leaving his tears to flow on to the pillow while he moaned with a

low-pitched rasp and allowed his strong body to collapse under the moaning of his soul.

He did this every night before lying down on his stomach, pressing his body against his small, coarse mattress and stretching his arms as far as they would go, just like a crucified messiah, a messiah sleeping on a bed of thorns.

Uncle Musa says that at first the sheikh's sight had just been weak. It was excess of weeping for the departure of women from his life that had sent him blind.

Samira

I didn't weep over her departure long enough to go blind, but I did come close to killing myself.

Perhaps if I'd put an end to my life so innocently, if I'd possessed the strength to do that, I wouldn't have ended up where I am now, and life would have been a lot more just, more forgiving, kinder . . . nicer.

I remember her, a grateful smile on my face, my eyes flashing and shining as they watch her phantom, my heart leaping in my chest like that of a guileless boy.

Samira was the icon of my adolescent years, shining down on my head like a little sun. I feel a great longing for her, a longing to experience those same heedless emotions once again. Remembering her, I return to things I've almost succeeded in rooting out of myself – innocence, integrity, idealism and the well-meaning good-heartedness that I lost long ago.

I can invoke her now and feel no pain, or heartache, or bitterness; just a long ironic laugh at the expense of that boy in his first year of secondary school, a laugh that rises from somewhere between my lips and my heart.

I think of her and am struck by a wave of nostalgia for those days that have gone for ever, and of joy that I can still picture the delicate features of her face, her honey-coloured eyes, her small fine nose, her short curly hair, the distinctive husky timbre of her voice.

The images I retain of her are many and dazzling. They follow one another slowly in my mind's eye like a reel of film that I've taken in my hands so that I can scrutinise it frame by frame.

She is sitting on the stoop and first stone step up to their house. Her trim body is settled on the clean stone of the stoop, her legs are a little splayed and her long toes peek out of plastic slippers with a green rose. Each morning Samira scrubs the steps with water and soap, using a piece of sackcloth. Her body is relaxed as she sits and leans at an angle. Her back rests against the yellow wall, and her face is buried in a book of poems that lies open in her hands. Her legs are long and slim and her sweet brown knees shine out under the hemline of her short house dress, a white dress with large red dots scattered over it. From the transistor radio in her lap rises the voice of Nagat el-Saghira: 'I wait for you . . . I wait . . .'

She is standing to the right of the open wooden door to their house chewing gum, hand on hip, her face tilted upwards, eyes on the second-storey balcony of the house opposite, chatting with her girlfriend Asmaa, who is leaning down, resting her budding breasts on the balcony railing. Samira asks her, insistently and yearningly, what life is like at Cairo University. 'What do the lecture rooms at the college look like? What do the girls wear, Suma? How do they walk and how do they talk? What do the professors say in the lectures? What are the boys like on campus? What are the latest love stories? Have you found one that likes you, skinny legs? Tell me everything, you little minx.'

Then Asmaa turns on the tap and nothing can turn it off again. While Asmaa gabs, Samira sighs, going 'Ah, ah' over and over and asking, 'OK, and then what? What happened?' She looks grave, and her eyes take on a far-away look, her hand arranging her hair, and she goes on chewing the bitter gum, unaware of what she's doing, her small jaws moving mechanically. After a while she gets bored, fed up, and falls into a state of gloom. Sorrow, trying to hide behind a wan smile, sketches itself on her face.

At the end of the conversation, before turning her back on Asmaa, she lets out a great sigh, perhaps because she has never seen the university and has failed the Secondary General Certificate three times and Boss Farag keeps her at home, waiting impatiently to be rid of her so that the honour of the twenty-year-old spinster can be preserved when he marries her off to the first man to knock on the door.

Some days, when I skipped school to saunter through the streets with Haris, we'd see her walking through the market in a tight-fitting green dress and high-heeled black pumps, strutting with the daring of a 'daughter of the neighbourhood', her fat buttocks shaking as she swayed, a bag for vegetables, large and empty, swinging to the motion of her right hand.

I'd just manage to drag Haris back, and we'd follow her from a distance, taking care she didn't see us as she made her way across the vegetable market without a glance at her father's store, buying meat from Gabr's butcher shop, bending forward and to the side, picking out tomatoes and greens and fruit, and returning to the house with a full heavy bag, not having spoken to or haggled much with the sellers. Most of them knew her as the daughter of Boss Farag and Mrs Teresa, and always addressed her as 'Miss Samira'. I called her by just her first name, which I loved very much.

She's on the roof on a hot, moonlit night, seated on a large empty metal can, her face in her hands, pensive and grave, silently raising her eyes to the sky, and Shawqi and I go into his room, with a 'Good evening, Samira' to her, though she doesn't reply. After a while we hear her sobs and quiet moans.

It's late afternoon. She and I are sitting on the stoop, in the light coming from the stairwell. She is reading quietly and I am sitting a few inches away from her. I rest my arm on the wooden banister and gaze at her, smiling. I have pretended I have to wait for Shawqi to come back from the store so that he can explain the difficult algebra lesson to me and she has told me gently, 'OK. Sit down,' so I sit down next to her in silence, stealing glances at the page from which she is reading and hesitating over whether to ask her why she likes poetry so much. I am on the point of speaking but the words turn to stone on my trembling lips and I fidget where I sit. She is unaware of my presence and doesn't raise her eyes from the book. I enjoy myself looking her body over from top to toe for long moments, flustered and almost shaking. My eyes settle on her gleaming knees and stop there. I am at rest and unafraid, and I look like any good, well-behaved boy (ho-ho), shyly gazing at the ground.

Shawqi's room, a month before the inter-year exams. We're sitting opposite one another on the rush mat, our Arabic language books and texts open on the low round wooden table between us, and I'm looking in the direction of the open door and reading out loud (with extreme listlessness) to Shawqi one of the memorisation poems:

Lodged am I upon unspeaking rocks,
And would that my heart like this unspeaking rock might be!

She enters carrying a tin tray with cheese and egg sandwiches and two glasses of tea. I'm suddenly overcome by ardour and my voice rises and rings out, and she smiles at me. I go on reading and try to jazz up my poetic performance with Quranic embellishments. My eyes meet hers and I get flustered and the blood rises to my face. I make a mistake and start stammering: 'And would that my . . . and would that my . . . and would that my head like this unspeaking rock might be!' She puts the tray on the table, leans towards me and winks. Then she says, 'You've got a nice voice but you're saying it wrong, sweetie pie. It's 'would that my *heart*,' stupid!'

And she leaves, her figure elegant, and I'm covered in embarrass-ment and shame.

I'm standing at the threshold of the door into her house, my sweat pouring off me from top to toe, my heart beating hard, my mouth dry, my face red, my ears burning, and she's staring at me in astonishment. I stammer without producing a single word, making meaningless sounds, summoning up all my courage to take from my pocket the thing that I've spent all night working on. 'What's wrong, Rabia?' she says. 'What's happened?' With trembling fingers, I place in her hand a poem in which I write of her and about her, for her alone. I give her a pallid smile and turn and flee. I run till I get to my room.

The next day, as I was climbing the stairs to Shawqi's room, she came out from their apartment on the ground floor and stopped me. Her face was rosy and very beautiful. She looked into my eyes without saying anything for a while and examined my face closely, then stretched her hand out toward my hair and stroked it, saying with unforgettable sweetness, 'I love you too. But . . . but you're still young.'

Then she gave me a single light kiss on my cheek, and that is all I ever got from her.

Her naked body shines and dazzles, her black hair is wet and undone so that it falls over her face and on to her shoulders, her lips are as delicious as cherries, her small breasts are in my hands, and one of her nipples is in my mouth. Her hands are in my hair and on my back as a flood of water falls on my head and body from the shower-head. I gasp and shiver with pleasure and the soap suds are thick and white and cover my left hand and the thing between my thighs.

Samira is in a white wedding dress, her right hand on Luqa's arm at the threshold of St George's. Luqa, her cousin, has his big jaws parted as far as they will go, and his whole repulsive black face is filled with joy and delight. His grey hair is slicked with oil and shines, and Samira is dwarfed by his great hulking body.

Samira's face is brown and beautiful on the water under Abbas Bridge, and a fifteen-year-old teenager looks at it and chokes as he weeps and tries to pluck up the courage to jump over the iron railings.

I neither laugh nor weep at that scene now. I just long to see her, but she hasn't come back to Giza even once since she set off with Luqa for the ends of the earth, aka Canada.

Why didn't I kill myself then and have done with it? Why did I have to come this far?

Translated by Humphrey Davies

from the novel

The Last Hanging Poem

Hussein al Abri

Abdallah looked at his wristwatch. It was already past eight o'clock and he was late for work. It dropped into his hand when he saw that his colleagues Muhammad and Salim had arrived before him. He was rarely late for work, as he had trained himself to always arrive a little before eight. This wasn't because he loved this job or loved what he did in his office all day long. Despite this, he wasn't able to hate his job either. The one good thing he got out of this job was getting to stay far away from the ruckus of the editors. It was neither his speciality, nor the speciality of his two colleagues, to do things that required fast-paced or urgent work.

After he said hello to his colleagues, Abdallah stood erect in front of the board, staring at the clippings hung there. The gallows rope stood erect in a large picture of Qurum Bridge, and then another rope, hanging off of New Bridge. He was nervous. He scratched himself more than once and felt light pains shooting through his shoulders and the top of his back. His anxiety began to show in the form of a thin line of sweat, first on his back, and then his neck. He resolved to try as hard as he could to get a hold of himself, and not reveal his worry to his colleagues. He thought this despite knowing that they must have noticed that, lately, he wasn't doing as well as could be. Today, however, is totally different. When it occurred to him that he was wearing the dark blue *mussar* that he wore on special occasions, his body temperature rose, while a prickle began to gnaw at him from within.

He was still standing erect in front of the board when Salim said to him, 'Abdallah, you've got to close the books on this issue!' Abdallah

looked at Salim with surprise, trying to understand what he meant by
'You've got to close the books. . .' Did something recently happen,
did his colleague know something new? Had he noticed the anxiety
built up inside him? Was he trying to advise him to take it easy – to
tell him that the time had come for setting aside this non-essential
work and looking into more important things?

The gallows ropes remained hovering in his mind, swinging in
the wind, while the newspaper clippings blended into one another,
making him miserable. What should he do? He couldn't really tell
his colleagues what was going on inside him, not so much because
he didn't want to, but because he didn't know himself. He gave his
colleagues a couple of dopey, meaningless looks, picked up a clipping
and removed its thumbtack. Then suddenly, he turned to them and
said, 'Yes, the time has come to close this case. I'll take down all of
these clippings. No doubt we need to do something new.'

His colleagues were surprised by what he did. At the same time,
they didn't usually disagree with him about anything. With the
passing of time, each of them had got used to respecting the wishes
of the others, realising their good qualities as well as their defects.
They had reached a state of both adaptation and collusion, which
made each one of them cooperate with each other, and with himself,
at the same time. Abdallah thought to himself that Muhammad and
Salim would ask him not to do that, or that they would object,
one way or another. Yet this did not happen, simply because the
two of them became engrossed in telling stories that seemed more
important.

He went back to his desk, carrying the newspaper clippings and
the thumbtacks, and started punching holes. He pulled out the folder
that had been filed away in one of the drawers and started to file the
clippings. His anxiety was clear from his restlessness – his inability to
sit still in his chair for a while, as was customary for him – and from
the quick, aimless fidgeting of his feet. Now, it crossed his mind that
something powerful was eating at him from within. He had to close
the books on this issue that had lingered too long. He looked at the
board again, picked up the folder and put it in the drawer where it
had been.

It didn't appear that Muhammad and Salim wanted to broach the subject of the gallows ropes, since for them the issue was over, even if something might happen in the future. They had no pressing desire to imagine and discuss possible outcomes. They had noticed that Abdallah was wearing a new *mussar*, different from the one he wore for a long time. They also noticed that he had done a number of things that were out of the ordinary for him, all in a single day: he had been late to work, whereas the two of them had made it in before him; the fact that he was wearing a different *mussar*; and, finally, he was clearly very nervous. Yet even stranger than all this was that he collected all the news clippings from the board without hesitating; all it took was a simple suggestion.

Something is eating at him from within! Could he be sick? Or could it be this grave issue preoccupying him to such an extent? It's not so far-fetched: he didn't go to his desk directly, as was his habit, but remained standing before the board until he set about taking the clippings down. This was a clear display of how sick he was over the issue. Yes, something was changing inside him. The two of them knew that he would not explain the matter to them, even if they asked him, so they kept colluding with him: they left it up to him whether or not he would tell them about what was going on. However, Abdallah nipped these musings in the bud when he got up from his desk and left.

Nothing of note happened after that. Abdallah wandered around the hallways of the ministry, truly unaware of what he was doing. The truth is that the gallows ropes had gone back to swinging inside him. This time, they took hold of anything and everything they could cling to: he saw them swinging from the bridges, from the billboards, from the balconies of buildings – to the extent that he imagined a gallows rope at every door of the ministry and on every stairwell. He went out to the wooden café standing behind the ministry twice; each time, he tried to eat, but he had no appetite.

He was thinking about that reckless man. He must want to send some message to the people, and to himself. No, the man's not crazy – everything he does, he does knowingly. He wants to say something, but what could it be? Abdallah thought the man would, no doubt, write something in the papers in order to finally deliver his message. Granted, he might not be able to do this, since the police would surely arrest him, but how would he be sure, after all these gallows ropes, that his message had reached everyone else? It seems that no one understood anything: they thought that this reckless man was mad, or possessed, or that he was playing some silly pranks. No one seemed afraid – on the contrary, people were excited just to find out the fate of the reckless one.

As for this issue of the gallows ropes, they didn't symbolise anything; it was never a part of the country's history. Condemned criminals were not killed by hanging. Not at all: they might have been shot with rifles, or thrown off a balcony, or buried alive, but killed by hanging? By rope? By stringing them up in front of a crowd? No, that kind of thing is a world apart from this region. Abdallah considered the possible endings to this matter: would the man send a message saying that he did all that for a particular reason, and that he was sorry? Of course, he could not say that he was sorry, and just leave his message on the bridge and go away; that way, people would know that the issue had come to an end. It wouldn't cost him anything, and he would have finished the thing he started. But to make things so suspenseful – no one could predict when or where the next gallows ropes would hang – that was truly the epitome of a reckless thing.

The whole day long, he had been thinking about the reckless man with a kind of grudge. But now he began to feel sorry for him, this guy with the gallows ropes. He must be a man of influence in order to do all of this. 'We're not being respectful when we call him mad, or reckless. Others might have been labelled this way, but this man would have to have influence in order to do all that he did,' Abdallah thought.

Muhammad got up from his desk and announced that he was leaving. The time was 2:10 in the afternoon, his quitting time. Salim looked at Abdallah before he started gathering his things from his desk. Before Salim left, he looked over at Abdallah and asked him, 'Is everything all right?' 'Everything is great,' he answered. Abdallah thought this strange. Was Salim embarrassed to ask him what was preoccupying him since the morning? Or did this mean that he actually knew what was bothering him, and just wanted to see how he was doing? No matter what, Abdallah repeated, 'Everything is all right', and that there was no need to worry, he 'was just sick'. Salim left the office after giving the board – now empty of clippings – a meaningful look.

For a few minutes, Abdallah stayed at his desk, alone in the room. He was deep in thought, considering the things that must be done in hard times like these. He was about to explode inside, not really knowing what was going on. Had he gone mad? A little crazy? If he was back in his village, like the rest of them, he wouldn't doubt that he was possessed, or that someone had put a curse on him – making him a body without a mind, a rudderless craft, or a machine operated by a magician from afar.

Suddenly, he pulled out the folder and flipped through the clippings, taking them out one after the other. He was trying to see if it was possible for him, Abdallah bin Muhammad, to find out who was this man who vexed him so, who heaped all this worry on him. How does his mind work, and what are the instincts that drive him? Why would he seek to destroy the world, to plant horror everywhere? Finally, without knowing why, Abdallah started pinning the clippings back on the board. He looked at them for a long while, until it was time to leave the ministry.

The action quieted his inner turmoil, and he got back some of his balance. Now, he was more in control of his senses; there was no longer cause for concern. It seemed as if the gallows ropes disappeared from his consciousness. He went back to the rehearsed, mechanical movements that were his habit: he shut the office door and walked to his car. He didn't see gallows or ropes hanging in the air, nor from the roofs of bus stops. He started the car and locked it as he headed home, thinking himself utterly free of this sickening issue.

The closer he got to Qurum Bridge, the heavier the traffic got. Frustrated, he thought, 'No, not again! The gallows man will not come now. It's not his time. It wouldn't be the gallows man if he came now. He would have changed his behaviour; we would all have been fooled!' Once again, thoughts of gallows ropes overtook him, more forceful this time, violently clashing inside him: 'Does it make sense that he could have done this, here and now? Does it make sense that the man had finally hung something on the bridge? At a time like this?'

The thoughts haunted him arbitrarily, and the issue began to rise up inside him. Then, all the clippings burst out before his eyes – all the pictures, events and names of their authors and photographers. The drivers were watching in their cars to see what would appear when they got close to the bridge. As for him, he wanted to get going, to get away from this place quickly, without watching anything. He thought he would be all right if he could just get away from all of this. He just needed to head right and get out via the exit of the road about three kilometres before the roundabout, then turn on the service road that goes through Sultan Qaboos City, and from there, retrace his steps to the main street via Compounds Roundabout.

He signalled, but the other drivers didn't notice him. All of them were staring off into space, trying to find out what was happening on the bridge. After almost hitting a car in front of him as he tried to turn around, Abdallah was finally able to get into the right lane. He drove his car through the exit in the direction of Sultan Qaboos City's inner road and headed east. There was a lot of traffic on the street, but he was able to drive through it to the nearby roundabout, from which the road leading to the bridge branched off.

It crossed Abdallah's mind that instead of getting away from the scene of the gallows rope – which might be hanging there on Qurum Bridge – he was now actually closer to the bridge, but he could not see anything from here. He had to just go halfway around the roundabout and then straight ahead. By doing so, he would have rid his mind of the matter of the bridge and the gallows ropes for the day. He would have been able to find out the expected ending by way of the TV, or the radio. He would have put all of that off until tomorrow morning and read everything in the papers. He would sit in his chair and, once again, he would be free of all the cares of this world.

It also crossed his mind that he could go three-quarters around the roundabout, then head left and get on to the bridge. There, he could get a closer look at what was happening, and see if gallows or ropes were hanging there. It started to appear worrisome: he had to decide immediately or miss it. He went halfway around the roundabout, then three-quarters of the way around, unable to immediately turn in the direction of the escape route. He also couldn't turn in the direction of the scene of the action on the bridge. He went around one more time, going halfway around the roundabout, and then three quarters around. Stubbornly, he stayed headed toward the bridge as he let his car hit top speed.

He wasn't able to continue for long: by the foot of the bridge, there was a police car. Two officers loomed over the horizon as they ran. Their car was parked on the side of the road, its doors open, blue lights flashing. Abdallah could make out what was going on: the two officers were chasing someone else. That was him, then: it must be that heroic man, the one who hung up all those gallows ropes these past months.

Abdallah grew very excited, hoping to get a look at the car next to him. The other drivers were taking in the scene with curiosity, while the more curious among them got out of their cars to see what was going on. Abdallah thought the officers would arrest the man for sure. He looked toward the bridge, but from where he stood, he was unable to see if there were any gallows or rope. He would have to get out of his car and go to the top of the bridge to be able to see the main road. He wanted to know if the man had come back to hang up a gallows rope – and if he was able to do it – or if he came to end the matter once and for all. No doubt he too, like Abdallah, was worried all this time and wanted to end the matter, but perhaps the police took him by surprise.

Abdallah saw the hero running down the bridge, the two policemen right behind him. Some of the drivers tried to block his way, but he was quick. He had got rid of his sandals and pulled up the end of his *dishdasha* in order to run faster. People watched the chase as the man was able to dash behind the cars and run in the direction of the trees and greenery along the roundabout, leading to the bridge. Behind him now were three other men who had left their cars in order to help the two policemen, despite the fact they were screaming at the men not to get involved, or they would get themselves into trouble.

Abdallah saw the heroic man coming in the direction of the cars and tried to look him straight in his eyes. For an instant, he was able to look at his eyes as the man looked at him. His face was covered in sweat and his head bare; locks of hair were stuck to his forehead. Now, Abdallah hoped to do something to save the hunted man – but how? If the street was clear, he'd be able to let him into his car and drive off at top speed. Then he could, once the man calmed down and wiped away his sweat, ask him about the significance of all this, and about the secret that spurred him to do it all.

But that would be difficult, and Abdallah wouldn't dare do something like that, even if the road was clear. That would be against his principles, not part of his character or what he was made of. Why was he involved in the whole issue anyway? If the man had come to kill himself, would he help him, throw him from the bridge, a coarse rope around his neck? He would help him satisfy the violent desire that had preoccupied him for so long. This running man was another news item on its way to being over once and for all.

'But was it really this man,' he thought. 'Couldn't it be that they were trying to arrest the wrong man? And that the man who hung up the gallows rope – if there was one there – was not this man, but another who was able to disappear before the police arrived? This hunted man, with his light beard and smooth hair, looks decent and kind-hearted. No, this is not the face of a dangerous man, or an evil one. It's a face just like one of us, a complexion just like ours. No, it's not this man who did all these things. He's not the man behind all these clippings. Yet it must be him, or they wouldn't be chasing him. They must have seen him hanging a gallows rope.'

Abdallah left his car and headed toward the bridge. At that point, everyone was facing the three men and the two policemen who were running after the suspect. Abdallah felt like it was the right time to take a look at the gallows rope, but he wasn't able to think at that point. He ran up toward the bridge.

The weather had begun to get hotter and the sun cast its burning rays on everything. Despite this, the view from above seemed bizarre: the cars had lined up in six crooked rows, gleaming in the yellow column of the sun's rays. Some of the drivers had left their cars, while a number of policemen in their blue-flashing cars tried to order the drivers to move. Yet most of them continued to stare at the bridge and the movements on it.

Abdallah was facing the street. He was facing this whole, strange gathering, amidst the crowd of drivers and policemen. The scene was barely there; the sweat in his eyes made everything blurry so that nothing could get through. He stood at the impact attenuator facing east, then stepped back a bit in the midst of the people's noise and confusion. Then, he ducked down a bit to get a look at the gallows rope, but he didn't find one. There was no long, hanging rope, suspended from the side. He stepped backward and looked at the other side of the bridge, on the west. He stared intently at the clamorous crowd, which was unable to find out what was going on, but was waiting. At that point, Abdallah was unable to realise what he was truly doing. That whole crowd was gathered, waiting for something from him. He had to do something.

From below, Abdallah looked like someone intent on doing something. Everyone watched as he untied his dark blue mussar; they watched him as he tied it to one of the columns of the bridge's roadblock. With a movement backward, he suddenly disappeared. Below, no one on the same side or the other side could see what was happening. Then suddenly, something was flung downward.

It was five seconds before one of them suddenly screamed: he had seen the man with the end of the mussar around his neck throw himself into the air. It was Abdallah bin Muhammad himself. He was bare-headed, eyes bulging, looking off into the horizon as he hung off the edge of the bridge. The others screamed and the police took off running in the direction of the bridge, while everyone left their cars to get a look at the man hanging by his neck. They all thought he was the reckless one, the one with the gallows ropes, come to hang himself, finally. Their mouths gaped for a few seconds, and then a few of them began to come closer to the bridge, and to the hanging body. Loud murmurs rose up, then screams. Then, some of the people below pointed their mobile phone cameras at the man hanging under the bridge in order to get a suitable shot of this shocking, sudden and important event.

Translated by Nader K. Uthman

Three Poems

Hussein Jelaad

A Little Sugar

Do you touch the New York moon from the tenth floor?
I still scoop water with my palm, search in the river for my friends'
   eyes
heedless of the letters, ink-flooded, tumbling from my top pocket.

*You tell me that I carried off the forest's honey left behind by bears, so now I
sleep dreamless in the light. Without you, my hand can't lift to wave or write
a letter. I expect no meeting in a crowd and don't lift my eyes as I walk: the
faces I know from the scent of streets and memories. As though we grow used
to the world passing in front of mirrors and fail to see our souls withering in
the passages.*

True.
   Our knees no longer tremble to see light pass across a naked back.
We've grown anxious before staircases.
   The trees we climbed by stealth when young left for the forests
when our hands grew slack, the nests embrace pebbles that neither
shine nor fall, and the breeze laughs all around us.

*Big cities are a trick of dreams, you say: so keep your small joys safe.
Check your wounds: the moons here are cold. But don't go all that
way. Isn't there more joy to be found on your doorstep than in dancing
with strangers? Do as we always do and drink my coffee with your scant*

sugar, or every evening lay your head across my knee so I can breathe
your face.

You won't find a little mat with the keys to Paradise hiding
beneath, not here. No doorway with 'I love you twice' inscribed
on the frame.

Fine.
Our old pictures aren't of anyone: we're no longer in the frame.
We won't grow back because some hand wipes the rubble's dust
from our sunken grins. In the original story the river runs to flood
and the earth's a female moon, but we leap from the world every
day and do nothing twice.

We're happy with the unseen, you say: content to be snatched away to the
world's end. But when all's said and done, we shall never reach ourselves in
mirrors: like making a reckoning of one's journey two steps down the road.
Before us, our eventide. Behind us, in the vanishing future, the weeping of a
child. We stumble on the truth just once: being born we wail at the hand that
slaps us into breath. The earth is broad: welcome to life.

I wasn't born in the bed itself after Achilles' death, for I fear perfection and polish my sword twice daily. I own a single shirt that
I remove before sleep, and, love done, leave hanging from the
lover's bed. Preachers curse me in the marketplace and behind the
shutters women wail for a boy gone mad before his time.

The song's lighter than a bridegroom's handkerchief, you say: and the thea-
tre's lights take up the task of bringing the film to an end. Stand and scream
your name: become the story's hero and exit wreathed in smoke. Are not our
names all that's left of melody? After us no one gets close to endings.

Windows are a house's metaphor for sky and light a proffered
crumb to help our souls step out beyond its gloom. I never mention
love twice: when I count beyond one thousand I go wrong. I
take the door with me whenever I travel so I can go into myself.

There's no geography outside my frame, and keys are a lie from legends to stop us sleeping soundly.

You play the fool a lot, you say: the mirrors have cut you, too. And you laugh: secrets can't be said, so how can you narrate the journey of creation (Genesis) as if it were a bedtime story or old memory. You never got between Adam and his soul to know what it is to weep between my hands, and I never donned the serpent's garb to taste temptation and lead astray each sea-close moon with scarlet eyes. Your first love-letters are my heart, which I forgot in ancient tongue. I know love from your shirt buttons, hastily snagging my downy hair in lifts, on park benches, sprinting between stations.

Secrets are told every day but we don't hear them. Who sees you in their heart save me? By day a thousand hands wave near you. So: the world's a personal affair (if you want) and the hymn grasped in the hand sets the shadows of the self to trembling and delivers harvest unto harvest so that footsteps may flower in a new hymn.

I don't speak of my soul, floating on heaven's sea, you say: I make do with wings that sprout when I embrace you and furl in rage. I slammed the door behind you. Leave me a small space in the margin that you might know I love you, when I do. Don't strike your brow in front of me each time you're late, trailing apologies in your wake. Your hands are your two hands. I have a past before you and after you, a purpose. I know that you watch the world through your eyes and lean over me with your heart. Go after your prophets as gently as the mad: leave their majesty unbroken. Scream my name whenever you long to kiss me; drop in on me to put flesh on your bones and commit whatever profanity you desire. No one will see you but me. Come, I shall pass you all my secrets in a neat handbag. Do you remember?

First Love

To love, two calls:
initial groan
and heart's croak.

Late night calls ring in dreams.
Of your distant voice I have only the ocean retreating from your
    silence
and the hand's preoccupation with the phone cord.
You have my old shirt, buttons sparkling in the steel sky.

Like the banks of a river
we walk together constantly;
the river gets there but we never reach the sea.
Have we suddenly grown so much?
That I sleep on the arm of a lover other than you?
That you bear our child by a Polish migrant,
A New York trader in Red Indian horses?

The sky belonged to us and the kites, but the dead made a pillow of
    the ancient church's gloom.
We were content to walk the earth like this, wingtips trailing.

A lock of your hair and a bottle of perfume: your present to me on
    my seventeenth birthday,
I planted them in the Garden of Bells fast by the priest's sermons
    and Sunday prayers.

I put away our old friends in a wooden box,
and entrusted to the monk, so when the angelic host passes by they
    might bow their heads in deference and chant:

Our rings
Your mirror that became our mirror
The perfumed eraser, watercolours and scribbles
Coloured ribbons in your hair
Songs of Abdel Halim and Edith Piaf
Abdel Nasser's picture, black and white
Nietzsche's moustache and Sartre's hell
Your school smock
Freckles on the shoulder's slope
Bellybutton
And my hands at summer's start!

To love, two calls:
softly it passes over us like scent,
issues from eyelashes like a final breath.

Royal Coaches

His coaches shine with splendour, robes embroidered with Hijaz
    gold.
We rushed to strike the land between his hands
and hide
(to curtail servants' reports of stinking sheep flesh in our braids)
and justify our bowing to a moon that came to rest in Sham
from Thaniyat al Wadaa.

We were brutal with women and children.
The horses did not escape our frown.
We lit no fire,
we did not wash for a thousand years,
until at last the prince grinned ear to ear
and in British barracks bedded down.

Translated by Robin Moger

Layla's Belly

Hyam Yared

B y the time Layla thought she had found love, it was too late. She met Will after having read Yourcenar. 'Love is a punishment. We are punished for not being able to remain alone.' It was in Beirut, on a busy street in Gemmayzé. The Rue Gourot. For a long time she had refused to indulge in the belly dance of this city surgically excising its own pain. Postponing its duty of memory. This renunciation to the sound of blaring techno music saddened her. It astonished her to see people arguing in bars over the bill. The will to power in the price of a lemonade.

She had extricated herself from this dance, from this war at the same moment. When all was said and done, she preferred the company of her tabby cat. Now grey, now white. Every time she fed it, she thought of the unbearable beauty of things. It doesn't kill you, she said to herself, you just come through with cuts and bruises. Layla was waiting for something more unconditional than life, but nothing trickled through the gaps in her being. At times, loneliness weighed on her, forced her out into the night to do the rounds – Elements, Gem, Ventral, Mynt, Bo18 – the nightclubs that vied with one another with eye-catching names, numbers, kitsch and flashy décor. Layla went out squeezed into jeans so tight they guaranteed the usual success. And the usual disaster. She had clothes for every occasion. Clothes in which she was a predator, clothes which made her a seductress. Now and again she allowed herself a brief fling with a foreigner. Better than with a native, as far as gossip and discretion went. Her cat was always waiting for her when she returned home.

Will thought he would play it cool when he saw her; take things slowly. He didn't talk to her about his desire at first. He talked about his soul — that flame banished to his veins, possibly to his bladder. She found this perceptive, almost clairvoyant. She had been constantly plagued by urinary tract infections. She had consulted a specialist who had advised her not to change partners so often. She had never worked out how to avoid making such attachments. One more man in her bed, one less ache in her heart, she thought. She felt compelled to drive out the inexorable loneliness of being in the world. 'I'm high on life,' she told her friends, 'I snort it, I smoke it, I don't need morphine. Life's enough for me.' Many men were attracted by her directness. She was knocked back at random, each time dying a different death and each time swearing, 'That's it, that's my last death.' Will must have noticed this, because he was careful not to stare at her hips. He communed with her in the language of the soul. He spoke to her of existence. She thanked fate which, until now, had always had her meet fuckers. Gimps. Cowards. Never a soulmate. That evening, careful not to rush things, Will did no more than give her a kiss on the cheek as he said goodnight.

Every detail of that night, every word was seared into her brain. Every gesture. The kiss they shared on the pavement. She couldn't sleep. She thought about Will as she lay on her back. And on her belly too. His kiss had left her every organ fit to burst. Until that night, she had lived as if one might accumulate a sum total of moments. As though desire, love, gestures were burnt *in-vitro* before fertilisation. That evening she had pulled away from his embrace, eager not to rush things. She felt as though she had sensed something rare in his restraint. The moment Will had walked away, she regretted keeping him at arm's length. She wasn't sure now that she wanted to postpone passion. Standing on her doorstep, she could run after him, catch him up, ask him to stay with her. She did none of these things, but went to bed alone, consoled by the comforts of hope. The following day, when he called, he told her that he was sorry not to have stayed with her. She was too quick to concur. 'I'm sorry too,' she said. Her heart was racing. She could feel the ground in the soles of her feet. Her vagina in her head. Her brain in her blood. None of her organs was where it should be. The next time they met, they made love. Will penetrated her. Her eyes closed, her body and her heart wide open, she thought this is how two bodies should be. Zero degrees of loneliness.

Layla loved in order not to disappear.

Will lit a cigarette. His body brushed against Layla's back as she lay next to him. The smoke traced a line along her naked form. He exhaled a cloud of smoke before asking her, 'Do you have someone in your life?' She couldn't understand the transition from his erection to this. She wanted to say that she couldn't possibly have someone in her life, and to gyrate her hips as she had done. Like the lyrics to the song by Barbara, 'A love one might die of . . .' She turned to him:

'Lots of people, but there's no one special. What about you, do you have someone?'

'Yes.'

His reply rang out like a sniper's bullet. Layla imaged a Citroën 2CV belonging to a bored, elderly couple. This, surely, was what his wife was like. A beaten-up old 2CV Will could not bring himself to abandon, out of consideration for her suffering. She adopted the detached air of a casual lover who is owed nothing. Will's revelation, immediately after sex, was like rape. He could at least have put his cards on the table before they fucked, she thought, disappointed to find that love and fucking were like a game of chess.

'Have you been together long?' she asked, clinging to the thought of spent desire, of a couple who had been too long together, convinced that he must be staying with this woman so that their time together might mean something. She would be well into her forties, she had probably met him when they were young, thought Layla. Childhood sweethearts. A mistake, probably. She waited for him to confirm what she thought. Fifteen years, he would say, maybe twelve. Ten at least.

'A year,' Will's voice echoed in the room. 'We've been together a year.'

Twenty-four hours had elapsed since, with platonic speeches, he had wooed her with carnal ends. Perhaps he did not love this woman he had met a year ago, she thought. She did not ask.

Will nodded just the same. 'Yes,' he said, 'I do love her.'

Her mind buzzed with questions. One too many men had used her body. She had to get out of here now. She resented him for dragging the soul into what was nothing more than a fuck, only to take both away as soon as he had had her. A soul with a beautiful back, she thought as she slipped on her shoes. A nice arse. She could make do with pornography when she had to. She was angry with herself for being in the wrong place at the wrong time yet again. She dreamt of free souls, in thrall, searching for the same thing. The reality was a tired aching body and a lie.

'The absolute is seedier than you think,' he said, as though he could read her mind. 'It's not reality that's abusing you, it's you demanding more than it can give.'

Meanwhile, she had a heart she wanted to give away, any way she could, to anyone who'd cherish it. Layla was tired of being the dregs of desire left behind on a plate; tired of the same spiel from the same men eager to use her crotch as a latrine to dump their seed. They say the only thing not to ride an easy woman is a train. Layla thought of the pain of the rails. Of bodies crushed beneath the passing carriages. However much she lied to herself, she could not trample her own face. To be used was a vileness from which she could not emerge unscathed. She would have liked to draw a line through the past. Come to terms with the remains of her love. Reading Proust, she had thought perhaps that was what Time was. A lost emptiness.

Every time she went home, more alone than dead, more in need than craving, every time she crossed the threshold Layla was accustomed to finding her flame intact, curled up in the armchair with her cat. Every time she turned the key in the lock, this part of her would recognise her and come to greet her. Her cat would shift in the chair and Layla's face would return to normal. The day after Will, this didn't happen. There was no sign of the flame. In its place was nothing. Nothing everywhere. She looked under the bed, behind the door, under the doormat. The flame had simply disappeared. Guttered out. She went back out on to the street, retraced her steps, carefully going back the way she had come. It was no use. She would have fumbled inside Will's body, but he was longer taking her calls.

She questioned passers-by, asking if they had seen something that looked like a haze. They said they had seen nothing. No flame anywhere. Long nights passed. She fell asleep with the absence of herself. One morning she noticed a swelling in her body. Her belly was distended. She pictured a pinhole, a condom, some night when she had had too much to drink. She rushed into the kitchen and stripped off her clothes. She longed to strip off her skin. She stood in front of the washing machine and stuffed everything she wanted to use into the drum. If she could, she would have thrown her body in too. She turned the dial on the machine to the *indelicate* programme, added a double dose of detergent and turned it on. As abrasive as possible. She waited. She hoped she might find amnesia when she opened the washing machine. A memory scalded. Frayed. Clogging up the pipes. Her heart, intact, sitting on the fresh laundry like soap suds on the surface of things. The clean smell turned her stomach. Disillusioned, she gathered everything up, folded her clothes and put them away, then went back out to face the street. Knocked up. That was what she had been, knocked up. As though by a sniper's bullet into a corpse. It was increasingly difficult to walk. In fact, she was no longer moving; life was moving through her, carrying her along. She found the strength to drag herself to the doctor, a backstreet abortionist by trade. He was categorical.

'Madame, there is nothing I can do for you. I cannot perform an abortion. You are pregnant with nothingness.'

Translated from the French by Frank Wynne

Who Are You Carrying That Rose For?

Islam Samhan

for Gaza . . . and all the martyrs

A lover stopped me and I said:
'Who are you carrying that rose for?
Your beloved will be snatched away by the shelling soon
and become a fistful of ash, so don't wager on love.'

A lover stopped me, and she said:
'I have a lover who will come . . .
Maybe during the ceasefire I'll manage
to get my hair done
and pin a brooch to my chest,
a rainbow-coloured brooch
and run, at the last hour,
to him.
I think that time will be on my side then
unlike my luck now, terrified by the sound of bombs.'

The little boy stopped me and said:
'A few days ago we were playing in Gaza's alleys
and a misunderstanding led to a fight with the little girl.
I didn't mean to release a storm of screams in her face
but the doll's business is mine
and the little girl could not convince me that dolls
come and go, like planes.'

The little girl stopped me and said:
'Ahmad died.
He enjoyed the phosphorous toys
that lit up brightly.
He didn't know
that he burnt up like a butterfly
without a sound.'

A woman stopped me, and I said:
'I see people carrying your son
as if nothing had happened to him
and I didn't see you.
From the boy's mouth flowed
a stream of flowers,
crimson.
I made out a shy smile.'

The same woman stopped me again, and said:
'The house was full to the brim with sons,
the middle one was fetching hot water
to sweep away the first early hairs off his chin
but in the blink of an eye they all left, carried on shoulders
like the handbag of a girl heading to her death.'

The sad man stopped me and said:
'I was arranging shells in the fish tank
and brushing Jamila's hair,
gazing at the spray of freckles on her breast
but the planes
did not wait for me to wrap
her bridal waist in its feminine shawl,
and the shawl and her limbs flew out the window.'

The man masked by his *keffiyeh* stopped me and said:
'What's the use of hiding or disappearing?
In a while, our cover will be blown

and the rockets will accompany us to our graves
and since I was unknown before, I will be unknown after.
But the deer will know me from my clothes and from a necklace
I have hidden in my pocket.'

As for me, I was stopped by the scene, and I said to myself:
How does death become a bread
that we hunger for?
We await our ration of death
and walk to the cemetery, family after family,
carrying our civil documents and family records.

Translated by Ghenwa Hayek

from the poem 'The Geology of the I'

in *The Book of J*

Joumana Haddad

'A poem is a naked person'
Bob Dylan

I am the sixth day of December of the year 1970;
I am the hour just after noon.
I am my mother's screams giving birth to me
and her screams giving birth to her.
Her womb releasing me to emerge from myself.
her sweat achieving my potentiality.
I am the doctor's slap which revived me.
(each subsequent slap trying to revive me quite destroyed me).
I am the eyes of the family upon me,
the gazes of father, grandfather, of aunts.
I am all their possible scenarios;
I am the curtains drawn, the curtains behind the curtains and the
    walls behind those,
and I am she who has no name no hand for what comes behind.
I am the expectations of me, the aborted dreams,
the voids suspended as amulets around my neck.
I am the tight red coat I cried whenever I wore,
and every constriction which still makes me cry.
I am the brown-haired doll with plastic eyes;
I am that discarded doll I refused to rock,
cast aside, still oozing blood from the base of the head
(two drops on ordinary days and three on days off and holidays).

I am the sad hole in my teacher's socks.
It still stares at me like the reproach of Abel in my soul,
staring to tell me of her poverty and my impotence,
the exhaustion of my patience and the terror of her despair.
I am the times table I haven't mastered to this day;
I am the two that adds up to one, always one.
I am the theory of curved lines, never joined up,
and I am their applications.
I am my hatred of history, of algebra and of physics.
I am my faith, as a child, that the earth revolved around my heart
and my heart around the moon.
I am the lie of Santa Claus,
which I believe to this day.
I am the astronaut I used to dream I would become.
I am the wrinkles of my grandmother who committed suicide;
I am my forehead pressed against her absent lap.
I am the boy (was he called Jack?) who pulled my hair and ran off.
I am he who made me cry, which made me love him even more.
I
am my little kitten;
and the neighbours' son's bicycle which ran me over and I did not
    protest.
(I sold the souls of my cat for a single glance from that handsome
    boy.)
I am blackmail, my inaugural vice.
I am war
and the corpse of the man the combatants dragged around in front
    of me,
and his torn-off leg trying to catch up with him.
I
am the books which I read as a child which were unsuitable for me
(which I now write and which are still unsuitable for me).
I am the adolescence of my right breast,
and I am the wisdom of the left.
The power of both under a tight shirt
and then my awareness of their power: the beginning of the descent.

I am my rapid boredom, my first cigarette, my late obstinacy,
and the seasons past.
I am the granddaughter of the child I was;
her lack of my anger,
my disappointments and my triumphs,
my labyrinths and my lusts,
my lies, my wars,
my scars and my wrong turns.
I am the tenderness I bear despite myself;
I am my god and my greed;
my absences filled with my dead;
and I am my dead who never sleep,
my slain who never sleep;
I am their last sighs on the pillow each dawn.
And
I
am my resentment, my contagion,
my danger,
and my flight from cowardice to worse.
I am my waiting around not knowing the time
and my not understanding space.
I am the silence which I have learned
and the silence which I haven't mastered yet.
The solitude which steps on my soul like an insect.
I am the granddaughter of the child I was:
My lack of her innate carelessness,
of her selfless perfection.
I am love's disaster
and happening.
I am the wolf of poetry coursing through my blood
and me running barefoot with it;
I am she who is in search of her hunter
not finding her hunter.
I am the frothing waters of my lust as it gestures on to lust;
I am the succession of tongues which irrigate its froth,
and my lipstick anticipating their thirst.

I am my fingernails too: what lies beneath them and what they sink
   into.
I am the memory of their wounds,
the memory of their anger,
the memory of their weakness,
the memory of their strength, beyond proof,
and I am the little pieces of flesh torn from men's backs
in each ecstatic moment.
I am my teeth
and my delicate thighs
and my bawdy desires.
I am my sins and oh how I love them;
I am my sins and the way they mirror me.
And I am my girlfriend who betrayed me -
And I thank her for that.
I am my spinal cord howling in the face of the traitors.
I am my eyes looking into a darkness which is mine.
I am my pain,
yes, my pain.
I am my scream in the middle of the night
(suppressed at the appropriate time.)
I am what I hide,
what I don't want to hide but do
and what I do want to hide and don't.
I am 'tell me how much you love me'
and 'I don't believe you'.
I am the head connected to the body, disconnected from the body.
I am my early death - I say that without drama –
and whatever devastation will be left behind me.
I am the madness and the absence which are before me
And the petty, little, revealing things:
The postage stamps, the clippings from letters,
the notes under the glass of the table, my smiles in old photos.
I am the composite of men who loved me and whom I didn't love.
I am those I loved who didn't love me,
those I didn't love and who didn't love me,

and those who imagined I loved them
and imagined that they didn't love me.
I am the composite of the one man whom I love.
I am the woman whose image cried in the photo of her wedding (but
    only the image).
I am my refractions, my defeats, my vain victories.
I am my salvation from drowning once (if it really was salvation).
I am the staleness of a breadcrumb on my table.
I am the seven days and the centuries which took me to create myself.
I am the fish and the birds and the trees
and the smoke of the factories,
and the asphalt of the road and the whistling of the bombs,
and I am the wind and the spiders and the flesh of fruit.
I am every volcano on top of every mountain in every country on
    every continent on every planet.
I am each hole dug in the earth of each country on each continent
    on each planet.
I am the second which took me to destroy myself
and all my bodies
and the humid streets of my city
and I am who was and I am who I could have been.
I am the blue dress that my mother refused to buy for herself so as to
    pay my school fees.
I am my father's library, his eyes and his petulant heart.
I am the glances I did not allow myself, the words I did not say and
    the lips I did not kiss
and the trails I will not leave behind me:
All the stupid things I did not do
all the departures I did not return from.
I
am my daughter which I did not give birth to
and
the woman I will be.
I am almost that woman
and I am almost that man
which I did not become completely

and who saves me from myself every day.
I am the woman that I am not right now,
all the things and the people who I was yesterday,
who I will be tomorrow,
and who create me.

Translated by John Peate

from the novel

The Scalpel

Kamel Riahi

Why couldn't the criminal be a woman?

Based on eyewitness accounts, the papers reported that the criminal was wearing a helmet and riding a red motorcycle. An investigation confirmed that most red motorcycles fitting that description belonged to wealthy young women. One of the victims said that she had heard a woman's voice shouting to her before the scalpel slashed through her jeans and butchered her backside. Another victim, before retracting her statement, said that the criminal was small, as if he was a slightly built youth, or even a girl. But the other victims insisted that, beyond a shadow of a doubt, the criminal was a man.

'It's impossible that a woman would do that to other women,' concluded Ms Layla Ghasham, professor of psychology at the College of Humanities. 'Such aggressiveness only exists among men. It's masculine sadism, there's no doubt about it.'

In her recent article on the concept of sadism, she offered further analysis: 'The term "sadism" entered into popular usage in reference to the French aristocrat the Marquis de Sade (1740–1814). De Sade's perverted reputation began after he won the affection of a young street girl, who he invited to his summer house. Once there, he held her captive and stabbed her repeatedly. He later killed two prostitutes after offering them lethal doses of Spanish fly aphrodisiac, a crime which earned him twenty-seven years in prison. The criminal, therefore, must be a man.

'According to works of analytical psychology, the sadist derives his pleasure from the humiliation of his partner, who he immerses in a sense of inferiority and filth. And because pure mental sadism thrives on the act of intimidation, in my opinion, this was what the criminal was seeking when he struck fear into the hearts of all those women, and that is why his crimes have come to claim a stranglehold on this secure society.'

I heard that professor Biram Rabihi, from the same department, responded to her remarks in a lengthy piece that was published in the same magazine. He argued that it was more probable that the criminal was a woman because, in moments of desperation, women become more aggressive than men and lash out at those of their own gender: nothing reminds a woman of her own failure as much as another woman's success. In his analysis, the professor noted that most of the victims were charming and seemed to lead successful lives. 'That is why,' he suggested, 'it is probable that the attack came from within the female unit.'

Dr Rabihi also argued that, contrary to the assumptions of Professor Ghasham, sadism is not an exclusively male trait. Rather, he ventured that 'female sadism stems from a woman's sexual frigidity. A lack of sexual satisfaction among women can turn into a sense of loathing, a desire for vengence or a destructive outburst, which can sometimes amount to sadistic tendencies.'

Readers caught on that the doctor was referring to 'the mediocre scientific knowledge' of Professor Layla Ghasham when he merely stated that nobody has the right to offer a conclusive judgment on such precise scientific matters, especially if they require further consideration. The press interpreted this as Dr Rabihi alluding to the fact that Professor Layla Ghasham had still not completed her dissertation, and that her previous research had not been of a sufficient standard to earn her a university teaching position.

At that point, the debate got bogged down by issues far from the original topic and even reached the point of slander. Dr Rabihi struck out at Professor Ghasham's civil status, being still single despite being over forty, and she retorted by alleging that he'd had an affair with one of his female students. The following week, Dr Rabihi responded by accusing Professor Ghasham of being a lesbian, saying that he had discovered her in the female teachers' room in a compromising position with one of the cleaning ladies. The doctor ended his article by stating that he was stopping this debate with the professor because, in his opinion, she didn't have the intellectual rigour needed to participate, adding that she should visit a psychologist before attempting to teach psychology. Only for her corpulence, he concluded, he wouldn't have been surprised to learn that it was in fact *she* who had committed the crimes, and otherwise warned her, in his mocking ironic manner, that she was at risk of becoming a victim of that scalpel, bearing as she did a few of the same characteristics as the victims. He was, of course, taking the piss, because Professor Ghasham wasn't exactly a looker.

After that article, Professor Layla Ghasham would only get out of her car directly in front of her house. She would turn and glance behind her a lot, as if someone was always pointing at her.

It was clear that she had become very nervous. She didn't leave her office any more, she began to dictate her classes from her chair and she never turned to face the blackboard. They say she started wearing a heavy, velvet coat at the beginning of autumn, even though the heat of summer had not yet faded.

I can't deny that I learnt a lot from that bizarre debate between Professor Ghasham and Dr Rabihi. I learnt about the case of Ibn Al Hujjaj, a friend of Bou Lahiya, who got kicks out of undressing next to the window so that women could see him, a case they call 'exhibitionism and nudity'. The most I ever knew about this category of men was that, contrary to appearances, they were sexually impotent. 'If, for example, a woman that he was harassing were to respond to his apparent desire to copulate, he would quickly conceal his arousal and appear resolutely in front of her as one who is sexually impotent. He by no means ever thinks about building true relationships, but seeks provocation and sudden, non-committal stimulation.'

When I initially read about him, I pitied Ibn Al Hujjaj, but then I wondered if he could be the criminal. In fact, all of my acquaintances seemed to fit as the perpetrator of the crime. Bou Lahiya's remarks, for example, seemed strangely forced, like that time when he told me that his father and mother died when his house was destroyed by a carob tree that had fallen on it. An odd story, which I used to listen to as if I was listening to a grandparent's fairy tale. Recently, he told me that his father died in a field after the hernia that had afflicted him for years suddenly split open. And when I said, 'You told me a different story about your father's death,' he got angry and left me, withdrawing to his books. I don't understand him any more, nor can I grasp his affliction. It seems like he has started progressively losing his memory, and I suspect that those yellow books that he returns to every night, reading and copying till dawn, are what's making him lose his mind.

Writing in bed and worried that I'll fall asleep, I don't know why I've carried this cursed notebook to my pillow. Bou Lahiya went into his room over an hour ago and I haven't heard his voice, but the light is still on, which means that he is in the company of his own notebook. I wish I could read what that strange man is writing! The curiosity is killing me.

From Bou Lahiya's notebook:
The story of Khadija that shook the world

My task has finished, I won't write anything else about Ibn Khaldoun today. I've become convinced that I'm delusional. Statues don't talk or move and are not infested by lice. Statues are statues. Shame on me, to disturb them in their peaceful slumber, even if I justify myself by saying that the matter is both metaphorical and symbolic. Because, in life, what is more remarkable than these wondrous snippets? That is what is butchering women's backsides. Isn't that story more wondrous than my own?! The story of a semiliterate Negro who became a book fiend?! And Shwarreb himself whom I never understood, despite the long months that we spent together under a single roof?

I can still remember the day he burst into our lives like a nightmare. As usual, myself and the Negro were in the kitchen frying eggs for supper, and I was accusing him of not doing it properly. He would spend the entire day in the house and at five o'clock he'd go to guard the macaroni factory. He used to say that the factory didn't need protection because people hated macaroni. He couldn't stand even speaking about it, and more than once he banned me from eating it, saying, 'Cook it at night after I leave the house and open the windows to get rid of the smell so that it doesn't disgust me when I get back'. Fortunately for him, he went back to working nights after the boss replied to letters of complaint that he dropped into the factory suggestions box.

He said that he couldn't sleep at night any more because he had gotten used to the vigils, which is why he took brief naps during the daytime in the guardhouse. He was punished on several occasions, and would defend himself by saying, 'I can't live during the day any more!' He came back that day happy because things had returned to normal. Days were back, and night was returning. The Negro suffered from weak eyesight, and light made him uneasy. I told him that he reminded me of the main character in Albert Camus' novel *The Stranger*, which he then insisted he wanted to read. That same day, he fell in love with novels, a passion which only increased after Shwarreb slashed his cheek and caused him to be sacked from the factory.

One day, the Negro told me that he had woken up late and was still under the spell of a nightmare. 'There was a hideous bird perched on my chest. It started to peck at my face, my body, even my belly-button, then it started to pull out my intestines. It chewed on them for a while, then it spat them in my face. It was a disgusting night-mare; I woke up straight after and vomited. I don't think I can even think of food ever again.'

I'm reminded of it now because it was that night that I wrote the story about Al Makakh, the brain-eating bird.

But more importantly, while the Negro was telling me about his dream and I was frying eggs, there was a knock at the door. He went to answer it, and when he returned his face was even blacker than before. Visibly shaking, he mumbled that the 'nightmare at the door' was knocking, so I left the eggs on the stove and went out to find an ugly man in a Berber robe. His long blond hair was pulled back in a tight ponytail, and a tattoo depicting a terrifying snake rose out from under his tight shirt, which was tied in a protruding knot above his satchel. The sleeves were folded back to reveal the undulating surface of his flexed muscles, encircled by the bulging green veins. A toned, hairless chest peeked through the open collar of his shirt and was adorned with a thick, black string, from which dangled the head of a pharaoh and a swastika. His face was long like a camel's which, coupled with his coarse lips, made him look like a dusty, beastly wretch.

After a few seconds' silence, he asked me if I was Malik Al Manfoukhy, known as Bou Lahiya.

'Yes, that's me', I replied, upon which he strode into the house wearing a wicked smile.

'Well, then, why aren't you welcoming me? Haven't you been expecting someone?'

'No, I actually haven't been expecting anyone,' I said, running behind him back through the doorway. 'Who are you?'

'Think hard,' he ordered, moving to take a slurp of water out of the tall crystal pitcher from which I had forbidden the Negro to drink.

'Drop that!' I exclaimed as he was about to drink. 'Get something else to drink from. I don't want anyone sharing my bottle with me'. Without the slightest regard for me or the glass I had placed next to him, the stranger put the pitcher between his big, disgusting lips.

'Who are you?' I cried, trembling slightly. 'If you do not tell me who you are and why you are here, I will call the police!'

He put down the bottle, which he had emptied of water, and burst into a lengthy fit of laughter. 'You seem like a very nervous person. I don't know how we will manage to live together.'

'You intend to live with me?! WHO ARE YOU?' No sooner had the words passed my mouth than something stirred in my memory. 'Are you one of Sofyan's relatives?' I murmured. He smiled that wicked smile a second time and nodded. 'But you are late,' I said, slowly recovering from the shock, 'and someone else is renting your place.'

This angered him. 'Why'd you go and invite someone else to live in my room?' he roared. 'I'm going to sever his head myself. And you, you were supposed to wait a while until we came back.'

'So who would have paid the rent?'

'I was going to pay you personally,' he claimed. 'Look, evict that thing and tell me how much he paid.'

'That won't happen. The man is a legal tenant, I can't evict him. Besides, I get along with him.'

'But I didn't take a liking to him!'

'Do you know him?' I asked.

'Wasn't he the lump of coal who opened the door to me and then ran away as if he'd seen a ghost?'

'Yes, that's him. And it doesn't matter whether or not you get along with him. The important thing is that I get along with him because I'm the one sharing the house with him.'

The Negro had reappeared, with traces of fright lingering on his face. The visitor examined him closely before saying, 'It's not a problem, we can be three. Just look at him, he's so simple and miserable. OK, I'm going out. I won't be late, but don't wait for me 'cause I have a key already, Sofyan gave me a copy. I don't want us to waste the entire day just trying to figure out the basics.' With that, he threw his leather suitcase and dusty coat aside and left with a cackle, leaving me to enter with the Negro into his nightmare.

Those were dark months, the ones we spent with that beast that stormed our house by force. When I think back to that day, I'm reminded of the snake that lived in my childhood home and used to force me and my family to sleep in the stables. That snake would roam around constantly in the ceiling shafts as if it were the master and we were but cumbersome guests. It used to caress dry palm fronds with its poisonous tongue and sometimes it would even catch an annoying canary.

That was over twenty years ago, well before the lightning bolt struck which took my mother and the house with it. For some time afterwards, my father lay weeping for her under the carob tree that he took such pleasure from, saying that it had protected us.

I remember one day he woke up angrily. He picked up his axe, headed out towards the gigantic tree and was about to cut it down when the hernia that had plagued him for so long flared up once more. He collapsed under the tree, twisted in pain, and died before any help reached him. Our neighbour, who was one of the first to reach the carob tree, said that he had been bitten, because his corpse had turned blue, and that the culprit was a viper or some other snake. But he was surprised by the location of the wound, which was on the back of my father's left hand.

For months, the snake had been ripping the backsides of women with its scalpel, and no one knew about it. There were thousands of victims; the streets were emptied of women, and for weeks I only saw old men out on the main roads. What I didn't understand was how made-up foreign women, whose red behinds peek out from under their mini-shorts, aren't afraid of the blazing sun of Tunisian beaches?! Sometimes, I think they're suicidal. Other times, I wonder how a woman can hide herself indoors when her only crime is to have a beautiful ass!

Apparently, the mosques in the city were uncertain about the big debate on the interpretation of the Quranic verse: 'Your wives are a tilth for you, so go to your tilth as ye will.' Prayers at the mosque would often finish with people squabbling over different opinions of the meaning of the verse, specifically the words 'as ye will'. It was said that dictionaries confirmed that they connoted 'how' and 'where', which is why foreign news agencies thought that the criminal was probably an Islamic extremist who had tried solving the matter in his own way: mutilating women's behinds so that men would renounce them and return to the word of God.

One fundamentalist group posted a photo on its website of a man slapping the backside of a foreign female tourist who was kidnapped in Baghdad before having her throat slit from ear to ear. Afterwards, the resistance issued a statement saying that the group was affiliated with the Tunisian jihadi fighter that had appeared in Tunis to combat immorality and debauchery, praising him as a young defender of the cause.

A TV station well-known for its opposition to legal and social reforms that have taken place in Tunisia since independence invited one of the fundamentalists on to the show and asked his opinion on the matter.

'Tunisians,' he began, 'have gone too far in defaming sanctity. Forbidding polygamy and granting women a set of rights which contradict Shariah law wasn't enough for them. It's got to the point where they have started referring to buttocks using the name of one of the Prophet's wives, the one who was closest to him. These are the signs of the times, and God's punishment will be meted out on this nation that, in its debauchery, has turned into a bunch of fags . . .'

Incidentally, the signal was cut and the show host excused himself, saying that the debate had strayed off the topic and that the traffic on the airwaves caused by the programme's listeners had disrupted the satellite connection. Telephone calls were cancelled and listeners had to make do with emails.

The channel moved on to a summary of the news: Mexican women had organised a peaceful demonstration held in solidarity with the Tunisian women who were being criticised for standing up against the oppression of their bodies. They considered anal sex to be a matter of personal freedom, and called for similar shows of support to be organised worldwide.

A spokesperson from the World Health Organisation said that they were very concerned about the consequences of the current crisis, particularly after they received reports indicating that the number of births in Tunisia had risen dramatically. Analysts claimed that this was due to men's aversion to the practice of changing sexual positions.

One of the sheikhs of the fundamentalist group offered his analysis: the women whose backsides were being butchered had strayed from God's path in an Islamic country. He who butchers the backside of a single insolent woman would be rewarded with a hundred praises on Judgment Day. Someone went so far as to accuse the followers of Malik Bin Ans of heresy because, in his opinion, Bin Ans was the one responsible for legalising the changing of sexual positions. He added that those who had theorised about promiscuity had already left Tunisia, mentioning such names as Tifashi, Tijani and Nafzawi, and argued that Muslims should forbid people from going on the pilgrimage to Kairouan this year on the occasion of the Prophet's birthday in protest against what was happening to Islam in that nation.

The Tunis Afrique Press discredited the dispatch of an opposition newspaper abroad which alleged that the Association of Khadija the Most Revered was forbidden from pursuing its activities and could not obtain work permits without agreeing to a set of legal conditions determined by relevant laws. Based on a statement made by a senior official, the agency said that no such association existed, and that the whole affair was nothing more than a pathetic attempt made by some expatriate activist traitors to betray their homeland.

Translated by Kristen Hope

from the novel

The Threshold of Ashes

Mansour El Souwaim

I have become a legend whose fame has surpassed that of the most notorious of looters. The whole city is uttering my name: the important officials, the dignitaries, the beautiful girls from the elegant neighbourhoods. A single man kept a close watch on me, doubting my integrity; he started questioning the meaning of the strange coincidence between the thefts that I succeeded in thwarting and those that I failed to prevent. He counted precisely and with a unique sense of security the number of operations I fought north and south, and then compared them to the number of operations that actually occurred north and south. He mentioned in his reports the perfume merchant and his unusual relations, and wondered about my connection to him. I will never forget that man, Major Issa. He used to pierce me with his look and would challenge me publicly, swearing that he would expose me, catch me unawares. The rumours multiplied, my fortune increased and I searched for a way to escape. The perfume merchant started to complain and plot against me, there were two attempts on my life and I found myself surrounded at the peak of my glory by Major Issa with his strange integrity and the perfume merchant with his dangerous scheming. Salim got rid of the unforgettable Issa for me when he appeared, and as for the perfume merchant, I prepared for him what he deserved . . .

That man summoned the perfume merchant and planned a major joint operation with him; he let him go north to the deserts and the arid lands, to the harsh mountains, the violent winds and the thirst, where the Angel of Death reigns; he then dispatched his private militia of twelve men and six camels, well trained to withstand death and the devastating winds, three cars and five barrels filled with water. All escape routes were sealed before the perfume merchant, nothing ahead of him but the vast ruthless sands and the mountains of death. He could smell the betrayal and started to spin among his men like a mad man, his ammunition wouldn't be enough for an hour's battle, his camels hunted down one by one, his men assassinated by thirst, hunger and the silent bullets in the midst of the desert sky, the motionless stones providing no protection now, and the lieutenant waving at him from afar, leaving him buried up to his neck among the vast sands, as he repeated despairingly . . . water . . . water . . . water.

The old and forgotten melodies expand. His old and broken *rabahah*, Umm Kiki, forces the strange tunes into the room. with the fingers of a veteran musician he produces harmony from a single string and a broken case, his lips muttering the inverted letters. The dark hidden spaces within me quiver and ripple with the echo of the ambiguous tunes. I try to leave but the melodies seize and imprison me, time slips away, I try to hold on to it, the place melts away, and the person sitting in front of me holding his *rabahah*, muttering those distant fading songs, does not resemble the old man with protruding eyes who drowns in apathy. Time slips away, and the darkness, my darkness spreads, and the sorrowful tunes sway endlessly. I manage to stand upright, I fight against the current of sorrowful tunes and swaying melancholy, I leave him holding Umm Kiki, recalling the songs of his ancient days that will never return.

I advance with my car, braving the city's jelly-like neighborhoods. The darkness envelops everything and spreads its dominance and tyranny over the whole city. The ghosts of old waning homes evade the car lights and are lost in the dark. The car headlights scan the insomniacs dreaming of impossible paths lying on the dirt, exchanging dead words and burping that evening's arak. The dark, my darkness is chiselling inside my head, hammering, hammering. An overwhelming migraine assaults me, and a fire burns my body as I reach the outskirts of a city drowning in sleep. I take my car away from the side neighbourhoods and I turn around, continuing to travel around the small dirty creeks and among the rocks scattered neglectfully. Something strange and meaningless leads me to them, I glimpse them from a distance, prostitutes disguised in the clothes of women selling tea, sitting in front of their straw and dirt homes, hugging their fire stoves, their tea and coffee pots, hopeful for some good fortune that the city's endless evenings might bring.

I approach them with my suspicious and hostile-looking car that belongs to the enemy, they are confused and flustered as I stand next to them; the prostitutes gather their clothes and short dresses, trying to cover their sinful bodies. I drag a stool and fling myself down on it. I observe their moist faces and I smell their timid odour. I watch them as they collect their belongings, to give the impression that their day has ended. I follow them in silence, and then I press my hand to my head saying:

'Coffee.'

I drink my coffee slowly and deliberately, staring with tired eyes into the face of the woman selling tea, and I am about to ask her her name . . . or ask her anything; I am about to ask her for one of her girls who would agree to sleep with a man whose mind has gone mad with fever and distant tales, but I remain silent, and they are silent. Nothing can be heard, only the sound of my occasional sipping of coffee and the scratching of my foot. A stubborn man, whose face is completely covered, sits close to me insisting on owning his evening, despite my vile and dangerous presence. I move my head slowly and travel with my eyes, contemplating the old shacks and dirty cabins, homes for stolen happiness and spoils of pleasure. I glimpse from afar skinny men passing like darts, then vanishing in the dark. I think again about asking her for a girl who will allow me to travel within her, my tired and sad self looking for comfort among the ruins, but then she speaks, intending for me to hear:

'We're late tonight, Amina, what time is it?'

'The talking distracted us, gather everything up quickly.'

I continue to drink slowly and deliberately, hoping that my migraine will disappear. I follow their coldness, as they awkwardly move things inside, and I hear my forgotten friend saying:

'There is no one better than a whore to raise men they should be left to exercise their sacred role freely in bringing up men.'

Now the great mothers are pale and frightened by my presence; me, sir, the master of fear, darkness and illusion.

I leave the miserable women behind and drive my car as fast as I can towards the city's farthest entrance. The lazy self-important men salute me, standing erect in front of me like a disaster. I salute them and wait for their reports while my head is one crushing pain. I sit in the nearest chair and the self-important men offer me their various reports to read. I hear their voices coming from afar, and I see their shapes dancing in front of me. They recite their reports and insist on explaining them to me. I complain to them of my headache, and my pains, and of the dark. They rant to my face about the suspicious cars discovered beyond the remote valleys, and about the amounts of smuggled arms that have leaked into the villages and rural areas. I hold my head with my hands and they tell me that the petrol crisis is getting worse and they foresee the signs of an approaching explosion. I moan, I throw up in front of them, emptying my insides, and I lie on the dirt, I hear them mumbling:

'Sir, you are tired, you can lie inside.'

They try to lift me up and take me to the rough dry bed. I stretch out there, tired, and feel the sweat oozing from all the pores in my body. I feel overcome with fever and a raging desire to mount a female body. I imagine the face of that woman selling tea in front of me, smiling; I smell her strange scent. I smell them, I imagine them facing me, I feel them next to me, glued to me, warm, scrubbing my body, pushing away this residing cold, then I feel myself travelling away in the dark.

They moved me to the mansion. I spent two days lost in lakes of fever and delirium. They tried to transfer me to the hospital, but he refused, and I refused in one of my wakeful frenzies. He took care of me with tenderness, and with a pitying heart he nursed me, spending long hours next to me, watching the saline drop through the transparent tubes. He remained stationed at my side, insisting the moment I wake up that I drink the bitter yellow herbal mix.

By the sixth day of my illness I was completely recovered, I was talking and had a reasonably good appetite. He appeared not to believe that I was talking to him again, laughing at his jokes and rebuffing the men in front of him. He was childishly happy with my recovery, and started prescribing the benefits of raw liver throughout convalescence, especially camel liver, and talking about the need to eat hard-boiled eggs, and fresh oranges, and grapefruit, and all kinds of fruit and foodstuff he could think of so that I could regain my strength quickly. He even offered me a glass of whisky, insisting that I drink it, describing it as medicinal above all else. But I was an exhausted body, and a frustrated soul, and infinite loathing.

In the morning he took me on a tour amid the trees and flowers of his garden, telling me that malaria was a paved road to emotional trauma. He sat me beside him beneath a jasmine tree and said to me:

'Smell . . . breathe the scent of heaven.'

He breathed deeply, closing his eyes. And I wondered what I was doing by this man's side!

I asked him:

'Your Excellency, during my illness . . . did anything new happen? I mean concerning you!'

He breathed deeply and patted my shoulder:

'You weren't out more than five days, and believe me nothing will happen, they will leave me like this another month . . . another year . . . then they will return everything to me, or reinstate me.'

He said this and laughed resoundingly, and I said:

'I don't think so, there are huge files prepared against you.'

He relaxed and yawned:

'They won't find anything, I know myself better than anyone.'

'The reports say that what they are preparing is worthy of your greatness, your Excellency'.

He glanced uninterestedly at me:

'Let them make whatever arrangements they want, regarding me, or regarding everyone, but they'd better make arrangements for themselves first – can't you see how they've started gaping like fools!'

He paused, then added:

'You are one of them, of course, but you are still a distance away. Get up, you are sick and need rest.'

I was angry and upset with myself. I wanted to tell him that they were going to send him to hell, that I was here to imprison him, to observe him, and that I was not staying for his amusement, or to partake in his drinking sessions. I wanted to tell him that he was garbage, and that he belonged to the dump site of history. But he propped me, and prepared the boiled chicken for me, and chose the cassettes with dreamy music, caressing me with it until I slept. He was as compassionate and kind to me as a mother would be.

On the sixth day of my illness he woke as usual at dawn, with the chirping of the birds and the emerging dew drops on the leaves of the trees. He came to my room as he did every morning since my illness, but he didn't find me in bed. He wandered through the wide terraces and looked for me in the creases of his huge upholstered chairs, and among his strange antiques and mounted animal heads. He roamed the empty unfurnished halls until he reached the garden, he expanded his chest and smelled the scent of roses, he exercised next to his rabbits and deer, then moved towards the men stationed next to the enormous gate and asked them about me. They told him I hadn't left so he went back to his many rooms to look for me again.

When he entered his favourite room, his warehouse of memories, he found me lounging in his rocking chair and holding one of his photo albums in my hand, looking at one of the photos. He raised his fingers like a veteran magician and lowered his head a little and said:

'I knew I would find you here. How did you get in?'

'Your Excellency, all the rooms, drawers and closets, anything that has a lock and key, we have a copy of it. Your Excellency, have you forgotten who we are?'

He seemed distressed sitting in front of me. He ignored my talk about keys and locks, and 'we'. He pointed with his hand to the photo album and asked me:

'What are you looking at?'

He smiled and added with sarcasm:

'Your Excellency, captain, sir . . .'

I talked to him with a strange and uncalled-for impertinence. I said:

'This is what you should clarify, your Excellency.'

'Clarify?'

He stared directly into my eyes as he said this, his face changing colour suddenly, the veins in his forehead jutting forward and his mouth shrunken. He looked strangely angry and said:

'I will not clarify anything and I ask you to return the photo album to its place, and now . . .'

We exchanged sharp looks, his face was getting darker and his eyes redder. He was extremely angry, and I really wanted to laugh, seeing him transform in front of me in such an unexpected and sudden way. I could have escalated matters then and settled my problems with him once and for all, ridding myself of the predicament of constantly having to accompany him. Just by instigating an elaborate argument with the clumsiness and cruelty of a soldier, I could have got rid of him and this pain that was renewed every day. However, and with the utmost politeness, I returned the photo album to its place and moved closer to him, patting his shoulder and apologising, promising him that this would not happen again, until his palm touched my hand on his shoulder.

He said:

'I hope it won't happen again . . .'

I said:

'Yes, your Excellency.'

He lit a cigarette and handed me one.

'Believe me, no one forces me now, after all these years, to do anything. All I say to you or recount I do out of a sincere desire to do so, without pressure or otherwise.'

He said this and was lost in his thoughts a little.

'I apologise again, your Excellency, and I repeat that it won't happen again'.

He was silent for quite a while until I thought he had forgotten me, but he surprised me by saying:

'Bring the photo album, sir.'

They were old black and white photographs, showing him in an old and distant past. With a straight body and irritable eyes, very different from those of this old man. But it was him, with his protruding eyes and the rectangular mole spreading the length of his neck, completely naked, a bright passion and fearful defiance radiating from his eyes. Between his arms a naked female with a beautifully shaped and lithe body, burying her face in his underarm in one of the photos, and between his thighs in another, and although there were several photos, her face was never shown.

I asked him:

'How did this happen, your Excellency?'

'This happened during a beautiful time, the days of tyranny and bullying, a time when the whole city was repeating my name.'

He would focus his eyes on my face then his gaze would pass me by and travel far away.

'Yes, after all those exciting storms that I used to raise following every one of those chases in the ancient times, they would surround me and create a buzz that did not subside during my presence in the city; all this made everyone seek me out, to see this legendary man up close, to talk to him, to drink a cup of coffee or a bottle of arak with him and then boast about it. But I used to choose those I wanted to know with care and knowledge. I met many men during the meetings of the city's dignitaries, during the long hunting trips with the sons of notables and prominent families; I met the outlaws and the reckless sons, the famous and noteworthy, during wild nights filled with alcohol, women and gambling tables. Among the many I met Salim El Sheikh Salim Ambady, you know him? Yes.'

The man met Salim during one of those wanton nights that the city used to witness in those times. They met over invitations for drinks with excessive persistence and deliberate attempts by Salim Ambady to get close, and then they met repeatedly after that – loud orgy nights that would last until dawn, invitations to grand dinners, and meetings with important people coming from the capital and neighbouring cities – but he always felt that Salim was hiding something mysterious, and carrying a heavy weight that he was unable to bear. He observed and followed him until they were alone one night sharing a bottle of arak, with heavy silence, and an apparent sadness and apprehension surrounding Salim.

'That night Salim was talking in a low, whispering voice, and the moonlight was reflected on his handsome face. He was in all his splendour with his wide eyes and the deep concern and regretful sorrow in his looks, talking and almost fading away with shame. A strange and unexplained reason that was unrelated to my affection towards Salim, or my sympathies towards the position he was in, something else very far from all this, mysterious and exciting, drove me to listen to him and support him – an unknown man who suddenly arrived in town, an imposter and a sorcerer treating barren women, and a clandestine pimp. Nobody remembers when he arrived or how he came to own that big house in the centre, married to a woman with diabolical beauty. He turned his house into a den for nights of eternal debauchery.

'He plots with malevolence to set up important men in the midst of his lowly schemes: he chooses with care one of the prominent men in town; he gets him to drink until he forgets even himself, then leaves him alone in the house a day or two with his wife of great beauty, and surprises the man with photos of him completely naked in the arms of a woman whose face remains hidden, and the blackmail begins.'

Translated by Rowan al Faqih

The Path to Madness

Mansoura Ez Eldin

I watched my neighbour take her first steps down the path to madness: the same trudging pace at which she put the rubbish bags out in the morning; the same painstaking manner in which she cooked those delicious-smelling meals that tempted me each time I walked past her flat, directly below mine.

When she moved into the building, I didn't notice anything strange or unusual about this woman in her early thirties. She was an energetic housewife and single mother who went a little overboard with her three kids, the eldest of whom, she told me, was nine.

She smiled at me each time we passed each other on the staircase as I was on my way to or from work. Her voice was faint, and her diminutive frame went together with her little face. Although she covered herself all over with a gown and headscarf, she was quite generous with compliments about my hairdo or my dress or even the smell of my perfume. 'How lovely,' she'd say, her gleaming eyes expressing an eagerness to communicate with others.

I was usually quite guarded when she spoke, and would then feel guilty about it afterwards. From the very beginning, I had been keen to keep a decorous distance between my neighbours and myself. With my lifestyle, I can't afford to waste time talking to people I have nothing in common with. To them, I'm a strange sort of woman, who treats her home as nothing more than a place to sleep, leaving at one in the afternoon and not coming back until around midnight.

It was not a familiar sight, a woman like me, over thirty and living on her own, no husband, no children, no family. But this lady seemed

happy to disregard all the preconceptions my neighbours had about
me. I saw in her eyes a kind of yearning to communicate with me.
I put that down to how different we were. To her, I was like the
stranger you meet when travelling far from home, to whom you spill
out your deepest secrets because you know you will not see them
again.

Maybe I've read too much into the way she looked at me, but I
was certain that this petite lady with the delicate features had something she wanted to tell me.

Something that confused me was her daily screaming, interspersed
with loud sobbing, as she punished her children. How could the
gentle, fragile lady that I bumped into from time to time on the staircase turn into this hysterical creature who would make my mornings
hell with her constant yelling at her children, causing me to get up
early even on my days off?

I can't remember exactly when, but she started to come out on to
the landing and call out to the doorman's wife at the top of her voice,
telling her to go and fetch some things from the shops, even though
there was an intercom from which she could have placed her order
without raising her voice or leaving her flat.

I pitied the doorman's wife when I heard my neighbour hurling
abuse at her and accusing the poor woman of ignoring her. I also
felt for my neighbour's kids (whom I never saw) when she punished
them for being naughty by locking them in their rooms, indifferent
to their pleading and endless banging on the door.

I began to picture her mind as a patch of dry, cracked earth in
desperate need of watering, and the water that found its way there
was the water of madness, seeping through, spreading slowly until
her mind became submerged.

I could not get out of my head that image of the parched earth and
the water flowing through. Whenever I bumped into the woman on
the steps or heard her voice, now hoarse from the continuous shouting
for no reason, I saw the cracks in her mind filling up with water.

One morning, I was surprised to hear her knocking on my door.
She was disorientated and her eyes were red, as if she had been up
all night crying. I opened the door and she walked straight into the

living room, as if she knew the layout of my flat like the back of
her hand. I was not quite awake, so I followed her in a slight daze,
uttering the usual words of welcome. When I sat down opposite her
I noticed that she was trembling and her eyes were darting to every
corner of the room, nervously checking to see if we were alone. She
carefully examined the ceiling and the walls, and then came and sat
next to me on the sofa, whispering:

'I hope you don't mind. Can't be too careful.'

I did not comment, just smiled encouragingly as she began to talk,
begging me to believe her and not to suspect her of being mad like
other people did. She said she couldn't go on living like this, that
her ex-husband was watching her every step, even in the bedroom,
so much so that she felt forced to sleep with her gown and headscarf
on. She asked me to come down to her flat to see the cameras that he
had planted in various corners. I felt obliged to follow her. When we
got to the door of her flat, she put a finger to her lips, indicating that
I should not speak. She went in on tiptoe, with me behind her. Her
place looked like a copy of mine in every respect: the furniture, the
colours of the curtains, even the pictures on the walls. Her TV had a
cover over it, just like mine. I didn't know what to think; I was deeply
unsettled and a fear began to grow inside me. I looked around me to
see where her children might be, but there was no trace of them. I
went into each room with her and she began pointing out what she
thought were hidden cameras and listening devices. My thoughts were
taken up with finding some trace of those three naughty children. She
left me for a moment to use the toilet, so I slipped into her bedroom.
I found a large tape-recorder and, next to it, a pile of tapes. Without
thinking, I took the one that was inside the machine, hid it inside my
clothes, and headed for the door.

Back in my flat, I played the recording and heard the voices of
the children, sometimes banging on the door and begging to be let
out, other times playing noisily, interspersed with periods of silence.
These were the same voices I had got used to hearing from my neighbour's flat, but there was no sign of her own voice. It seemed that she
had been playing the recordings and then adding her own voice on
top.

So the three children I had never seen were nowhere to be found. Everything I knew about them was taken from the few words exchanged with my neighbour whenever we met on the landing, and from the delicious cooking smells as she prepared food for them, and also from the children's clothes she would regularly hang up on the washing line.

I felt bad for her and decided to visit her the next day on some pretext, even though she would probably think I was some kind of spy acting on behalf of her ex-husband, seeing as she evidently suffered from paranoia, and especially as I had left so suddenly the last time.

In the morning, I found myself standing in front of the flat above mine. I knocked on the door lightly three times. It was opened by a woman of about fifty, wearing a cotton house shirt and beaming a warm, welcoming smile. I asked her about . . . I realised that I didn't know my neighbour's name. I ended up describing her and said she lives in this flat.

This older lady informed me that she had been living here with her daughter, a university student, for the past ten years, and that she did not know what I was talking about. She seemed to be running out of patience with me and her look changed to one of suspicion. Embarrassed, I apologised to her and left.

I kept an eye on the rather odd woman who lived in the flat above mine but didn't say anything. I'd usually see her from time to time on the steps of the building, always in a rush about something or other. She'd go up and down the staircase in a right hurry, as if someone was chasing after her.

She was thirty-something, slim, and had a small face. She had this long black hair that hung down over her shoulders. She wore quite short dresses and these really high heels. I did my best to steer clear of her from the very beginning because she didn't seem like she was all there. I'd often see her talking to herself as she went about. I'd just say good morning or good evening when we came across each other, and she'd reply without so much as looking at me, and then she'd carry on rambling to herself about I don't know what.

She could have been just like any of my other neighbours. Her being a little bit mad and all was her own business, so as long as she didn't go bothering or hurting anyone. But I began to get really irritated by the constant racket coming out of her flat. I knew she lived alone, but there were all these noises of children crying and fighting with each other, and then the voice of a woman who sounded like she was their mother, always punishing and yelling at them.

When I complained to the doorman and asked him to tell her that she was disturbing her neighbours with all the loud noises coming from her flat both day and night, I got a right shock: he said that demented neighbour of mine had just been complaining about the same noise, saying it was coming from *my* flat!

One day, I was about to go up and give her a piece of my mind, and how I couldn't sleep with all that noise, when I heard a knocking on the door. It was her. She asked me if I had seen a skinny woman who wore a gown and headscarf, claiming that this woman lived in my flat.

I was speechless, her saying these terrible things. Now, I had seen a woman in a black gown and headscarf. In fact, she looked quite a bit like my neighbour, and I thought they might be twins or something. But the doorman had told me he had never seen the two of them together, not once. He thought they might even be the same person.

I calmed myself down and told her that it's just me and my daughter here, that we'd been living here for ten years now, and that I had no knowledge of the woman she was asking about. She seemed really surprised when she heard me say this, and she was about to ask me more questions, but I made as if I was about to close the door and put on a friendly smile. She got the message and went away.

I am not really sure who's brought me to this awful place, but I have a feeling that delusional woman with the black gown and the little face must have something to do with it, or it could be that older lady that I found living in her flat instead of her.

I want to go back to my home and my work. I won't bother anyone next time, not that I did anything wrong the first time. Why won't anyone believe me when I tell them it was that nutcase who lived in the flat below me all along? It doesn't prove anything that they found her gown and her children's clothes in my wardrobe. They have to believe me. They can ring her ex-husband. He was given custody of the kids. He'll tell them that she's the mad one, not me.

Translated by Haroon Shirwani

Haneef from Glasgow

Mohammad Hassan Alwan

I was crossing Al Khaleej Bridge when he phoned. My eyes clouded over a little but my wife didn't say anything.

'Congratulations,' he said, and in his voice was the smell of wool you'd expect from a man whose throat was woven in Kashmir. It seemed he still felt the same loyalty to me that had defined our relationship for twenty years and had today inspired him to send his best wishes via a telephone call that must have cost him quite a bit over there in Glasgow.

The call came unexpectedly, right in the middle of the bridge, and that's why the conversation seemed hesitant, awkward, ready at any moment to tumble over the edge into the surging coldness of formality which I did not think appropriate. I slowed down and tried to be as kind to him as he was to me, in the hope that my sins would not proliferate. It was a strange situation, trying to be intimate with a friend whose Arabic is still very broken, and whose English is in its rudimentary stages, and switching between the two languages was the last thing my affection needed, for it was cautious at the best of times and not used to expressing unexpected sentiments like this.

I had last embraced him two years ago when he told me that his immigration visa to Britain had been issued at last, ten years later than in his dream. His suitcase, admirably prepared for the journey north, reminded me that we had been no kinder to him than that promised land. Twenty years he'd been pacing the streets of Riyadh, until the city was as familiar to him as the mountains of Kashmir, and neither of them any longer held precedence in his memory. His life had been divided between the two places so exactly that bias towards either one of them at this turning point of forty threatened to cripple his memory, which was the last thing he needed, especially as he was on his way to a third, new city with no idea what it would have in store for him.

When he left Riyadh for the last time the visa in his passport was no different than the one he had entered with twenty years before, and although his status had not changed after he left he took with him the many experiences that were written on his days here. I remember when I was five years old happily celebrating the arrival of the new family driver. He was very tall with black hair and thick lips, and skinny, although my mother's cooking soon put an end to that last attribute and caused him to develop a rounded paunch not entirely in keeping with his extreme height. I remembered our farewell two years before. He was still tall but his hair had whitened gradually in a methodical kind of way, and he had recently begun to look tired. His sense of humour was depleted, his carefree laughter gone altogether; I couldn't even be sure that I had heard him laugh for years!

For a long time he occupied the middle ground between family and servant, unable to cross from one to the other. He went home and came back a dozen times, and every time his humble suitcase would be bulging with small textile gifts, marble ornaments and fruit from Hind and videotapes that he'd filmed in his village. We'd all gather round in the living room, Mother wrapped in her *khimar* sitting at the back, and my brother and sister and I in front of the television while he sat unobtrusively next to the video player, stretching out his long arm from time to time to point to an alleyway on the screen, or a shop, or a twist in the road: 'Walk on a little, that my mother sister house. Two street after on left my big brother house.' He would be interrupted by all kinds of questions which varied according to the age of the person asking. I, having ignored all the family history he was trying to explain to us, asked him: 'Is there no tarmac?' Haneef laughed, as did my mother and my big brother while my little sister waited, like me, for the answer.

His childhood had been postponed for a long time. His father had become mayor of their village in Kashmir two years before Haneef was born. With the government position and the status afforded by his rank he had married a second wife, to enhance his prestige. Haneef and his younger brother were born of this second wife. There was every indication that the two brothers would eventually reap the many benefits befitting the sons of a great sheikh and his favourite young wife, and a new position. But none of that happened, for his father died, as sheikhs tend to, and most of his older stepbrothers were of an age where they could leave the village and head to the four corners of the earth in search of work.

So his childhood was put on hold like all orphans. He left school when he was still young and sold woollen gloves which his mother knitted for the soldiers stationed on the border. The road between the village and their barracks was filled with the noise of distant bombs and the songs of children mocking the Indians, inventing vivid stories of their cowardice and weakness. When he turned twenty, a recruitment office picked him up and brought him to Saudi and he felt his life was just beginning, just as now he felt the same sense of beginning in Glasgow, father of three girls, forty years old, making halal hamburgers for university students and waiting for his British naturalisation to be completed.

When Haneef came to Saudi for the fist time, Riyadh was like a pleasant oasis in the middle of the desert, strange but comfortable. The sound of the call to prayer emanating from dozens of minarets over microphones inspired a sense of awe in his soul and reassured him that the people were Muslims who loved Allah and the call to prayer and that they would take good care of him. He earned a wage the like of which his pocket had never seen and ate three square meals a day in exchange for which he drove a new car in a modern city and watered some trees in the garden. It was exile without teeth. The good life was all around and people had no worries, and few expectations. His heart was reassured and, remembering that he had not yet lived his childhood, he decided to savour it with us, like a ruminant brings the cud back into its mouth to chew a second time.

Then a midlife crisis struck. It suddenly dawned on him that he had been traversing the streets of Riyadh for twenty years and neither he nor the city had changed. His fortieth birthday hammered him

like a tent peg unwilling to descend any deeper into the sand in case
he'd be lost there for ever. The three little girls, whom he had given
Arab names, were still far from his arms, in Kashmir, rearing peacocks
and spinning wool, waiting for their father, the hero, to come home.
They were growing up so fast his distant heart could not bear it.
Akbar, his Pakistani friend, who had worked as a driver in Riyadh for
thirty years, died from diabetic shock near his employer's house in Al
Wuroud. He collapsed in the middle of the street, dropping the eggs,
newspaper and tin of oil he was carrying. It wasn't the way Haneef
wanted to go.

The damned steering wheel crucified his shoulders as he drove us
wherever we wanted, and nowhere he wanted. Meanwhile the children of the family he worked for were changing. They were growing
up and beginning to speak a language which was too difficult for his
humane dictionary compiled over twenty years of intimacy and loyal
service. It became apparent to my mother's compassionate eyes that
the strong and honest man she had hired to serve her and her children
when she became a widow was no longer strong, even if he was still
honest. I heard him once having a terribly sad conversation with our
Moroccan maid. His tearful eyes looked like glistening green olives.
He was taking the cup of tea which she usually made for him after
sunset. On this particular occasion he was sitting with her by the
kitchen door, telling her about his daughters. He said he could smell
the mud off their feet thousands of miles away. She was telling him
about her sick mother and her daughter whom her ex-husband had
taken with him to Italy. She hadn't heard from the girl for years.
These unexpected scraps of sadness fell on the kitchen floor, strewn
about the doorway like lumps of wrinkled, pungent-smelling cheese
past its sell-by date.

He went back to his room, and the maid went home. Their similar
pains remained scattered at the kitchen doorstep to be chewed by the
cats that circled there throughout the night. My mother increased
his wage by a few hundred riyals after securing a promise that he
would make more careful arrangements for saving his money and
stop buying the modern electronic gadgets which took his fancy. She
would tell him off like a child as he shook his head in embarrassment,

not uttering a word. And she gave him the freedom to work week-
ends, transporting fruit and vegetables with some of his compatriots
so he could make a few hundred extra.

He told me he wanted to move with his family to another place,
far from his Kashmiri village where he could never be sure that they
would not be attacked by the Indians and their stray bullets in that
contested border area between the two countries. He told me he
wanted to buy a small pick-up to ferry passengers between their
homes in the mountains and the train station. That would be sufficient to make a living. He also told me, later, that everything he had
earned in Saudi he had spent on his expensive wedding and the generous remittances he sent to the wife he had left behind and whom he
visited every year, sowing in her belly a baby girl the colour of wheat.

Haneef the bachelor, in his first fifteen years with us as a driver,
had been different from this preoccupied distracted character whose
presence in our house now almost went unnoticed. His smile had
been wider before and he had lived life to the full. We were his
family and it seemed he would never leave one day with a final exit
visa. But during the last five years Haneef the father was gloomy
most of the time. He had a little family in Kashmir to worry about
and his smiling features disappeared to be replaced by a tense face and
troubled brow. His usual smart appearance slipped and he started to
appear in traditional dress, looking just like any Pakistani labourer.

Now, with his voice crackling over the airwaves, the most enthusiastic I could be was to take as long as possible with my greeting and
ask about his children, and because that did not require more than a
couple of questions at the most I was obliged to repeat them several
times, and then as the questions dried up I asked him about Glasgow
and its people. He laughed, 'Lot of Saudi here ya Muhammad, study
university, come to restaurant for halal meat. I tell them I in Saudi
twenty years, they no believe.' I didn't know if seeing the Saudis,
who had become his favourite customers in Glasgow, delighted or
annoyed him, after he had spent exactly half of his life in their country. Certainly they could not all be pleasant to him and Haneef would
never have expected them to be as kind to him as they were now
being in Glasgow.

I remember one day when he called us in Riyadh from the police station and we had to go and take delivery of him. He was covered in blood, having had a fight with five Saudi lads who had tried to cut him off while driving. His face looked like a burst ball despite his nonchalant grin and the dried blood on his forehead and moustache, which indicated that the altercation must have lasted several minutes before it was broken up by passers-by. The five Saudis were in no better state than him, having learnt that life in Kashmir, in a border region contested for decades, forged proud hearts and strong fists!

It pained me that I found it so difficult to move along the conversation with a man who had played such a major role in my childhood memories, if I were to be honest about it at least. I still remembered them with total clarity, in their natural colours, and at the same time I couldn't come up with spontaneous words for the telephonic ether to transmit. All the memories were there in my mind but they were incapable of speech: playing football in the sultry summer heat, watering the garden on poignant afternoons, the wrestling match on the TV on Tuesday night, the national team's matches in the Asian Cup of '88, the crowded Ramadan *umrah*s, swimming at Half Moon Bay, changing burnt-out light bulbs, barbecues during the boring winters, Eid prayers with all their *Allahu akbars*, singing in fast-food restaurants, taking the mickey out of the fat Moroccan maid, and lots of other memories you'd expect from a child as he hurtled from five years old to twenty-five. Haneef was present in them all, right in the thick of the action, for they would hardly have been possible if he had not been there. It was he who taught me to clean the heads on the old video with drops of petrol, and how to tell the difference between Hindi and Urdu, and how I could blow up the football using the insect repellant, and how to stop the buzzing of the neon lights without having to change them. That was when learning those simple things was interesting, before I grew up and the pleasures of life gradually receded.

Haneef bade farewell with the words that his limited Arabic vocabulary allowed, and I bade farewell to him as I crossed the remaining metres of the bridge. I gripped the phone for a moment in irritation, trying to imprison some of Haneef's voice inside it in order to hold a more decent conversation later, one in keeping with the refined humanity he deserved, not one that grew more uncouth the older I got.

I opened the window, hoping that the air blowing in would explain my watering eyes, and waited for a question from my wife who'd been watching me closely since the conversation began:

'Who was that?'

'Haneef, our old driver.'

'Why the tears?'

'I miss him.'

'The driver?!'

Translated by Anthony Calderbank

A Boat That Dislikes the Riverbank

Mohammad Salah al Azab

I

Amm Samaan is Amm Samaan; that's all there is to it. With his olive-coloured skin and wide-sleeved jilbab, he's forever smiling – as though he wants to show off his gleaming white teeth.

'That's how it is!' he'll say. 'The world's got no time for scowling.'

He's seventy years old, but there's not a bent bone in his body, or a single white hair.

'So how do you do it, Amm Samaan?!'

'I'll tell you, sheikh's grandson,' he says. 'It's all a blessing and a miracle. May God let you in on the secret!'

He's worked for my grandfather, the sheikh, for thirty years.

For sure, he's liable to stutter, veer off the point and forget things, but he's still the focus of the story. Amm Samaan is the narrator here, so anyone who wants to hear the way the whole thing starts had better be patient and take heed.

'So, Amm Samaan, tell us Amm Samaan's story.'

He grows bashful and refuses to begin. Instead, he tells me other endless tales. But I'm not going to let him get away with it. I keep on at him. It's only this particular story that he's reluctant to tell.

Samaan's poor, and he's not from around here. As far as he's concerned, the yellow sands of the desert are totally alien; and he doesn't even care. It's the strange taste of well and spring water that's in his mouth. Every time he finds himself confronted by the rugged faces of the Bedouin, with their shrouded eyes and whitened lips

– emblems of eternal thirst – he longs to be somewhere else, that other place where the brown earth recognises his tread. Samaan comes from the farthest reaches of the river, where the water's just like sugar and there's green stretching as far as the eye can see. The tawny girls sing wedding songs in voices as sweet as the muezzin's. Even so, the abundant livelihood out there, offering its bounty to every extended hand, eventually wears poor folk down.

'"Listen here, pauper," they said, "take a boat, hitch a ride in a car, get on a train. There's money to be had in lots of towns for people who are prepared to move." But many people, including me, didn't realise that if a poor man can't find a living where life is good and things grow, then it's going to be even harder in the cruel desert environment.'

'Mother,' Samaan said once, 'every day there's a wedding ceremony here. Young folk grow up and get married. But Samaan's getting old, and he doesn't have a single penny to his name. He can't go around saying things like, "Here's a dowry for your daughter," or "Hey, Samaan would like to join your family!"'

All he owns is his jilbab and a mother who's even older and really tough.

'Don't worry!' she told him, as she hid her tears and rubbed her departing son's back with her powerful hand.

'Lord of our universe,' she prayed, 'shed some light on the path of this poor man!'

Once he'd begun telling the tale, he ignored my interruptions, gesturing with his hand or clasping my knee to get me to shut up.

'It's as though everyone in the country keeps cuffing me,' he said.

His livelihood went from bad to worse, so much so that it managed to murder the modest dream the poor man had of finding a little olive-skinned girl with long black hair and black eyes, and skin as smooth as rose petals, someone whom he could sit on his knee in a little boat that disliked the riverbank and didn't rock the little girl too much so she got scared.

'You're deluding yourself, Samaan. How on earth can you be dreaming of getting married when you're starving?!'

'So who was it, sheikh's grandson, who dragged me along by the scruff of the neck? Nobody but the lord of the road. Did anyone else say, 'Keep cuffing him, you people in the country! Throw a lack of livelihood at him till he gets there!'

'So, Samaan, beg for forgiveness for your dumb ignorance when you always used to bitch and moan about your empty stomach – you ignoramus! You need to apologise for such bad faith, you idiot. You kept your dream to yourself so no one else would find out about it. That's why nasty people whose evil ways you didn't even understand were able to trick you so easily. 'OK, you people,' you told them, 'not spending the night hungry, that's all I want!'

'I was worried you'd stay that way, marking off the days as the sun rose and set. But you know, grandson of our master, there's nothing faster than time itself. With every wedding that was held, I was worried you'd come back and find that all the girls were already taken. There would be none left to sing you a marriage song and say to you, as you left the house with a girl on your arm: "Don't hang around. Mind she doesn't get scared when the boat starts rocking!"'

'No, Samaan. You need to be grateful for your hunger, your poverty, and the way everyone kept cuffing you. In particular, you need to thank that honest lad to whom you told your tale of woe and who brought you to the desert in his car.'

'I got out of the car,' Samaan said, 'and they fed me. I heard every-one talking about the sheikh. I asked about him. I told him I wanted to drink deeply of his blessed presence. Actually, I told myself that what I also wanted was to find something to eat and somewhere to live.

'Your grandfather welcomed me. He was the one who gave me somewhere to live. I stayed with him for a while.

'"You're just at the beginning of the road," he told me after a while. "You've crossed the threshold. You'll be halfway there when you manage to get the picture of that little olive-skinned girl out of your mind. The road finishes where the river ends."'

'Well, Amm Samaan,' I said, 'you must have abandoned that dream long ago.'

He looked off into the distance. There must have been a puff of wind. I didn't feel it myself, but I noticed the edge of his garment flapping.

'Yes,' he said, 'a lot of time's gone by, and I've still not reached the halfway point.'

2

I was thrilled to see the large house that would adjoin my grandfather's property. It was some distance away, but it was clear that it was a mansion. I can easily see it from my rock overlooking the river, while I'm sitting there listening to Samaan's stories. It took two full years to finish building this mansion, with its three storeys and a stone wall with embedded lights.

Two whole years it took, and the builders would come and go, to and fro, from our property to the new mansion. Every night they used to come and sit reverentially in front of my grandfather the sheikh. They would bow and kiss his hand, whenever they saw him, but he would withdraw it quickly. They would ask him to pray for their livelihood and to look after people far away till they could go there themselves.

'This is the sheikh's grandson,' Samaan would say, pointing at me. 'He's acquired some of the sheikh's own radiance and blessing.'

That made them all treat me very kindly. One of them brought a bottle of perfume and daubed my hands with it. He then got me to rub his face and neck with it. They all lined up single file behind him, expecting me to do the same for them. The perfume had a nice scent, and my grandfather loved smelling it on my clothes.

Another one brought me a small tortoise, which I liked a lot. It used to hide its head and tail and turn into a piece of stone. That tortoise of mine used to eat greens and smile a lot.

One of them brought me a new pair of shoes, another one gave me a watch, and yet another some old coins with holes in them. The man who'd given me the tortoise brought me a hedgehog as well; it was the first time I'd ever seen a real one. He put it on the ground and then placed a cage over it. That hedgehog was really funny; it used to roll over and over inside the cage. It would splay its quills and roll up into a ball each time I put the tip of my cane through the bars of the cage.

I loved those workers. There were a lot of them, but I remembered all their names and what each one did.

Every day after work they would go down to the river and spend ages there swimming and yelling. At dinner time they would come back to our enclosure. Samaan used to make them tea in tiny cups after evening prayers. Their hair would still be dripping as they sipped the tea and listened carefully as he told them stories about his village far away. I felt happy because I knew more than they did, and he would tell me even more stories. They had their own stories to tell as well, but they never managed to finish them. Just one more cup of tea, then they'd be on their feet again.

'We've got lots of work in the morning,' they would say as they bid farewell to Samaan and me. 'We'll get together again tomorrow evening.'

They were forever talking about far-off towns where their loved ones were. They would all swear (although no one ever asked them to do so) that, if it weren't for the need, they would never have left them behind. They'd talk as well about the chief engineer who was their supervisor. I would often see him there, but never up close. They used to chat, as well, about the owner of the huge mansion who'd chosen this spot for his retirement.

I really liked those workmen, with their friendly expressions, and I enjoyed the presents they gave me and the jokes they told. But the fact that they were constructing a huge mansion weighed heavily on my mind. Day by day I felt anxious as I watched the way the building was progressing, almost as though it was my own.

The workmen eventually departed with fond farewells. Behind them they left a superb mansion, the genuine article. It was even more spectacular than the mansions I'd seen in my dreams based on your stories, Amm Samaan!

But I had no friend with whom I could share the story about the mansion. My fellow pupils at school didn't hate me, but they avoided talking to me because I was scared to get too close to them. I could see that in their eyes, and it made me feel sad. I used to move away.

The mansion remained locked, empty. There was just a silent guard, who brought his chair out during the day and sat in front of the gate. At night he used to lock up the mansion and disappear.

Every morning, before I started the long trip to school, I would walk around the mansion, stunned by the sight of its three lofty storeys, the glass windows that reflected the light like mirrors and the stone wall with embedded lights that remained lit even in broad daylight.

More than once I made an effort to talk to the guard, but he seemed scared. He would grab his chair and hurry back inside without saying a word. Then I'd hear the sound of doors being closed inside.

After the guard went crazy and ran away, the mansion remained empty. There were lots of rumours, of course, but no one dared go in. They had no idea that I was sneaking my way inside after sunset, feeling as happy as any owner of a huge mansion that no one else dares come near.

3

One morning, after thirty years in my grandfather's service, Samaan looked happier than I had ever seen him.

'Today I'm going back,' he said.

I was stunned.

'Going back, Amm Samaan?!' I asked. 'Where?'

'I'll call her "Nur",' he replied. 'Do me a favour, hand of the road, and shorten the distance so I can go home to my aged mother. "The pauper's come home," I'll tell her, "but he's not a pauper any more. Now Samaan has enough to pay the dowry for the olive-skinned girl. Now the light in his room will reveal a young girl with long black hair and black eyes. He'll be able to sit her by his feet in the boat which knows no shore. This time the girl won't be scared when it rocks."'

'So you're leaving, Samaan?'

'Your grandfather sat me down in front of him after the prayers,' he said. 'He told me to go back.'

'"Have I done something to annoy you?" I asked your grandfather.

'"No, it's not that," he replied. "The long road's worn you out, and you've done the same to it. You've lost the will to carry on."

'"I've tried every way I know."

'"So go back, Samaan, and start afresh. There are many roads you can take, and your destiny's the harder one."'

'So are you leaving, Samaan?' I asked him.

'There's a niece who's nice,' he said, 'and another who's really pretty. And the weird one is still alive . . .'

'Are you really leaving?'

'I've got the dowry now,' he said. 'Your grandfather's been really generous. I've got enough for four . . .'

'Are you going? Are you really going to leave me?'

'I'm going to choose the olive-skinned one,' he said, 'then Nur can provide for me. I'm going to choose my niece. Her father's a fisherman, and he has a boat which I can sit in and Nur can sit in my lap. We'll follow the river's undulating waters all the way to the joys of married life.'

Still staring off into the distance, he didn't notice my tears falling and producing prickly pears all along the road. This time I was the one to take him back, clinging to the mule's halter and walking ahead. He couldn't stop smiling.

'I'm going to take a car to the train, then ride in the train until I'm hugging my mother once again.'

'"I'll get lunch ready," she had said. "I'll be waiting for you by the front door."

'I can see her now sitting there, waiting for me to arrive. As is her custom, she won't eat anything until I get back. I've been away for too long.'

'"Mother," I'll say, "you'll have to reheat the lunch."'

I said goodbye and gave him a hug, and he suddenly came to. As he closed the car door from the inside, the car began to move off. But, just then, he leaned out of the window.

'Sheikh's grandson,' he said, 'I'm just afraid that my niece, the fisherman's daughter, may already be married.'

I shook my head and waved my arms to say that wasn't possible. The dust stirred up by the car's wheels hid his broadening smile as he pulled himself back into the car and disappeared from view.

Translated by Roger Allen

four poems from

Like the Blade of a Knife

Nagat Ali

Electra

He was not as bad
as she thought
he was.
More likely that
he loved no one
in the first place.

His work as executioner
meant he loved nothing
but the sight of his hands
stained with them
even after the show
had ended.

She too did not fully
play the victim
– as was required –
but fled whenever
he confidently pulled her
towards the final scene
and mocked him
when he spoke to her of Electra
'her ancient double',

she who gave her
deep scars
in the head
and taught her how to live
with disabled parts.

The Competition

She did not curse her, never, on the contrary, she recognised
her misery. Her beautiful adversary, who watches from centimetres away, with a sharp gaze, and prepares for the next round
to win back the precious prey. She was like her in everything;
the deep eyes, the senses damaged by love, the body blinded.
But anyway, she, her adversary, was more innocent and wrote
no poetry.

The Beggar

for Naguib Mahfouz

Mad she must be
to let him pass
– not moved
by his indifference –
'the teenage vagabond'
whose scrawny fingers
unintentionally scratched
the wound that runs
between her flesh
and her bones.

He told stories
– passing his hand over
her long locks –
about the history he lost

among buildings
that mostly burnt down
in the centre of the town.

He saw her as nothing
but a child
whose confused eyes
dig relentlessly
into every being
she encounters,
she who trembles at
her own name
if called
too loudly
and resents the boys
for telling of the beauty
of her breasts.

She stood still
as a lame statue
and observed him.
In her eyes he was nothing
but a wretched man
drooling over the breasts
of plump women,
stumbling in their midst and asking
– half-consciously –
about the meaning of a truth
without head
or tail,
about the necessity to stay
alive,
he who is no longer capable
of wonder
or weeping.

He wished for nothing every night,
walking alone
in the company of stray
dogs,
but to stone
all the lampposts
in all the streets
so that he fails to find
the way home.

Glass Tombs

I

I like these tombs dark and noiseless, where I can roam at leisure, covering distances and killing time in my own way. I can, for instance, enjoy the company of the dead, 'my father's good neighbours'. They – only they – do not interrupt when I talk about him, when I dig their graves in search of his body, for often I tried to guess the spot where I had buried him, to see what remained, when I came to visit him on Saturdays in the winter, the winter that he too had loved – although he died without telling me anything about the purpose of my existence in this filthy place. He in fact gave no clear answers whenever I pressed him about anything, and I inherited nothing but a handful of obsessions, and a few old commandments that my brothers – with amazing consistency – keep hanging next to his big portrait on the walls of the house. For years I confidently awaited the fall of the commandments and his picture and the walls.

Would you believe: one wish only occupies me . . . do you want to know what it is?

To lose consciousness – if only for a few minutes – then to wake up and find the boy who betrayed me – shamelessly

– a decomposing body beneath my feet, the bones of his skull devoured by these hordes of ants that crawl after me to devour me too; and to forget that old man after whom I ran tirelessly for five long years – in the hope that he would love me. He really did resemble my father, the scratch marks he left on my breast confirmed it.

I know I have ruined your solitude with useless disturbing chatter, but we could still talk about better things, a less painful subject. We could talk for instance about the spiders that swarm around me, whose dreary caves I shall enter to discover why they have eluded me for so long, to watch the ruins of ancient skeletons and the snakes ringing their bells in my head. Talking about spiders has great advantages that the likes of you do not appreciate, known only to my friends, who are fools and poets all.

I follow their movements with mounting enthusiasm now; they are predominantly triangular and black, and never look at me when I 'call' them. I am happy when I sense the movement of the fallen in the battlefield of life or when I see the ones lying still in glass-covered coffins.

Poor spiders indeed. They are honoured by no one so far, not even me.

It is enough for me then to observe – in ecstasy – those scorpions taking their time to sting me. Naked of everything but this whiteness that surrounds me, I observe, and receive the successive stings with an open mind that you envy me for. Although you, like me, wake up to this nothingness with no beginning and no end, and to these indolent eyes, and this body stretched out alone in the dark, and this silence weighing on the chest.

2

Maybe I have now become a ghost capable of moving lightly in the dark and avoiding the old furniture that filled the house and made a great graveyard of it.

I will be content with the virtue of lies that I have earned and will praise my sitting here among the bats that drop from neighbouring ruins, and strive towards the much-discussed inferno, and eavesdrop suspiciously on those who say 'If you learn too much you lose all your intense passions'. Maybe because I no longer trust anyone.

I will try then to wipe away this dust accumulating on the walls and caress the snakes that ring their loud bells, then inscribe my name on water and fake things to make them more beautiful. And naturally I will rise above all the red stains that made a bloody creature of me, and I will pity no one, not because pity is linked to nihilism – as they say – or because it leads nowhere, but because I don't see it as a virtue in the first place.

I will go back to my solitude and become more ferocious and cruel, even though the light in my room has dimmed considerably. I will listen only to heavy hammer blows while wiping away the painful stories that flow from my head. No sense in talking about them now; they will turn into pitiful jokes and take us nowhere.

So I will entertain myself by watching – just watching – these coffins after failing to become even a cemetery guard. You will see with your eyes my real features and know that words are the least deceptive of mirrors.

With you I will be released from my body, this 'moveable grave'.

Believe me when I tell you openly that I am like you, I have sharp fingernails that will soon deface you.

I will scream as I remove my lover's picture, now a terrifying skeleton, and then destroy my senses as I must do to become all-seeing and all-knowing.

I will see my hanging body half-Christ and half-Judas and, like you, will mock all the tragedies of life and confidently repeat 'What doesn't kill me makes me stronger'.

I will laugh contemptuously at that drunkard – who is rarely awake – when he calls to me from the next room, and will proudly tell him how I have become like grave worms that turn on each other after feeding off a lifeless corpse.

Translated by Nariman Youssef

The Pools and the Piano

Najwa Binshatwan

I

We took time off our classes to clean the school of the black ashes left behind from the burning of the foreign-language books, on a day in the 1980s, a day like all the others except for the lingering memory of ashes.

The foreign-language book bonfires were happening across the country, and our school was one of four in the neighborhood that complied with the orders and dragged all the foreign books out of the stockroom, along with the hearts of those who'd loved to read them, and executed them in the school yard, with our whole-hearted participation.

Some were delighted by the fires; they had hated foreign languages, finding them difficult to learn. But one of my brothers, a student at the nearby secondary school, who had loved and excelled at English, became despondent and refused to go to school after the books were burnt, stayed at home; ill. The only person who consoled him was my mother (who is illiterate, incidentally) because the rest of us had just excelled in failing at that language spoken by our enemies. In short, we all resembled the education minister, except for my brother, who broken-heartedly compared the loss of his books to the death of a family member. We mocked his effeminate sensibility, and would often mimic him to a group of fellow pyromaniacs in our street: 'You ignorant cretins; you'll know the size of the catastrophe later'.

Frankly, at the time, we thought that the biggest catastrophe was having a brother like him.

2

The rain blocked our street as we walked to school on the first day back after spring break, so we made a makeshift bridge from rocks and spent rubber tyres from the nearby rubbish dump, throwing them into the murky pools so we could cross on them. Those who had rubber boots, the kind that made your feet smell, rushed to put them on and pick up mops to go clean up the school.

Our school was maintained by the students; we had to sweep it and clean up the ashes left by the incinerated foreign-language books. While the fires raged, the school would inhale black dust and sneeze out a strange alphabet. We spent ages sweeping and cleaning the school, supervised by our teachers. Sweeping was a great socialist opportunity to discover our teachers' human sides; their faces and ours were black, and their hands and ours mixed in the same fires!

Ceaselessly, we swept up the black ashes of the books that had settled on everything, until our school finally re-emerged, free and careless, returning to us spotless. In our school uniforms, we scrubbed the dust accumulated during the holidays off the stairs, the blackboards, the doors, the chalk and the supervisor's glasses; we also cleaned the bulletin board, which had nothing on it save the obituary of the deputy supervisor's grandfather, who had died two terms earlier. In our quest for complete hygiene, we sprayed the flag-pole with detergent, and also decided to clean the flag after getting the administration's approval, so that everything at school could be spotless.

4

I got into a fight with a Chadian student not in my class over the flag-washing. I told him that since it was my country's flag, I was more qualified than him to clean it. He replied in a slurry of strange words, but I made out a panicked glint in his eye that almost made me take my words back. I felt like keeping my country and my personal map

of it to myself, but I eventually soothed my nationalist pride by telling myself that ours was a land of peace and calm, and that there
was no harm in giving up a small part of my country to be washed
by an outsider or a naturalised citizen. Then the supervisor shot me
an uncommon glance, compared my dark skin with the black skin
of the Chadian boy and decided that I was closer to the flag, so she
handed it to me. I took it straight away to our house, which was
near the school's crooked fence, so that my mum could clean it. My
mother was busy, with one eye on cooking dinner and the other on
the clock, trying to spare her cheek from my father's palm. When I
rushed in with the flag, she told me to put it in with the wash, so the
flag was washed in the washing machine's last cycle.

5

The school was finally ready to let us in again, so we lined up before
the sturdy post. The Chadian student and I, and all the students from
other places, saluted the flag that was flapping gently, the smell of
soap wafting off it into our nostrils. We went back to lessons and left
the flag flapping alone in the large school yard; it made a noise like a
thunderstorm, so we shut the windows halfway before beginning to
study. Our class began with recitals, the class next door began with
maths, the other started with the history of conflict, and the last class
had an absent teacher, so chaos reigned for a while until the lesson
turned into a PE class. But when the PE teacher's pregnancy began
to show it became a drawing class. One of the students in that class
coloured in all the drawings in the children's copybooks; we envied
them because their sports class had become an art class, and because
their teacher had got pregnant, and because of the colours that had
blossomed like trees on their class windows, the hard work of the
student who had coloured all the copybooks.

When we met up with them in break, our envy doubled; they had
got used to doing art in sports class, and so the teacher's pregnancy
was just another lucky break.

6

Our street's gutter became blocked by the neighbourhood's garbage, and our wash water seeped out and made a mud-coloured pool that got in the way of our games every time we ran back and forth across the street. In spite of my best efforts, my foot splashed into the brackish puddle tens of times, and my trouser legs became soiled with wash water.

Due to our mothers' neglect (according to the civics teacher's announcement), the supervisor confiscated our trousers the next day, and the only people who got to attend class were those students who didn't wear trousers in the first place, and who didn't carry around the pool's history on their legs. Some birds built their nests in the trees drawn by a class of students who had all gone to sports class wearing jilbabs.

The rickety ambulance car came to take Hajja Masyouna to the clinic, after a terrible bout of coughing had left her unable to breathe and had drawn a trickle of involuntary urine from her. I should point out that the ambulance didn't usually come to anyone's aid unless the driver was personally related to the victim or to one of their acquaintances. For the former reason, the car parked in front of Hajja Masyouna's house, and its driver (Khalifa) waited impatiently, his lit cigarette dangling from the side of his mouth, for her to be brought out dead or alive, so that he could do his job, which consisted firstly of turning the siren on and then off again and then parking the ambulance on the sidewalk in its slot and collecting his pay cheque.

For a moment, the siren wouldn't start; also, the patient's legs wouldn't fit into the car. Khalifa jumped up and down several times, slapping the siren. It let out a hoarse wail at the same moment that the neighbours managed to jam Masyouna, who was taller than Khalifa's car was long, in.

This was the first time an ambulance had been in our neighbourhood, and we would have missed out had the tallest person among us not choked on the noxious fumes in her home, which bordered the school bonfires that were lit noon and night. We watched the neighbours rescue their tall neighbour, crowding around the car to watch. We got in Khalifa's way, so he stuck his shaved head out the window and sent a string of curses in our direction, then parted the pool's water by stepping on the accelerator. The stagnant waters splashed all over us, drenching us as well as Hajja Masyouna's feet, which were sticking out of the ambulance door that had been tied shut by Salem Hamd's trousers, which he had offered to the cause of saving Hajja Masyouna from her crisis of asphyxiation.

Khalifa's acceleration scattered some of the insects that had begun breeding on the pool's edges, and the crowd quickly dissipated, since the insects could only be washed off with acid!

The Chadian student screamed like an African gorilla whose children had been murdered when a frog's limb hit his eye. We left him screaming and ran off, in order to escape a similar fate.

On the edges of the pools spread out near the schools and between the houses all the way to the end of our street, many water creatures were spawned, the same colour as the pools that housed them. The more mischievous children developed an entertaining game from this. They would place a lit cigarette in the mouth of a frog, which would breathe in the smoke, its lungs expanding until the entire animal exploded, splattering its guts on everything around it. The kids would let the frogs smoke and expand, then take cover and watch the creatures blow up like firecrackers, so much so that the kids from the other neighbourhood thought that our street was celebrating one of the festivals that filled up our calendars, which was only partly true.

7

One of the advantages of wearing zippered trousers was that a rapist would have a harder time reaching his prey; after trouserless jilbabs became mandatory, the Devil found his chance to whisper in the townspeople's ears and turn them to sin, right in the middle of the school day during siesta time. Gossipers talked about such things, and alluded to other sly molestation attempts. Within the lexicon of honour crimes, these were described as crimes of acquaintance, in order to distinguish one group of predators from another.

The local police caught certain jilbab-wearers who were not students at the local schools. They were security guards and shop-keepers and truck drivers and teachers and retirees who had taken advantage of the schoolchildren's new nudity to quench their instincts. But the eagle eye of the law caught them, and they received the harshest of punishments at the time: to wear *two* sets of trousers under their jilbabs, in the name of preserving public decency from devilish acts.

8

Even before the books were burnt, my mother was a Libyan citizen whose Moroccan origins no one in our neighbourhood recalled. But the incident with the books brought my mother back to square one, as far as her battle against the neighbourhood women's perceptions of her was concerned. To them, she was an outsider, a Moroccan who wore a tarboosh with her djellaba (a disreputable form of dress because it was associated with the Moroccan women who worked at cafés across Libya) when my father brought her home, in blatant defi-ance of all social norms that dictated he choose a wife from among his close relatives. At the time, honour was a Libyan speciality, cheap and abundant, despite the expensive price it exacted!

I'm bringing up my mother's origins because of the story of Kenyan (or Sudanese) Aisha, as she is known across the Maghreb, that my mother used to frequently tell us. The book bonfire was one of the occasions that the Maghrebis felt was an appropriate time to bring her up again.

Lala Aisha, Lady of the Swamps, is a water genie who comes from wet or humid places and exacts a quick and brutal revenge. Sometimes she takes the form of a hag, sometimes she is a beautiful young maiden, or an insect, or some magical water creature. Our mother claimed that Lala Aisha had burnt a European philosophy professor at one of Morocco's universities to a crisp and scattered his ashes because she didn't approve of what he had said about her.

Lala Aisha was invoked at our school for two reasons: the first was the presence of all the black and green pools and puddles in our midst, and the fact that a Moroccan entity lived close to these aquatic forms, in the form of my siblings and I. The second reason was the disappearance of some copybooks from our bags, and their re-emergence on the pyre of books written in our enemy's language, despite their having been written in our language by our own hands, as God is my witness!

Truly, this was something astounding; for who would steal our copybooks and burn them?

When we failed to uncover the criminal, enemy of knowledge that he was, and since we didn't want to keep the case open, using our best didactic reasoning, we decided it must be Sudanese (or Kenyan) Lala Aisha, who may have been irritated by several things inside the copybooks.

This conclusion led to a fight between me and a Sudanese student, who became upset that Aisha's origins had been attributed to his country. He considered this to be against Libyan policy, which rejected the idea of his nation interfering in the affairs of any of its neighbouring countries; and he based his objection on the same logic we had used before!

It took quite a while for us to convince the angry Sudanese student that we were not accusing his country, and that it was not part of the deductive sequence that we had used; for, despite it containing a large chunk of the Nile river, Sudan was innocent of exporting water spirits to the swamps and puddles of neighbouring, friendly lands, since it could barely satisfy its own local market share of water spirits, and the swamps and pools of its friendly neighbouring countries produced their own spirits who ruled over the water and burnt any research or information they did not approve of.

The Sudanese student was convinced, and he sat back down in his seat drenched in sweat, his skinny body finally beginning to relax.

But the discussion about Lala Aisha went on, since we were in sports class (i.e., art class) and not a single one of us could draw a tree, a cloud or a fire.

My brother, still trying to calm the Sudanese student down, said, 'Friends, people say that Lala Aisha is also Kenyan, and that she was brought to Morocco as a slave; then, when the Moroccans came here and made their puddles, they needed their own water spirits as well.' My brother had barely finished his mathematical demonstration of the presence of a Kenyan spirit in Libya who had arrived via Morocco, when we began a new fight with a student who for three years we had just assumed to be Libyan, but who turned out to be of Kenyan origin, and who, as a Kenyan national, considered the potential accusation of setting fire to our copy-books an issue that could result in executions, and which would require the mediation of international peacekeepers between one puddle and the other, and between the classroom and the school. We just managed to sort the matter out with him by bribing him with sweets and sandwiches in exchange for his silence – luckily for us, he happened to be hungry, but unluckily for us, we watched him gulp our sandwiches down as the ashes of our burning copybooks fluttered about on the fire and billowed in through our classroom windows. Our hearts were filled with frustration, our mouths speechless; and at the end of the day, we walked back to our homes disappointed, shutting the door behind us and Lala Aisha. Our mother filled our stomachs with Libyan food as she asked us what the matter was. My brothers and I exchanged glances, worried that nationality problems had followed us home, so we decided not to talk about school matters. In the evening, when we went out to play, we discovered that our shame was enormous (bigger than the green swamp even!), since the neighbourhood parents had told their children that our mom wasn't Libyan, and that, like other foreign elements, she must be got rid of immediately!

9

Her shadow emerged first, and it was black, like the shadow of everything else. We recognised her from her enormous height that spread all over the wall, bending when it touched the ceiling, until it covered the wall and the ceiling of the school's bathroom, where my brother and I were taking a break from geography class by pretending we needed the toilet. We were both washing our hands after leaving our stalls when her shadow filled up the bathroom ceiling and covered the walls, drenching the bathroom in darkness. I called my brother, and he cried out to me, 'Where are you?'

'I'm here, but I can't see you, what's happening?'

'The lights went out.'

'No, it's an eclipse or something, maybe it's a curse because we're ditching geography class.'

'No, that can't be, because today's lesson is about different climates in Africa, not about eclipses; forget about it, and hold your hand out so I can find you. Put your hand in my hand, brother'.

The darkness gradually faded, and the shadow produced by her height receded, and Hajja Masyouna appeared before us, tall and skinny, but – to our surprise! – her skin, which was amphibian, like one of the swamp frogs – or not just one but several, since one was definitely not enough to cover all of Hajja Masyouna – had exploded all over her, covering her entire face.

She scared us, so we screamed and ran back to our class – I'd found my brother cowering behind the toilet bowl when the shadow lifted, his skin the same colour as a frog's, and I followed him when he rushed off like a bullet towards our classroom, swung the door open and threw himself shivering into the geography teacher's arms. The teacher and our classmates were frog-faced as the Hajja followed us silently, taking one steady step after the other. Her breathing was normal, her health and height were both good and Salem Hamd's trousers dangled from her neck. She peered into our classroom, and the wailing got louder as a mass evacuation through the windows began, since the classroom's only door was blocked by her shadow.

She walked towards the geography teacher and strangled him (which was a rather good deed, since no one at school really liked him much, unlike the English teacher, who had been fired despite being loved by all). Some of the braver students stood over the Hajja's shadow at the door, watching the geography teacher getting strangled and egging her on.

Then they scuttled away before they saw the teacher's eyes swell, just like a frog's eyes did before it exploded, but their exit was blocked by the swamps outside, so they could not escape, hemmed in by frogs, snakes and crabs. They began to scream, screams that reached far beyond our solar system to distant planets, ricocheting off them and back into our earshot like bad arrows.

Hajja Masyouna hung the geography teacher up on the green chalkboard using Salem Hamd's trousers, then disappeared as suddenly as she had appeared. The police were never able to find a trace of her, despite examining the webbed footmarks she had left behind everywhere.

My brother asked: 'Hey, why are you screaming for Masyouna, who's at home; isn't Sudanese Aisha enough for you?'

At which point I woke up and made sure to tell him: 'Don't call her Kenyan, though; let's avoid geopolitical problems that cost us our sandwiches.'

Then I scrutinised his face: strangely, his skin was not as froggy as it had been just a few minutes earlier.

10

One of my brothers was a book-burning leader, working hard to get rid of every last one. He would poke at the fire with a broomstick handle and urge students to turn the burning books over, to make sure that the fire wholly consumed each one. He did not let a single word in English or French escape, wholeheartedly participating in cleansing our education of them. He thought he was setting fire to real enemies, and has not surrendered his big stick since that day. His pyromaniac tendencies also prompted him to burn our school's

Western musical instruments, so he and his friends dragged them into the large schoolyard and set fire to them using the barrel of local petrol they had brought. The instruments did not make a sound, burning in silence and quickly turning to ashes, as if willing themselves to do so, out of a love and respect for fire, an 'I do not play, therefore I do not exist' of sorts, an escape from participating in the formation of a band of players that no one enjoyed listening to anyway.

When only their charred skeletons remained, the instruments were thrown outside the school wall; the piano, being large and heavy, had taken a long time to burn. My brother and his minions had thought about dragging it into the fire with the help of some Nigerian labourers. Then the school caretaker from Taba suggested that they wipe it down with kerosene in the music room and then saw it to pieces, in preparation for burning it outside.

I have never ever seen a piano as defaced, amputated, fingers butchered and silent as that piano I saw at Tarik bin Ziad school, which the beautiful and graceful Lebanese teacher used to play. The teacher disappeared from the school, for obvious reasons, shortly before the piano did.

The Taban's decision had been a good one, and the stick-holders approved, as they brandished their broom handles at the fire and the burning piano's scent rose up in the air and mixed with the scent of the incense that the neighbourhood girls burnt every Monday and Thursday to invoke the spirits of potential suitors. The smell of burning piano ruined the spells, and the guardian angels in charge of relaying the message couldn't make it through the tongues of fire. And as the souls of suitors clamouring for girls to marry encountered the piano's spirit emerging into the ether, they wailed and screamed in terror. So the last sound that came out of the piano contained all the swear words in the language, which was definitely strange for a Western-made piano!

That evening at home, a domestic battle erupted between my stick-wielding brother and my other, effeminate brother, in which the latter's teeth were broken and his face bruised. As my stick-wielding brother's hand rose, he said, 'Let me at him,' and we suggested that he give him up to Internal Security, because he was a traitor and they were specialised in extracting a person's inner thoughts and would be able to find out our brother's secret intentions. But one of us said no, don't give him up, just throw him into the darkened bathroom and let the imps get him. So we did, and then heard him crying bloody tears as he thumped his head against the bathroom mirror to the rhythm of a foreign beat that made us laugh out loud when we heard it.

What still makes me laugh after all these years since the fight that turned one of my brothers into a power broker and the other into a toilet imp is that the bathroom did not even have a mirror to reflect the weeper's tears or the laughers' guffaws!

Translated by Ghenwa Hayek

Six Poems

Najwan Darwish

Our Feathers

Chicken cages . . . no one knows how they became a hotel
or how I came to be there wrestling with cages
in search of those the aviary had swallowed into its vast gullet,
or perhaps it swallowed me
so I would wrestle with chicken cages
in the form of ceilings and beds and rooms.

Abandoned cages . . . in some we come upon human feathers
   and remains of clothing.

Chicken cages . . . no one knows how they became labour camps
   and relentless trains.
No one knows how they became settlements.

Chicken cages . . . we found no traces of chicken, only our own
   feathers.

Kol Ha Musica

I

Our enemies call the piano 'psanter' . . .
how long have these psanters been striking in the wakefulness of
   the sleeping dead?
How long have they continued their transmission from
the station Kol Ha Musica
while their planes shell the southern Al Dhahya
and bomb a three-room home in Jabalya Camp?

The psanters . . .
that hunt him down
to the darkness of the other bank.

The psanters . . .
that now strike with their same icy drone
the psanters . . .
the psanters . . .
   .   .   .   .   .   .
   .   .   .   .   .   .

He will carry on calling them in the enemy's language until the
   musical instrument
desists from partaking in the crime.

2

   'The piano is the grandchild of the Qanun.'
   This is a historical fact,
   it has nothing to do with these psanters   .
   that now slash my face with razor blades.

The occupiers do not care for stories of blood or genealogy,
to them the piano is but a foundling they call the 'psanter'.

3

Sometimes I imagine that soldiers killed the pianists,
and generals are now playing instead inside the records.

A Profile of the Sea

You would rather think of this breeze coming from the
      mountain
of birds beating their wings by the sea,
of trees shading pathways
of these residential blocks that lack in taste.

You would rather watch this crow taking off a lamppost;
how he resembles a monk expelled from the monastery
preferring to be a beggar!

You would rather look at your foot catching the breeze.
You say: this morning I shall leave my heart asleep
dreaming it's in Haifa and that boats
were coming and going from Tyre and Tartous and the star of
      the Fertile Crescent . . .
that boatmen in the sea are calling out to me
in the accent of Alexandrians
and I would laugh in disbelief and say: 'an invitation from boat-
      men at sea.'

You would rather think of this breeze
coming from the thirties of the last century,
think of a woman of Sudanease ebony and Egyptian sycamore
who stands to sing in Jaffa

as they offer her a silk handkerchief and tell her: You are the 'Star
of the East'.
You would rather think of this breeze coming from the mountain,
of birds beating their wings by the sea.

The Women of Lod

Tall women of dry wood,
memory can only compare them to spears,
spears craning out of buses, coming to visit Jerusalem.
That was before the arrival of short women settlers
whom memory can only compare to dumdum bullets.

A Clown

Today is Saturday – today was Saturday,
it became Sunday and tomorrow will be Monday
and the day after tomorrow will be Tuesday.
After Tuesday Wednesday always comes before Thursday
which comes before Friday.

The week is a clown
juggling a single ball.

Reserved

I tried once to sit in one of the vacant seats of hope
but the word *reserved* was lurking there like a hyena.
I did not sit, no one did.
The seats of hope are always reserved.

Translated by Lubna Fahoum

Thirteen Poems

Nazem El Sayed

The Advice of Others

I do nothing except write the advice of others
I write it on small pieces of paper
and put them in the dark drawer
after a long or short time I go back to their advice
and am not surprised to find
that they don't resemble what they gave me
so I write it down
and leave it there to change on its own

This Waiting

I dug for a long time
in the same place
not to find a thing
a trace, a chair, or even bones
All I wanted was
that with persistence
my hands would change

A Day There

From my spot in this sea
I raise my hand and say:
hey Earth!
I was born there
so that I can now accompany your stride
by swimming and greeting
I am in the water
and nothing links me to you except this floating mouth
a memento from the shore

Oh, I Am So in the Middle

I have used all my promises
and here I am
sitting with my present
shivering and clinging to it
like a repentant swimmer between two banks
measuring what is before him
by what is behind

Partner

Come, breath
I will take you along
to see with your own eyes what I told you about
our end together

Everything Is the Same

When I returned
I found that everything was the same
including
the tired shadow my last farewell drew in the air

Affection

You almost discovered my tenderness
when you suddenly entered
and saw that kitten we had taken in from the street
sleeping on the couch next to me
how it was slowly shutting its eyes
under my hand which had left me
and declared its affection

oh, I forgot to say
all the things in me
have left me and gone to tenderness
left me alone and harsh
like the tooth of a man who had died

Shadows

At noon
the shadow of a tree
rests under it

the shadow separates from the person
but walks behind
silent and cold
repeating every move
in its own clumsy way

this shadow lies
on the ground
tired
of playing a lamppost

'I was born all of a sudden
big and rough'
says the shadow of the post
'at least you,
neighbour,
tree shadow,
have a childhood'

the bird soared
but its shadow
clung to the earth
an illusion standing for an original

a bird's shadow in the sky
returns to earth
frightened,
having lost its true colour

A Sock after a Day's Work

After it bathed well
and dried in the air and sun
the sock returned to its house
curled up
a warm fist
a jolly ball
a planet without feet

On the Clothes Line

Socks on the line
dripping
the footsteps
washed this morning

The Bus Cemetery

I passed by it
that cemetery
where buses
are left
to the wind and sun
and the moon too
which descends every night
to make sure
that they are dead

What Happened to the Two Sole Survivors

The two come daily to the café to drink coffee
the mother is approaching seventy and the unmarried son just left
    forty
as they do, they quarrel
they always quarrel
the son, whose forehead betrays deep wounds, always gives in
then the two get up
the son walks first, followed by the mother
he is a few steps ahead
turning back each time towards the angry voice behind
The two make a turn now
alone

final
hiding from destiny what it missed
returning to the house
where until today
one shell still falls
killing an entire family
of which only two survive

The Young Sister's House

There are dried remains of apricot jam
in the glass jar
at the door
orange peels
guiding the ants to an empty house

Translated by Sinan Antoon

from the novel

America

Rabee Jaber

Going to the Great War

Sapped by her coughing and bruised by fever, she huddled inside, while outside the snow and ice were melting and birds twittered in the trees. She was immersed in the odours of sickness and wool, caught helplessly in a fever like a locked cage from which she could see no past or future. She turned to glass after glass of mint tea, hoping its heat would kill the microbe that had assaulted her chest. As she bent double, nearly throwing her limbs out of joint in Philadelphia, her cousin Joe Haddad – Khalil, he had always been – was struggling for a breath of air three storeys beneath the sea's surface, somewhere in the Atlantic Ocean. Innumerable soldiers were massed in the hold, as one steamer chugged on in another's wake, a caravan of steamers guarded by frigates, reconnaissance planes and gunboats. The fear was of German submarines slipping into American waters: they had tried firing torpedoes into the harbour at Newport News in the state of Virginia, where army ships were now being manufactured. And German spies in America – wrote one of the newspapers – had tried again to blow up ammunitions factories in New Jersey. They had succeeded once before; the exploding factory had shattered glass on the opposite bank of the river and windows fell out all over lower Manhattan. The reverberations of the explosions caused general terror and panic; many believed the German attack had begun.

They lit lanterns in the hold of the ship which scared off the whales. Joe Haddad, as fearful as anyone of the lethal German submarines, wandered down the rows, along the mattresses. He was searching among the endless faces and masks for his friend Jeffrey Thornton. Before stumbling upon him, he was to encounter three Syrians from Massachusetts. (Three hundred and twenty-two Syrians from Massachusetts alone joined the ranks of the American Army during the First World War.) They were searching for their comrades-in-arms, they told him; most hailed from the seven villages of al-Kura, having arrived in America just a few years before. The transatlantic crossing remained alive in their minds: they had not forgotten tight chests, meagre air, the feeling that you were enclosed in an animal pen, one sheep among others, utterly powerless.

Joe Haddad laughed. 'Don't worry,' he told them. 'We'll find your buddies, and you can help me too. Call out my friend's name – Jeffrey.'

He shouted it, startling them and others around them, but they caught his good cheer and laughed, calling out the name once along with him. They spread out among the rows, moving between the mattresses and faces, repeating the name again and again as if chanting in a church chorus. 'Jeffrey! Jeffrey!'

They would not find him here. But months later, he would see his friend again, and were it not for a chance encounter he would not have recognised him, for now his face would be disfigured. The burns had melted and deeply scarred his ears, his nose and his neck.

This was how it happened. On 28 May 1918, the Americans went into their first real battle on the Western Front. Four thousand Americans from the First Division, 28th Battalion, nearly a full complement (though some fell before reaching Cantigny), advanced under the protection of twelve French tanks. The tanks were in front and the soldiers marched behind. There had been an intense rolling bombardment involving 368 heavy guns, a newly developed technique with the aim of burning the territory ahead as the attackers advanced, pursuing the defending troops as they attempted to withdraw, chased by shelling. Cantigny's fortifications could not stand firm. The Americans successfully occupied the village. But the battle did not end then and there. They were sitting down to a quick meal in one of the houses that had escaped total destruction when the

German bombardment began. Shells were exploding. '*Gas!*' they shouted, whipping out their rubber masks. At that very moment a spray of bullets from an Austrian Lewis gun shattered the glasses on the table in front of them. Some Germans who had escaped had fixed the gun on the window sash and fired into the house. The Americans were unlucky; they hadn't had time to put on their gas masks. German gas annihilated them.

Joe Haddad came out crawling. Getting as far away as he could from the yellow cloud, he pulled off the suffocating mask. He was panting. Everything looked rose-coloured or bright red. He suddenly sensed he was submerged in water and the thought frightened him into paralysis. It was not that he was afraid of the water itself, but rather of the gas, for he had discovered some time during the months past that gas collects at bodies of water: lakes, rivers, drinking-water reservoirs. He put on his mask again and crawled on, beneath bullets raining down from three directions at once. He fell into a crater made by shells and stayed put. The space was cramped, for he had to share it with severed limbs and rigid corpses, but he did not move. By now, none of this came as a shock. Why not? Had a crocodile's skin somehow grown over his own skin in the past few months? He had fought under English command in Picardy, when the German attack had begun at the start of springtime. In a different division then, he had witnessed the flames that attacked like a volcano, consuming the entire trench. Like wild hares chased out of their lairs by smoke and burning straw they had fled the trench. The bullets mowed them down as they fled the jets of flame. This had become his own private terror; it chased him mercilessly if he were to fall asleep for even a moment. He escaped, but how? He did not know. His feet stank with rot as they sank into the mud. But he was still alive.

In Cantigny, swallowing a gulp of stagnant rainwater as he wallowed amidst German, French and American bodies – old corpses and newer ones whose limbs still held a touch of warmth – he prayed that the Lord would bring him safely out of this pit. Out of this wrecked village on the blackened hill, out of this cursed land called *the Front*. He prayed to stay alive. He yanked the mask off his face – and saw a figure standing over him. His hand searched for his bayonet;

he pulled it out and sank it into the body, which collapsed directly on top of him. This was a German; he knew that from the grey uniform and flat cap. He rolled him over, to the side, and jiggled the bayonet to work it out of the body. Where had he trained? When had he developed this skill? Was it in far-off America, attacking scarecrows at a military base that seemed more like a kids' camp? They would stab at those straw dummies, the trainer shouting at them, 'Not in the back – underneath, into the kidney! And don't let the whole blade go in or it will never come out again. Don't try to pull it out directly like that; roll the metal around, work it out. The bastard dies and the steel comes out.'

He hadn't really learnt anything at the military camp. Here, in the trenches, as the bullets threw the helmet from his head, he had learnt. But had he learnt anything? Enough to survive? The bullets moved further away as evening fell. He heard his mates calling out. They were searching for each other. He looked hard and saw three shadows. He made out the blue Prussian uniform. He pulled out his rifle and aimed. One shadow fell, dissolving in the evening murk. His two companions faded away amidst the darkened hills. The rifle barrel stung his fingers as he dropped back to the spot he'd been occupying. He searched the corpses for something; he didn't know what he was looking for. He discovered a wounded man, moaning almost voicelessly, uniformed in green and blue. A Belgian. He gave him some water and asked him his name.

'Jean-Jacques,' said the Belgian. 'Jean-Jacques Simon.' He closed his eyes and didn't move again. Later, his name would be carved on to the monument at the entry to Cantigny, one of 526 names, half of them killed in that battle and the other half from gas after occupation of the village.

'I'm Joe – Joe Haddad,' he said to the Belgian.

It took him a while to realise that the man was dead. He raised his head from the crater and saw shadows gathering blackly overhead. Far away on the horizon the sky blazed red. There was no pause in the bombardment: the sound of the guns reverberated, and the sky was on fire, but Cantigny – for the time being, at least – was silent.

He clapped his hand over his right ear to stop the ringing, whereupon the sound moved to the other ear. His whole head was reverberating and he didn't know who those figures were, those shapes gathering in front of the demolished cathedral. Friend or foe? He returned to the shell hole. He heard a voice. The voice was talking to him. Somehow he thought it was laughing.

'My name is Nathan, I'm Australian.'

He realised the man was stretching out his hand, wanting to clasp his. He put out his own hand and took hold of the dark fingers. They were sticky, and then he saw that blood was coming out of the man's arm and chest. In the night-time that was spreading like ink and filling the crater he heard the laugh again, but it was interrupted. 'Water,' the voice croaked in English. He had not been asking for Joe's hand. He wanted his water canteen.

He tipped some water into the man's mouth. As the man coughed, spitting blood from his lungs which had been assaulted by the gas, the explosions started again. Had the Germans verified that the village had fallen and started the bombing? Or was it the other way around? Was it that the attack had failed and now the Allies were bombing Cantigny? In this crater he was not even particularly concerned about the answers.

The Australian said to him 'Stay' when he noticed Joe moving. Joe wanted to stay with him, but the man's lungs filled with water and he stopped breathing. Joe Haddad saw the moon, yellow and completely round and full. At the edge of the blackened, bombed fields stood a tree, white and flowering, like a spatter of pure paint in this blackness. The horizon flamed into light again and faded. The echoes were appalling in their loudness and yet he heard a call coming from the other edge of the crater, which opened on to a scattered series of other holes. A shell fell nearby, slicing off limbs and body parts that went flying. He was covered in dirt. But he was not harmed. He felt across the parts of his body and knew he was still alive. He heard it again, someone calling out. A man coughing, gurgling blood as though he were washing out his mouth with water and salt. Coughing, and calling out.

He crept toward the voice. This one was an American, like him, and he told him that he was from the 28th Battalion.

'I know who you are,' said Joe Haddad.

The man asked for water, and Joe poured water into his mouth, emptying his canteen. The man asked for chocolate. Joe fumbled through his pockets and came across a bar of chocolate from which he broke a piece off. The man opened his mouth and Joe dropped the chunk between his teeth. He settled the man's back against the crater wall. When the moonlight poured over the bodies he saw another one move. This one was in blue. He crawled over and aimed the pistol he held at his head. Before he could fire, the German said 'Kamerad!'

Was he surrendering? What was he saying? Joe was always hearing this particular screech when they advanced across a trench. Once he had gone into a German trench that had just been abandoned and he had seen a table in a fortified chamber below ground: cups of coffee, bread, cheese, meat and a box of luxury cigars. In a corner he stumbled on a carton of apples and citrus fruits. He stared, unbelieving. Here he had just come from a muddy trench overflowing with corpses, the stench of decomposing horses crushing his brain, and now he was seeing fruit and ordinary life in a room below ground, where steam still rose from the coffee cups! He ran out into the passage, shooting ahead of him randomly as though he were insane. Germans fell even as they lifted white underwear in the air, pleadingly. They were shouting that unintelligible stream of sounds, *Kamerad*, as they fell on both sides of the passageway.

A voice called him. He crawled on and saw an American from his own division. He must give the man a military salute, for the man was higher in rank than him. Before he could do so, the wounded man spoke.

'Can you carry me?'

He sounded as though he were simply asking Joe how strong he was. As if they were a couple of lads on a playing field. Joe nodded, reached out and pulled the man strongly by his shoulders. The man screamed at once, as though he had been hit. Half his body – his back – was completely crushed, dissolving and mixed with the black stuff that coated the bottom of the crater. Joe let go of him and said he would return.

He crawled on and on and then lifted his head to look. Inside the demolished cathedral he saw soldiers huddled around a small fire. He could not make out either uniforms or faces. They were too far away, and that cloudy red haze assaulted his eyes again. He wiped his forehead and checked to make sure it wasn't bleeding. Once again the explosions were coming intensely thick and fast, and smoke covered the face of the moon. Darkness came over the pit and the moaning quietened. He sensed something moving. He turned and made out a man with a burnt face. Blood was pouring from the face, and when he raised his hand Joe could see that his fingers were bleeding too. Then he collapsed on to the ground. Joe came up out of the pit and walked to the cathedral, going inside without a weapon. 'Hello,' he said. They were Americans. They were dipping ration biscuits in tepid water and preparing the evening meal.

He lost consciousness but only for a moment. Opening his eyes, he saw them spreading out behind barricades that the Germans had put up and then abandoned.

'There are wounded men in the pit over there.' Before he could get to the end of what he wanted to say, a mortar exploded at the cathedral entrance and blew apart the sole remaining statue of Jesus Christ. Someone brought him a lemon to suck on, to keep away the thirst.

'The water's been contaminated by gas,' the voice said, moving away.

The place was vast, like a castle complete with arches and moats and pillars. They must have built this edifice centuries ago. In America it was very rare to see such ancient structures. The explosions were still reaching him. They were growing more distant, but the rocky ground shook and poured like water, and he was slipping . . . he slid, slid as far as the beginning of the crater, where the corpses were talking with the wounded, and the wounded were asking for water and chocolate and milk, and a dying man would say, 'Stay with me,' while someone else put out his hand and asked for his water bottle. He slid further and saw the cherry tree growing at the heart of hell. He slid still further and saw a green mountain, birds, and nests heaped with eggs. He could hear the chirping. Then dust came down over his eyes and nose. Was he being buried alive?

He heard the sound of bullets now inside the cathedral. Had they returned? What was happening? Where was his strength? He opened his eyes and stumbled over his rifle – but hadn't he come from outside without a weapon? He shot at the man who was shooting at everyone. Had he gone mad under this shelling? Was he firing on his own comrades-in-arms? Fever was crushing him. After an eon, he realised that he was being carried on a stretcher. And so he knew he would not die.

In the field hospital – rooms deep underground – he was afraid he would suffocate. There was little air and he saw a man without arms standing beside him, looking at him. He coughed and spat out something black. A woman in a Red Cross uniform came over and said he had breathed in a little gas, not enough to kill him, but enough so that he must take leave and go to the back lines and rest. She was smiling and speaking words she'd become accustomed to saying over and over as time went on. Behind her, beneath lamps, they were injecting the wounded with drugs.

So it was that in another hospital – above ground and behind the lines – Joe Haddad found his friend Jeffrey Thornton again. They exchanged news. They smoked. And then they separated for ever.

Jeffrey hopped on his one remaining leg to Paris. And Joe returned to the front. On the way there, the military train made several stops. At one station he left the train – the railway lines had been destroyed and they were being repaired. He went into a buffet bar where soldiers were the only clientele. He drank half a bottle of wine, all the while rolling cigarettes that he smoked one after another. In his coat pocket he came across a Field Service postcard that no one had written on. He recalled the nuns of the St Martin Convent swarming like hens around him. He had been lying on his back. Two beds away, they were injecting a wounded man with morphine. A field of white assaulted his eyes as he faded. This moment was one of the strangest experiences of his life: he felt as though he was leaving his body behind and floating above the beds. He was gazing at the faces and recognising each in turn, as if he had always known them. And he was speaking to them, even though most of them were asleep. (He was recalling the corpses he'd crawled over, the corpses he'd slept on, through all of those months that had passed. They had been sleeping in a trench near the German lines when the shells dropped over them, gouging out fearsome craters and bringing up rotting bodies from below ground.)

He was completely immersed now in the cloud made by his tobacco. He got up and walked out of that darkness, approaching the bartender. Did he have a pen?

'*Ah, oui,*' said the man, turning to him.

He drew a pen from beneath the bar and, before handing it to him, requested that he would return it. Joe nodded.

'Sure, don't worry.' Taking the pen, he went back to his table. The door opened, admitting soldiers and mechanics, the latter covered in oil stains, and letting in the odour of burning. They were setting things alight that no one outside of this world would recognise by the smell – that stink of burning bones, for example. He drank the rest of the bottle as he wrote Marta's address in Philadelphia on the card and then read it to make certain he hadn't got anything wrong. He signed his name. He raised his head and yelled out into the room asking for today's date. Voices answered from all directions, but the dates that reached him were conflicting. As if he were living in a singular moment not defined by dates; as if he were not here on one particular day. He swore and laughed. The others echoed it, as if they'd agreed on it all in advance. They were like one big miserable beast with innumerable heads all split in halves. Drying a glass with a towel, the bartender directed him to the calendar hanging on the wall. He went over, carrying the card and feeling slightly dizzy. The French guy, with his laughable accent, asked him where he came from and where he was going. His English was lamentable but it was just enough for Joe to understand what he was talking about. He wanted to laugh but he didn't. In that moment, Jeffrey was in front of him, hopping on the remaining leg, swearing and slapping his hands together. Why did he do that? In the hospital garden, he had not asked. He was praying to be saved and to return to America, to see Marta, to have a conversation with her. But something strange happened to him as the bartender smiled, put out his hand and asked for the pen. He felt as though he had died, as though this were the very end.

He didn't send the card.

After this he fought with the US Second Battalion in Soissons, and then in Fère-en-Tardenois. (A cemetery there held six thousand gravestones, for six thousand American soldiers, in addition to a memorial erected in honour of 241 names, names without bodies, without graves.) The Germans had occupied the area in the spring campaign four months earlier. One of his comrades flew up into the air and fell, still alive. He carried him on his back to the hospital and returned to battle. The same thing happened three more times, and when the fighting ended he was panting as heavily as if he had been running a marathon that lasted years. The staff sergeant requested a medal for him and when it was delayed, reassured him that it would certainly arrive. Joe listened to him without interest, told him not to worry, saluted him and walked out. In the village of Sergy the Prussian Guard shot him in the hand. They treated him in a field hospital on the banks of the Marne and he hoisted his rifle once again.

It was only a light wound; it did not hit the muscle. He walked in a field of black, and then a field of yellow and then one of green. The fields were being harvested and when he saw bullets reaping the ears of grain and heads he sensed that he had not been vanquished. In one of the villages near Ypres he saw German prisoners locked inside cages and shackled like animals, up to the knees in mud. They were like hippopotami in the river, their lower halves beneath the muddy surface and upper halves in the frigid blue air. The sun shot out its rays as he was approaching them. He stared into their light-coloured eyes and tried to comprehend something. One of his company took a medal out of his coat.

'Look.'

'What's that?'

'A Victoria Cross.'

He told him that he had found a chest full of medals in the trench and now he was handing them out to everyone. He was laughing.

He started to cough and pounded on his chest and said something unintelligible about Flanders.

They transferred Joe to another battalion and he fought in St Mihiel. In the attack, he stumbled and fell and went unconscious. The bombardment was decimating them. The machine guns mowed and chopped and sliced, but he slept through it all. After the battle he asked for more pills because his hand was hurting. He was not given pills. 'There's a shortage of medical supplies.' He lost his helmet in Meuse-Argonne but plundered another from a German.

'This is very dangerous,' they said to him. 'Don't put on the enemy's helmet.'

But he did. He fell in an attack. He fell on to barbed wire and bled. They gave him leave and sent him to the demolished houses in Château Thierry, which had earlier witnessed a fierce clash.

He walked among the wounded men, dotted across the landscape drinking alcohol and smoking. The food was abundant here but he found himself incapable of eating. The sight of the drunken soldiers stirred up anxious feelings in him. He tried to pinpoint his emotions, but then realised that his mind had travelled elsewhere. His thinking no longer had anything to do with what was happening to him or happening around him.

A man he had seen before came up to him and asked in English, 'Aren't you Joe Don't Worry?' He nodded and said nothing. The man told him he'd been in the Battle of Belleau Wood and had seen too many dead men to count, and they were hanging from the forest trees like monkeys. He waited expectantly for Joe to laugh but Joe fended him off and walked away without opening his mouth. Where was Khalil Haddad going? What images did he hold before his eyes? What had he forgotten and what had he remembered?

Translated by Marilyn Booth

The Story of My Building

(After Isaac Babel's 'Story of My Dovecote')

Randa Jarrar

I was ten years old when card night was moved to our apartment in al-Zarqah, the poorest neighbourhood in Gaza. We lived in a sprawling compound of buildings which housed grocers, teachers, nurses, tailors, cooks, cobblers and, on the top floor of the third building, a translator of Russian literature – my father.

The men gathered in the living room, which soon filled up with smoke and the smell of bourbon, and the wives sat in the sitting room, which really was perfect for sitting since it was set up like a diwan, with rectangular pillows on the tiled floor and low wooden tables upon which small demi-tasses of tea were placed. My cousins and friends all piled into my bedroom, which I shared with my sister, who hated the fact that she had to live with a boy.

The men guffawed and clinked their glasses, and every few seconds we heard an eager smoker clicking the metal wheel of an old recalcitrant lighter. We had a trick we liked to play with lighters: we'd empty the invisible gas into a closed fist, quickly flip the flame on and open our palms, which then appeared to be on fire. Our female cousins and friends taught us the trick, and for weeks afterwards we worshipped them openly.

A few hours into card night, the women would be so immersed in stories and shishas, and the men so drunk, that we would roam free in the buildings' courtyard, which was sandy and surrounded by fake limestone walls, or climb the steps to the roof, where the doorman's wife kept her pigeons. We loved the rainbow one, which we dubbed Magic, because of the shifting iridescent colours on its blue-black neck.

As we unhooked the cage door and brought Magic out, passing him from hand to hand, he looked like the opposite of flames in our fists. Majduleen, the youngest of my cousins, observed that when his neck was gold he looked like the poster of the Dome of the Rock that her grandmother had plastered on to their kitchen wall. We agreed with her out of politeness; most of us deferred to Majduleen because of her exotic name.

Magic cooed in Majduleen's fist, and a glass broke in our apartment. We heard men shouting. I ran downstairs, not wanting to miss the argument, and when I flung the front door open I saw Uncle Fawzi, the cobbler, brandishing his walking stick at my father.

'Why are you defending them?' said Fawzi, 'You son of a whore! You traitor!'

'I am simply telling you a historical fact,' my baba said, his hands and arms shielding his head as confidently as possible. My mother and her friends were still in the sitting room; I could smell the scent of apple tobacco wafting in like phantom fingers stroking the men's shoulders.

'No! You are defending the Zionists! They use these things as an excuse to steal our land. Why do you believe them?'

It was a discussion I was somewhat familiar with, although I was unclear who exactly Holocaust and Pogrom were. I imagined that they were friends of Balfour's — his name was brought up often, too, though I had no idea who he was either.

The other men put down their blue-backed playing cards, but my father still held his like a fan in his left hand. I wondered if he thought they would defend him from the blows of Uncle Fawzi's walking stick, which was brown and didn't appear to be all that flimsy. The men were exhorting Fawzi to calm down, but they slurred their pleas and his anger seemed to grow from them. They were the invisible gas to his fiery fist.

My baba spied me from the corner of his half-blind eye — he liked to remove his glasses on card night because he felt he looked manlier and more intimidating without them. Apparently he was wrong about that. I stepped forward as he said, 'See, here comes Muhannad,' and cowered behind the cards. 'Son, go to the library and bring me the Babel. The Babel, *ya* Muhannad!'

I ran to the small room which my sister wished wasn't lined with books but with her posters and her bed (preferably a canopied one, with white tulle). This bedroom was made into the library when we moved in. Its windows were obstructed by the shelves, which towered within an inch of the ceiling. When Baba first moved the shelves in (he had bought them in Jordan) and saw that they fitted perfectly, he felt it was a good omen, like a *bashoora* moth, and set about his work.

I dragged his writing chair, which was small and wooden, to the *Aliph–Jeem* section and sang the alphabet song in my head until I got to *Ba'a* and realised I didn't have to sing for long. I found *Ba'a*, *Aliph*, then *Ba'a*, then *Laam*, and seized the Babel. I jumped off the chair, which creaked in protest, ran down the corridor and gave my baba the book. By now, Uncle Fawzi had retreated a little, and my friends were standing in the doorway, Majduleen still holding Magic in her hand.

My baba opened the book, which he had translated, and began to read. At first, Uncle Fawzi made spitting sounds whenever Baba said the word 'Jew'. Then all was quiet, and we listened while Baba read the story of Babel's first dovecote, clapped at the story of Babel coming first in class, and ended with, 'And so with Kuzma I went to the house of the tax inspector, where my parents, escaping the pogroms, had sought refuge.' The men shifted in their seats and said '*Allah!*' the way they do after they hear ladies sing beautiful songs on the radio. My baba and Babel were one beautiful lady singing.

The men went on smoking and drinking and dealing cards, and I was told to return the book to the shelf-lined library. I went in and turned Baba's reading lamp on and sat under its small light and read. The title I liked was *My First Goose*, so I read the story, but afterwards I was sad for the goose and for the landlady, and put the book back hastily. I ran to the roof and brought out a pigeon and held it in my palms until I was sure all the men had left and my room was quiet enough to sleep in.

All the men in my family were lazy, and slow to any action, whether ill- or well-considered. That is what my mama told me, but she was unhappy with our lot and with the lot of the men who showed up at our door, my great-uncles and older cousins who had no jobs and no homes. Still, I had two famous uncles, famous in our family at least. One had hijacked an aeroplane and got himself killed, leaving behind six girls, all of

whom eventually married under the auspices of the Palestine Liberation
Organization. One of the girls moved to Tunis and became Arafat's press
secretary. She wrote a book about her father's life and it was translated
into French, and my baba was proud of his niece, even though she was
older than him. The other uncle, Mustafa, had boarded an aeroplane in
peace and taken it to Detroit, where he bought a small market which
was attached to a petrol station. He did not own the petrol and did not
make much money, and all his customers were Negroes. Uncle Mustafa
had to carry a gun in the market, but one evening he was robbed and
killed by a Negro. The American police sent us some of his things in
a box from Detroit, which was held by the Israeli Defense Forces for
eight months before it was finally released to us. The box was silver and
looked like a metal version of my baba's briefcase. Inside, we found cards
with numbers on them, American dollars and pictures of naked ladies,
one of which I slipped into my pocket and took up to the roof with me
and showed to the pigeons. The only men left in the family were Uncle
Hassan, who lived in Beirut and taught at the Lebanese university, and
my father. Mama thinks they are lazy because she believes intellectuals are
weak. 'Have you ever squeezed a poet's arm?' she asked me once. 'It is
thin like a small girl's, and soft. It's not a man's arm. They do nothing but
think, and the heaviest things they lift are pens.' 'When did you squeeze
a poet's arm?' Baba asked in mock-jealousy. Mama clicked her tongue
against the top of her mouth and said she had been alive for two and a half
decades before she met him and had squeezed some poets. He laughed at
her. She said he was too lazy to be really jealous, or to enforce any sense
of propriety in the house. To this he didn't answer at all, and once again
was called lazy.

I spent the months before my final exams studying, to prove that I
am not lazy. I memorised three diwans of verse, from Mutanabbi to
Darwish; I paced around my room to the beat of the poems because it
helped me learn them faster. It sometimes left tears in my eyes when
I repeated the Darwish lines, 'So leave our land / Our shore, our sea
/ Our wheat, our salt, our wound.' By the fiftieth or sixtieth repeti-
tion I did not weep at all, but recited with anger and conviction. I lost
my voice and found it a week later. I ate cheese sandwiches Mama

left outside the door for me. I woke up in the middle of the night because the sentences and verses tangled themselves into my dreams, and everything in my head got knotty like my sister's hair in the morning. I rarely saw my pigeons or went to the roof. I heard Majduleen practising her flute on the roof one afternoon. Her mother hated music and Majduleen was never allowed to practise it inside the apartment, so she took the chipped old flute – which she had begged her father to buy her, and which she took free lessons for at the Gaza Centre for the Child – up to the roof where she serenaded the birds.

On 20 June 2006 a list was posted outside the headmaster's office with the names of all the students and their rank. I was ranked first. My father went to look at it every day, and on card night he made all the men walk down to the school with him to look at my name on the white piece of paper. They came back singing, and I heard their victorious song of victory echo from the courtyard. I prepared myself for their drunken congratulations so that when they arrived in our apartment I was ready. They carried me on their shoulders and sang and danced in the makeshift dance-hall that was our living room. Uncle Fawzi said I was not to become a martyr. He said I was too smart and the homeland needed me alive. The other men agreed with him and soon my feet were on the ground again. The men said they would build me a dovecote to celebrate my success. I told them I had a big cage on the roof, and they said it was small and not worthy of a prince. Uncle Fawzi wanted to go up to the roof and look at it, and I pleaded with my eyes and told them to stay in the house. I imagined them drunkenly falling off the roof like cartoon characters that keep walking after their feet have left the ledge, then, after staying in the air for a few seconds, fall swiftly, leaving a small white cloud where their bodies had been.

They went up anyway, climbing the steps in single file. They stood around my cage and crossed their arms.

'No, no; a thousand and one times no,' said one.

'No,' said another.

'No,' said Uncle Fawzi, who seemed naked without his cane.

'No,' said Baba. 'We will build you a real dovecote. From wood. We will paint it and there will be enough nests inside for ten pigeons.'

This excited me, so I jumped into Baba's arms and thanked him. We walked back down to the apartment and, as soon as Uncle Fawzi stepped down, we heard shots out on the street. We went into the apartment and waited. Shots were exchanged again a few minutes later, then all was quiet and still.

Early the next evening I set out to look for wood and paint for my dovecote. The water carrier was walking around without any water, cursing loudly, and a few blocks away from my apartment two boys were flying a blue kite they had drawn a peacock on. The blue peacock was brilliant against the grey sky, its fanned tail a cloud, the long string running from its drawn claw to the boy's hand. The kite swirled and bobbed in the wind.

At the hardware store, Abu Allam sat in a rickety chair and fanned himself with his white handkerchief. I told him the men were building me a dovecote and he said he would have wood and paint for them early next week. I asked him why it would take that long and he told me to look around me. 'Things are terrible! Open your eyes!' I did just as he said, pulling my eyelids away from my eyes and looking up and down the street, but everything looked as it always did. I shrugged and walked around the block, past the hair salon and the bird market, which was closed, past the fluttering robes and blouses at the souk, past old Ammu Khadr in his black wheelchair. He was trying loudly to hawk the single packet of cigarettes in his lap. The sun had vanished and I began to make my way back home before Mama began to worry.

At the mouth of Mansura Street, the neighbourhood's main thoroughfare, I saw a small line of green tanks. I turned around and stopped. Then I turned again and walked towards the soldiers on the ground.

'I live in the building,' I said. 'I live here. On this street . . . can I go home?'

'No,' one soldier answered. He was tall and skinny, and his booted legs looked like giant green beans in shiny black pods. 'This street's blocked. No entrance. Go on!'

'Where can I go? I have to go home to my mother. My family is inside.'

'These people,' he said. 'There's a devil in you! Didn't you hear me? No entrance here!'

I turned towards the mosque. I passed Ammu Khadr and saw that he had sold his pack of cigarettes and now had a mobile phone in his lap. I asked to use it and he pushed it towards me with his curled-in hands. I called my family but there was no answer, so I tried again, and again, but no one was there. I gave the phone back to Ammu Khadr and ran to the mosque, whose minaret was dull and grey in the night sky.

The men there covered me in a blanket and I slept on a straw mat like the prophet Mohammed once slept. Halfway through the night I heard bombs and shots. I was scared and I wanted to go to the toilet, but I peed on the straw mat instead. I woke up damp and ashamed.

In the morning, I walked back towards my street. The tanks were gone now, but I saw Magic the pigeon on the ground, bleeding and still, its rainbow feathers spotted red. I picked it up and held it against my heart and ran to my building. I saw, from a few yards down, that the building was no longer there, and I turned around and ran down the street again, as though I was rewinding something on a video, as though if I tried again the building would return. Grey bricks littered the earth, and there was soon a mountain of grey and charred concrete. Everything looked like pale colouring chalk under the brush of the blasted grey bricks and their powdery cast over the mountain. Chalky fabrics and pieces of shoes and curtains and beds and chairs and desks and tables and shards of mirrors and floors and walls and, soon, people. I was standing in a huge cemetery, clutching Magic to my chest.

The smell of bombed concrete and charred flesh made me drop to my knees and, as I lay on the rubble, Magic's guts trickled down into my yellowed lap. His tender insides spread on to my body, and on to the bodies and pieces of home that sat beneath me. I shut my eyes tight, my lids pressed together, my eyes which Abu Allam had asked me to open yesterday at the hardware store. I did not want to see the grey and pastel world that spread out around me. I felt something against my cheek and tried to see it with my skin; it was sharp and jagged like a beak; maybe it was Majduleen's flute. A cold slab of brick jutted into my hip; a corner of a room or a part of a ceiling. Wires tangled underneath my feet. Magic's feathers were soft in my palms as they once had been. I kept my eyes shut and pressed my body down into the rubble. This rubble did not look anything like real life, like the white piece of paper with my name on it outside the headmaster's office, or like Baba's voice when he read from his translations, or like Mama teasing him, or like Majduleen's hands. I sat there and wished the rubble would swallow me with its jagged and wiry mouth, wished I could belong to it. The earth beneath me smelled, I sniffed it in and began to weep. I lifted my hand from Magic and wiped my eyes, then opened them and saw the mountain on which I sat. I left Magic on the mountain with everyone else from the building and walked down the rubble. It reminded me of walking through the cemetery where my grandfather was buried. There were no markers, except for tombstones, and my sister and I were always worried that we were stepping on dead bodies. I stepped over all the grey and chalky rubble and wept as I walked up the street.

I passed Ammu Khadra and I wanted to call my family again. I imagined the muffled rings of the buried black telephone all through the dead mountain of our building. Ammu Khadra suddenly called to me, 'Muhannad! *Ya* Muhannad! Fawzi has been looking for you. He is waiting for you at Abu Allam's.'

I made my way to the hardware store, where Uncle Fawzi sat leaning on his cane.

'Where did you go, all night, flying about like a stray hair? Did you see what happened?'

I nodded.

'Don't worry,' he said. 'Everyone is waiting for you at my building. They all thought you were dead!'

I went over to Uncle Fawzi and hugged his crooked shoulder, and he patted my back. He heaved as he stood up and dug his cane into the brown earth. We walked away from the market, and I envied the cane in his grasp and wished it was my hand in his.

And so I went with Uncle Fawzi to his building where my parents, escaping the bombing, had sought refuge.

Written in English

Guardians of the Air

Rosa Yassin Hassan

There was a commotion in the embassy's long corridor. Her oriental-style shoes were made of cowhide, with soft soles. They barely touched the polished floor, and a ponytail swished playfully behind her head. She most resembled an odalisque from the age of the righteous Caliphs, tripping through the corridors of the palace, wearing flowing, floaty, purple *sirwal* trousers gathered at the ankle. I really have no idea where one can buy such garments in a city like Damascus at the beginning of the third millennium!

By the time I had managed to catch up with her, right at the end of the corridor, the breath had almost been ripped out of my chest:

'Madame! Madame Sophie!'

She turned, surprised, as if nothing else had existed, and smiled a greeting.

Whoever ends up looking upon the face of Madame Sophie, Director of Public Relations at the embassy, wouldn't have known from the back that she was a full-grown woman. From behind it is hard to believe that she is more than fifteen or sixteen. But her face is scored with fine lines which have transformed its smoothness into what resembles a war zone.

'*Bliize*, Madame Sophie, I wanted to ask you something.'

'Yes?' she asked in English.

She did not invite me into her office. In a rush as usual then! She stood waiting for me to speak, sleeved arms folded across my chest. I seized the opportunity. I began in *fus'ha*:

'*Bliize*, Madame Sophie, we must change our translation of the word "officer". The word "*daabit*" makes the poor wretches shiver and the blood drain from their faces. No Arab can imagine a civilian *officer.*'

'Uh . . .' She looked both exasperated and querulous.

'It is a word with a long history. It's entrenched in our brains in a way that's not easy to articulate.'

'*Well, I know that!*'

'Precision is the first requirement in translation. But I can hear the throbbing of their hearts from afar when they hear it, like a bird's heart in a hunter's fist. Do you understand me, Madame?'

Surprise was all that occupied Madame Sophie's face. No other expression disturbed the concentration there. Perhaps it was a lack of clarity on my part. To be able to change the translation of any word, I would need to find a surer way of convincing her, short of putting my request in writing to the ambassador's office. Madame Sophie looked gravely for a moment at the fist I was making in front of her as I clutched my imaginary bird. Her face showed that she was listening, but it was grim and unusually serious. I thought for a moment that she was going to continue to rush away from me down the corridor. But barely had my fist relaxed its grip than she came right up to me. She slowly smiled, stretched out her hand and patted me on the shoulder.

'Bravo, Annat, bravo, you are wonderful!'

She continued in stilted Arabic:

'For me, this love in your heart is more important than the literal accuracy of the translation, that compassionate heart in that petite frame.'

She probably meant my *tiny* frame.

When she stopped speaking, she gave me a broad smile which showed a full set of gleaming teeth. A white smile, like the white face that housed it and that bore no Arab features.

'*Do whatever you think best.*'

Her hand gripped my shoulder, then she was gone, leaving me trailing behind her on that long corridor, her hair swishing behind. I called out after her:

'Madame, what do you think about the word "boss"? Wouldn't that be better?'

She gave it the thumbs-up without turning round. She continued on her way, the lightness of her brisk steps only audible between these cold walls. For a moment I felt fresh and alive. A sense of joy suddenly came over me as I stood in that long corridor, lined with symmetrical rooms.

Madame Sophie had accepted my suggestion, as simple as that! I do not know how this chilly, whitewashed Canadian has such a spirit. She has a pure, sincere heart. Maybe it's the only thing she has inherited from her Lebanese father. She told me once that he had spent his life travelling the world in Red Cross ambulances. He had been there for every international conflict, a medic in every war. She may have exaggerated a little but she did tell me he had been in the war in Darfur, in Bosnia–Herzegovina, even in Afghanistan.

'Then he died, ironically enough, in an outbreak of malaria in Africa.'

I could not see at the time how that was ironic. Did an old man like him have to die by bomb or missile for it to be a tragedy, not an irony? Anyway, Madame Sophie believed her father had been buried in one of the mass graves which proliferate in Africa.

The important thing was that this success of mine would transform this bad day full of black thoughts I had had since morning. It would disperse those imaginary clouds. Being able to use the word 'boss' would mean I would no longer have to watch the panic in their eyes as they saluted in front of the 'officer', slamming their feet down on the floor with all their might as if they were privates in a comedy sketch.

I was late for the interviews. No doubt the Canadian officer – sorry, boss – would resent waiting for me. So too would those who had their interviews today, those who had to wander up and down the corridors, waiting outside rooms, their anxiety probably deepening, before the pistachio-coloured doors opened and the interviews began.

She felt like vomiting. The instant joy of her little language victory had already been forgotten. She was nauseous as she pictured crossing this threshold. Perhaps the sticky warmth was making things worse.

The air conditioner was pumping heat into the room, as was the little electric fan heater which the director had placed near his feet. The smell of coffee emanated from the copper pot on top of the heater.

The director was from Citizenship and Immigration Canada, delegated by the High Commission for Refugees to study all aspects of refugee life in Canada. As he had done every morning for the last two and half years, he was studying the mountain of multicoloured papers and pictures on his desk in front of him. He seemed particularly oppressed and miserable this morning, sipping his Arabic coffee from a fist-sized cup. Coffee was the one thing Jonathan Green liked here, besides the dark, kohl-eyes of the Damascus girls, as he put it. Annat greeted him.

'Hi, Jon, how are you?'

He did not reply. He raised his head from his desk, gave a sorrowful smile which turned into a grimace, then buried his face back in the mountain of paper. He must have been reading a medical report about some new refugee claimant he would be interviewing afterwards and for whom Annat Ismail was to interpret. She drew up close to him so that her metal chair touched his behind the desk. She glimpsed in the neat pile of papers a sheet covered with signatures and, next to it, the photograph of a charred body.

'Uh, how's the baby?'

He spoke in his elongated way while shuffling the picture back into the pile of papers. He laughed as he patted her stomach. Perhaps he sensed her shock at the photo which had been in front of him or how evidently disturbed she was by the expression which had been on his face. The smell in the room seemed to her a mix of purulence and coagulated blood.

'Fine.'

She manufactured a smile and felt her stomach, where her baby was growing into its third month. A new report, in English, from the High Commission for Refugees was on the desk: in it, a number of people reckoned to be deserving of the attention and action of the Commission. Perhaps Annat wanted, by reading for him, to overcome her nausea, to go beyond the confines of her little world – a world which bore down on her spirit – and into a bigger reality.

The estimated number of refugees from Asia was the highest, quite noticeably so. Europe was next: Bosnia and Herzegovina, the former Communist remnants and the like. There was no index providing dates, but it clearly didn't cover a long period of time. It would be passed around and around like a useless piece of paper until the maid disposed of it in the wastebasket. But it certainly wouldn't have been received in other parts of the world with such indifference and negativity.

Jon snapped out of his mental wanderings and gave her details about the first refugee claimant of the day. She read out for him what was in the report.

His name was Salva Quajee, a young Sudan Christian from the south. He had been a member of the Sudan People's Liberation Movement, the John Garang Movement, as it was called. He had then joined the troops of the Sudan People's Liberation Army, who manned rocket launchers in the North-South civil war, a war which had been going on for over twenty years. He had been held prisoner by Bashir's soldiers for many months before being released in a prisoner exchange deal. Unmarried, Salva lived alone, most of his family having died in the course of the war.

Jonathan was as intense and preoccupied as always on hearing these new stories, while all I wanted to do at a time like this was vomit. All I felt was an evil headache crushing my brain, forcing me to haul myself, staggering, out of my black leather chair. My face was deathly pale, so pale that he turned to me anxiously and grabbed my hand, drawling his English even more: '*If you are tired, Annat, we can postpone today's interviews.*'

'*Don't worry, I'll be fine.*'

Jonathan Green, despite his annoying coolness, had been my almost daily companion and friend for the past three years. I would be saddened by his departure, which was to be soon. His temporary project in the embassy was coming to an end. When we had first met he had seemed like a giant compared to me. He had silver-grey hair with tufts of black, and blue eyes surrounded by large expanses of white. When he glanced at you, his regard seemed the prelude to the hunting of prey. Nowadays Jonathan's hair was completely white, with not even a hint of grey.

The day after we met for the first time, he invited me for dinner and tequila. He said, trying to seduce me, that he would make me drink it the way Mexicans do. His mother was Latin American, from a little village on the Gulf of Mexico. His genes were more South American than North.

Although I had been unconvinced by his tales, I accepted his invitation. The air was filled with Julio Iglesias singing 'When I Need You'. I felt a sense of embarrassment I had never felt before. We ordered a dish of chicken with onions, peppers and mushrooms, Mexican-style of course. Sitting next to Jon, I had to empty the little glass of tequila into my mouth, exactly as he did, then suck a slice of salted lemon which had been stuck like a lid on the glass. I chewed on its harsh bitterness. The fiery liquid which burnt my whole stomach turned Jonathan Green, the giant with the bulging, glassy eyes, into my friend from that moment on.

To deflect his staring now, I pulled myself together. I struggled to form a smile and to get to my feet, supporting myself on the desk, so as to get things ready for the interview with the Sudanese. I did not want to feel overcome with guilt now. I did not want to feel guilty about those waiting outside, those who needed me. I kicked the heater away from the desk and sipped a little cold coffee from Jon's cup.

Instead of the entrance of a young man with a defiant expression, as I had imagined with Salva Quajee, the door opened and a small, black head appeared around it. The only thing that stood out from this round mass of flesh was the glimmer of humble yet fascinating eyes. Their dewiness shimmered like star clusters. Salva looked around the room, scrutinising us and the furniture with fear and suspicion, as if he was entering his place of execution. We waited a few moments while this young man took in all the little details. Then he hesitantly slid in and stood before us in silence, his eyes looking anxiously around him.

Seconds passed. Then his features seemed to become animated. He stood in the centre of the room, legs apart, palms at waist-height like a footballer about to shoot past a goalkeeper.

'*So, your name is Salva Quajee,*' Jon smiled encouragingly.

The young man nodded. His cheeks were fulsome and clean-shaven and they dominated his face. I explained to him in *fus'ha* that Jonathan, the Canadian boss, was one of the people who would decide on his refugee status. I asked him to sit on the metal chair with the purple leather seat near the desk. Salva relaxed. His features slackened and he sat down. Then suddenly he noticed the little electric heater by the desk which I had kicked away earlier. Shocked, he leapt to his feet and pointed at it in horror. He rushed out of the room like a maniac, muttering strange words. He took me by surprise; indeed, I was stunned. Jon seemed unfazed. He tossed his head back unhappily then asked the maid to give Salva something to drink outside. Perhaps it would settle his nerves. Then he said in laughable Arabic, '*Illee ba'aduu.*'

He drew his head close to mine and whispered, '*They tortured him with an electric heater similar to this one. Look!*'

He showed me a photograph of Salva's black, glossy torso. There was an oblique, crimson circle scorched on to it, scoring his emaciated belly and a little below. The lines were so precise it was as if they'd been painted on. So that was the burn that I had noticed the tip of when I arrived.

I felt even greater nausea than before. The room became narrower than a tomb, pressing down on my chest. The world had turned into a torture chamber. It wasn't surprising that I had thought of death all morning when this situation felt even worse. I was surrounded by degradation and death when all I yearned for was beauty.

The physical symptoms are always included in medical reports on would-be refugees. The physical symptoms of what they had been through, perhaps even the obvious mental consequences, for those who were clearly psychologically damaged. Many refugee claimants had been abused, their insides torn and their spirits corrupted without any physical mark as evidence. And their chances were few, their words for ever doubted.

Translated by John Peate

from the novel

The Scent of Cinnamon

Samar Yezbek

That slanting beam of light!
    The door was ajar. If it hadn't been for the thin shaft of light
streaming out towards the corridor mirror, Hanan Al-Hashimi would
not have noticed the whispering.

She was walking barefoot down the corridor. Moments before,
she had jumped out of bed like a woman stung, waking from a
dream in which had seen herself with five arms and three breasts.
Still somewhat delirious, she kept touching herself all over, patting
the burgundy lace nightdress clinging to her chest, seeking out any
sign that she had grown new limbs. Not believing that she was still
her natural self, she ran down the wooden staircase, towards the long
mirror she had kept on from her old house in the Muhajireen district.
She trusted that mirror. Only it could reassure her that a new set of
dreadful, snake-like arms, were not dancing around her body.

But that slanting beam of light!

It was that beam of light, dividing the corridor in two, which had
stirred her from her nightmare. She realised that she was barefoot.
And she heard whispers emerging from her husband's room.

She stopped dead. She stared, her eyes wide open now, but she did
not make any move to see what was happening in that room. She had
not been inside it for years, could not even remember its contents.
Never had she felt any curiosity about what took place in the room
that her husband slept in. She had only looked forward to the day he
would leave the house.

She took a step towards the mirror. Switching on the corridor light, she stood there, wearing nothing but the short lace nightdress. As she stared into the mirror, a bizarre thought flickered in her mind: it was ridiculous, but she wanted to know what her husband was doing. Had she gone mad?

She inspected her face in the mirror. Her eyes were sparkling. She massaged her hips and breathed in slowly, then laughed out loud from the depths of her soul. Happy. For a moment, the sounds heard from the bedroom were forgotten, consumed as she was in the pleasure of contemplating her body in front of the mirror. She lifted her nightdress and gazed at her buttocks with great curiosity, as if she were looking at the body of another woman. She ran her fingers along the surface of the mirror. Then she brought them to her face and stroked her cheeks. Delighted by their smoothness – so similar to the polished surface of the mirror – she began to giggle, covering her mouth like a coy schoolgirl.

She reached out, switched off the light, and, having checked her face, gazed at the shadows in front of the mirror. Darkness suddenly enveloped her; she noticed that the light streaming out of her husband's room had disappeared and that the door had been closed shut. She began to shake.

She tried to get a grip. There could be only one explanation: a thief must have broken into the villa. A scream dried up inside her throat. In the dark, she felt her way to the wall; touching it gave her a sense of security. Breathing became difficult. She began thinking about where the nearest phone was. She was sure it was not her husband – he wouldn't be up this early. Even if, by some miracle, he was up, it was not like him to switch off the light all of a sudden when he heard her footsteps.

She clung so closely to the wall that she became a part of it. She gathered in her body and her arms, and held her breath. A few minutes had elapsed with her standing like this, when the light in the room began to flicker, and the whispering started again.

Gentle whispering; subdued laughter; passionate moans. Slowly, she began to walk over, trying to figure out the source of the noise. Her body was shaking furiously. She stopped in front of the door handle. She clung on to it and then, in one violent movement, flung the door open. She came face to face with the dimly lit scene that was playing out in the dark theatre of the bedroom. The colour drained from her face, and her skin bristled as if a hundred thousand sharp knives had burst through the pores, from the soles of her feet to the parting in her tousled hair.

Her husband was stretched out naked on the bed, with lines of what seemed like pain visible on his face. Not quite pain – she had not seen that expression before. The man she called her husband no longer seemed himself. And over there, like someone trying to burrow their way out of the light, was Olya.

Could this be a dream? She wasn't lying in bed, drops of sweat trickling from a nightmare. It was Olya, whom she knew better than she knew herself. It was her!

It was Olya, whose teasing foreplay with the husband had come to an abrupt stop as she froze at the sight of her mistress, but who steadfastly continued to stare into her eyes. Both women were trapped in a stream of light that caused their eyes to gleam even as it cut through their bodies like a sword. Neither uttered a word. Separating their bodies was the motionless, naked and, to her, unfamiliar body of her husband. She had lived with him her whole life but had never thought of his body in any detail. Even when she felt its bulk on top of her, it was not as a woman feeling the weight of a man on her. It was just a feeling of heaviness. But here he was, naked! Exhausted, staring into space, he seemed untroubled by what was happening around him. He clasped his hands over his stomach and breathed deeply, as if he were getting ready to dive into a deep ocean. Hanan's eyes slid quickly over his body. They returned to Olya, staring into her eyes and contemplating the details of her body. Those fingers which she knew so well now clasped a limp piece of flesh; they were dry and pale, trembling as they struggled to loosen their grip. Hanan put her own fingers together; she could feel that they too were dry.

Olya looked like she was about to set off on a race, bent over, ready to leap over the bed. She did not dare straighten up, and yet she felt that her body would snap if she stayed like that for another minute. The air was trapped inside her lungs. She was scared to breathe, lest it bring the walls of the house falling down upon her head. Hanan, who could hear the sound of her heartbeat quicken, and was breathing so loudly it was more like she was choking, grabbed hold of the side of the bed and advanced a step. And in the moment that she raised the palm of her hand in the air, Olya slid under the bed, and crawled past her feet like a lizard, eyes glistening in the light, and ran to her room, coughing fiercely, having tried to take a few breaths and almost choked.

Hanan gazed at the ugly sight of her husband's member, dangling like a rag, and screamed: 'Olya!' She did not know where her voice was coming from. Was it from her throat or the pores in her skin? Or was it from the breasts and arms which had suddenly started to fly around in the emptiness of the room?

She knocked violently on the locked door of the servant's room, screaming and gasping and panting for breath. All of a sudden, she decided to pull herself together. She drew her hands away from the door and, in a stern voice, ordered her servant to leave the house.

She turned around, went back to her bedroom and closed the door behind her. Sitting down, she tried to gain control of her panting and gasping, which had started again. She made a decision to erase Olya from her life completely, as if she had never been here. She would wipe her out quickly like a word written in faded pencil. She heard the sound of her footsteps in the corridor as she slipped out like a thief. She was heading back to that filthy little alley from which she had emerged, amid the piles of scrap and the wailing of barefoot naked children who lick their own snot as they rummage around in the garbage.

She felt relieved, like a woman waking up from a nightmare, as she heard the creaking of the door at the outer fence. And then silence. She scrambled up to the window, threw back the curtains and peered out fearfully. She looked out at the ghostly figure of Olya, wishing that this figure was a dream too, just like that slanting beam of light. She tried to open the window with her trembling hands, but went stiff like a statue. She could not bring herself to shout Olya's name and ask her to come back. For a moment, she thought about it, but the next moment she drew back. She placed one hand in the other and squeezed hard until her knuckles cracked, just to check that she was still a creature of flesh and blood.

She continued to peer out at the figure of Olya in the blue dawn, her eyes following her stumbling gait into the distance, where flocks of strange birds gathered, as if to bid farewell. When Olya had completely disappeared from view, she drew the curtains, slipped into her bed and sank her face in last night's bed sheets, savouring the scent of cinnamon.

That slanting beam of light! The light which plunged all her nights into darkness, after she forgot to close the door to the mistress's bedroom, as she went down from the top floor, to the master's room.

As Hanan Al-Hashimi came down the stairs, Olya was shaking with fear. She thought that her mistress had finally caught up with her. She stopped moving and waited for the door to open, gazing at the shadow that flickered behind it. Her hands went dry and her body went limp, as she lay on top of the master's body. She slid herself down beside him. She felt a cramp in her fingers and could not let go of his thing. She thought about jumping from the window, or hiding under the bed, but she did not have the strength to move, as if she were caught in a dream. That beam of light, however, was all too real, and it caused her to scamper like a lizard past the feet of Hanan Al-Hashimi.

She was amazed at the way she fled from the master's bed to her room. The moment her head hit the floor, she thought she had entered a nightmare in which she was falling into a bottomless pit. But the sound of footsteps approaching her room left her in no doubt that this was real. When the mistress started pounding on the locked door, she woke up and saw that the time for games was over. She knew that her mistress wanted to tear her apart with her teeth, because she could hear them grinding like the screech of an old gate. The mistress had gone from sobbing like a baby to screaming and calling her an ugly, black-pimpled tramp.

She thought back to those times in her mistress's bedroom, when she was about to put her nightdress back on and, at Hanan Al-Hashimi's bidding, return to her own bed. A secret pleasure would fill the depths of her soul, and her body would tremble with delight, while Hanan's eyes shone with happiness and love.

How could she now call her an ugly tramp? How did those beautiful eyes turn into a blaze of fury? As she got her clothes together, her lips were quivering and she felt a strange, cold wind blow over her delicate frame. This was strange at the height of summer. An icy cold feeling overcame Olya's body and she began to shiver as a jumble of images – of death and disease, of filthy sidewalks and desolate streets – ran through her mind. It was for that reason that she would spend her days dreaming of the night-time, when she turned into a queen. She would think through the details of the night, which she loved, which she waited for. The night in which her mistress would call for her after returning from one of her soirées. The night where two moved as one in a concert of passion that touched the very core of her being.

As the night fell, her reign began, and she donned the crown of her unseen dominion. She would slumber a short while and then lie awake in her bed, waiting for her mistress' summons . . . For the second half, she would slip into the master's bedroom. Naked, she would doze next to him, fondling his flabby body parts. She would then leave him for her room. He did not complain about the way she fondled him. She did not succeed in arousing any part of his manhood, but this did not matter to her. She preferred to lie down in his arms and listen to his parched breaths. A little before dawn, she would return to her room, wash herself, and sleep like a corpse, for she knew that the daytime was coming and she would have to cast off the magical garment of the night, and go back to taking orders.

She had failed to notice that thin beam of light. Little did she know that it would turn her kingdom to ruins. Staying on the throne had not required much skill, now that she had learnt a thing or two about the facts of life and how to take charge in the bedroom. She had never imagined that her mistress would rise from the slumber she had left her in and slip down to the floor below.

The moment she saw the rage burning in her mistress's eyes, all those memories of living in fear came flooding back. It was a deep fear of things unknown and unknowable. The taste of that fear had lodged itself inside her a long time ago. It was as if a thin, fragile cloak had been keeping trouble at bay. Yet the passing of all these years had not taken away that twitching anxiety in her eyes, or that trembling in her cheeks, which Hanan Al-Hashimi found so charming. Now that trembling turned into convulsions of terror, viciously moving the muscles of her face, so that her right cheek rose, her left cheek sank, her lips rose to expose her teeth, and her teeth bit her lips, then her eyes started to twitch. She tried to hold back the tears, and ended up choking on them.

In that brief, fleeting moment which had felt like a hundred years, as she ran naked from the old man's room, the light went out from her eyes and she felt like she was falling into an abyss.

She locked the door, threw herself on to the floor, and broke into loud sobs. She stopped only on hearing the voice of Hanan Al-Hashimi, commanding her to leave the house.

She wondered if she had left her room and threw herself into the arms of her mistress, maybe she could have enchanted the enchantress, and softened her heart towards her. The night was still night, and the sun was not going to shine any time soon, and she was still the one true queen. Things would change only when the new day would dawn and she became a servant again. She really believed in the magic of the night, and thought she might have stood a chance. But the vicious look in her mistress's eyes had stopped her. She picked up her bag and meekly stepped out of the villa, without looking behind her. As she set off, she could not know that Hanan Al-Hashimi was standing at the window, watching.

Translated by Haroon Shirwani

Nine Poems

Samer Abou Hawwash

The Ones Who Have Departed

My friends
who have glistening eyes
that tenderly gaze
from behind the clouds
suddenly rose
in their real clothes
and casually exited
leaving life for me
like a generous tip
on the table.

Metallic Things

For the love of God and metallic things,
grant me, oh Lord,
before Hell,
some fleeting happiness
by the seashore.

After Bob Dylan

I watched a man drag a house he said he wanted to place by the edge of the sea, and a beautiful limping woman drag behind her a nation of limping children. I watched barking words, and varying degrees of silence dragged by horses. I watched black nylon bags fly in the desert, and a long-haired blonde woman lift her breast to the sky and cry. I watched the friend who died in his sleep smile through the rain. I watched the rain too. I watched trains raid bedrooms, and lightning mirrors that break with looks. And looks that break by themselves. And there was a boy in shorts jumping to touch a butterfly he thought was a cloud. And old black women practising rap by the constant gritting of their teeth. And there were philosophers trying in vain to explain coconuts. I watched clay pitch a tent, and mud dig secret tunnels. I watched the sixties approach me with extended arms, two black crows on their shoulders. And happiness jump rope in the nude. I watched my grandmother swim in a cup. I watched my father grow on a wall. I watched the nineties become a kite and dissolve in fog.

Photoshop

With two Photoshop hands at the height of imagination I try to repair a passing elderly man's face in the Centre of Commerce, as I think of the meaning of 'a passing elderly', contemplate the physics sphere of life, cut up the photo into squares and rectangles, place within each one an object or a person, and wait for the meaning to come by itself, as I repeat to myself: it will come, the meaning will come, and you only have to wait and wait. I make a wolf howl in a frightened child's face, and don't care to analyse the wolf, the child or fear. I place a mirror on a walking beauty's behind, and sketch on the mirror a dolphin's eyes and a clown's nose. I leave the spot for the mouth empty. And consider the tears a kind of mysterious sweat. My hand, resting on the trunk of an old tree, can also cry. I explain, and define; crying: my hand is resting on the trunk of an old tree. It is always possible to extract something out of a dead moment. It is always possible to confirm something with the press of a button.

Reconciliation

I'm thinking, Love, to help you reconcile with yourself,
to buy you a bicycle
and invite you to the seaside
where we can sit together on an abandoned chair
and contemplate the simple waves
as they wash with their eyes the feet of those who pass
through the water's secret sunset,
and we would need no more than a sigh
to forgive
your soul's slip-ups,
and no more than a gaze
to fill with stars
the pockets of your forlorn children.

Before the Buildings Begin to Collapse

We didn't know anything
we conversed with the air in complete imbecility
drew ambiguous shapes on water and in clouds
and pinned coloured pins on maps
without a care
for which city heart might bleed at that time
or which nations would become extinct

We were moving ahead
from all directions
towards one hole.

The Man Who Ponders Faces

He must, in the end, come away with some conclusion
a man like me
who doesn't tire of pondering faces
not because he loves it
but because it is some kind of secret
that makes him unable to cease pondering the faces
he knows
at the end
of the matter
will say nothing.

Alone with a Song That Overlooks the Shore

The little fish races its shadow in the pond,
dreams of a loan to start up a private business,
makes love in the bathroom with an Asian drug dealer
who makes love with a long tattoo at the base of her back;
the friends fufil the dream of their footballer friend who died of an
   overdose
come true, and so they go to the beach
and throw themselves in the sunset
while their
dead friend's smile
casts whole shadows
on the sand.

The Lonely

On park benches
or toilets at home
the lonely sit
completely lonely
no one knows them
they don't know each other
and no one knows
they are lonely
because they alone
are always
lonely
of everything.

Translated by Fady Joudah

A Crime in Mataeem Street

Wajdi al Ahdal

If Sana'a is the capital of the country then Mataeem Street is the inner capital of that multi-dimensional city. If anyone claims to have visited Sana'a but hasn't heard of Mataeem Street, then you know they haven't really been there. As the name indicates, the street is made up of a row of restaurants which specialise in popular dishes, and a cluster of cafés visited by countless numbers every day.

It was in one of those cafés one day, when the sun was unable to shine through a visiting dust storm, that an unfamiliar face appeared. It belonged to a man wearing an expensive brown suit and pink tie and carrying a Samsonite briefcase. He sat down near an old poet-turned-literary-critic and asked something very strange of him. He asked him to come with him to a bank near Mataeem Street to make a statement about one of the café's customers. In return he would receive a tidy sum of money. The critic doubted the seriousness of the whole affair and a sarcastic smile appeared on his lips, which were chapped owing to his diabetes. But the stranger, who presented himself as 'an emissary of the bank', took 20,000 riyals from the briefcase and tucked them into the critic's pocket. He promised him the same amount again after he had filed his statement. The critic cleared his throat and a gleam appeared in his eyes. He took hold of the stick he used to intimidate young writers and ambled to the bank.

The emissary led him to the bank manager's office. The critic, upon entering, was astonished that such a vast salon could be called an 'office'. He was in awe of the place and felt a sense of shame at the shabbiness of his clothes. In his hasty approach towards the bank manager – a short man as thin as bamboo – he tripped and nearly banged his head on a censer which was emitting scented smoke. The bank manager welcomed him and asked him to take a seat. A glamorous young woman gave him a sugarless coffee. He tasted it and took pleasure in its bitter taste. The bank manager addressed him, a broad smile traversing his face.

'You are a literary critic?'

'Yes. The best literary critic in Yemen.'

'Is it true that you take money from writers in exchange for praise?'

'That's a lie. The Zionists and the CIA peddle such falsehoods.'

'Do you know Abdullatif Muhammad Ahmad?'

'Abdullatif . . . Abdullatif . . . ah yes, I know him.'

'Excellent. I want you to tell me every detail you know, small or large, about this person.'

'Why, are you connected to him in some way?'

'That's none of your concern. Just do as I request, no questions asked.'

The manager reclined in his comfortable chair and indicated that the critic should begin. A moment of heavy, disquieting silence followed in which the critic sought the right place to start. He sucked in the air until his cheeks billowed, then exhaled as he gathered himself.

'What I know is that he's a civil servant in the Ministry of Information . . . no . . . I'm not a friend of his . . . but a café brings all sorts together, from mankind to *jinn*. He comes to drink tea every day. His majesty is there from early morning, and he stays in Mataeem Street, grazing here and there like a wandering goat, until the shops shut at ten at night. He has three or four bread rolls for breakfast and a cup of tea with milk. He lunches late. He slips into a restaurant owned by one of his acquaintances from the same neighbourhood to eat the leftovers, after the kitchen has closed. I don't know what he does for dinner because I go home before it gets dark. He is said to be an interior decorator. He seems to me more like a giant sea monster that has crawled from the sea, unsuspected, into our world through the drains.

'It seems he has studied abroad. He's one of those skulking pseudo-Europeans who are dazzled by the foreign country they have studied in. They are so swept up in a new, unfettered way of life that, when they come back to Yemen, they fail to fit back into society, fail to honour its customs and traditions. It is as if they are suspended in the air, cut off from their roots, unable to reintegrate. It is as if they are divided from their surroundings by a thin membrane. They are enveloped in their own self-obsession, their contempt for others, the disdain and arrogance that takes hold of them. They are wrapped up in their own pretensions, their unbending ego evident in their eternal scowls.

'He sits in the café as though he were a genius, a star attraction. He is deluded enough to believe himself a famous personality, obliged to address the mob from on high. Yes, he indulges himself in the belief that he is a celebrity. It makes him go to great lengths to disguise himself, hiding his true appearance so as not to be troubled by his alleged admirers. He supposes that his minions mimic his measured movements for, after all, he is an international star!

'From the very dawn Allah grants us, he is out drinking cheap country wine. I have seen him sitting in the café with a government newspaper under him. Though it bears Quranic verse and the symbols of our nation, he uses it to keep his trousers clean. He gradually wakes from his drunkenness as the evening wears on. Yes, he regularly curses the system. Indeed he starts his very day with a fiery invective, cursing our nation shamefully, our nation of five million heroes and five million delinquents. He remains like this all day, turbulent and moody, petulant and aggressive. He thinks everyone is out to insult and belittle him. If you listen to him a little, you realise he bears a grudge against those who are successful. He rants on about the wealthy and famous morning, noon and night, using foul language that reeks of revulsion.

'One time, a composer, somewhat dark of skin, visited the café briefly. After he had left, our friend spouted to one and all: "Allah Almighty, the *Akhdam* are trained in music now, are they?!" Is this not racist in tone? Is this not the phlegm of a failed man, a wretch wracked by his own inadequacies? It was I who had to point out to him the error of his ways.

'At other times he loses his temper when he sees a talented artist receive approbation and respect, diminishing the achievement by referring to the artist's class origins. I suspect he has a pent-up violence within him and dreams of destroying the world, of laying it to waste. I draw this from his praise for Osama bin Laden – a strange thing to hear from an interior decorator, one would think! Though he is not religious, not remotely connected with Islamic movements, he looks to bin Laden, considers him his saviour, pins his highest hopes on him. I once heard him zealously proclaiming that "Osama bin Laden is the only man who can put an end to the chaos in the world!"

'And if anyone else's words attract attention in the café, he becomes consumed with jealousy. He turns man against man, turns things on their heads and says, "Go take your wisdom from the mouths of goats!" He is deluded. He believes himself a very important man indeed and acts towards others on that footing. So he is not one to respond to a greeting or enquiry. He styles himself a king, one who disdains conversation with those of lesser status. He walks around with his face raised aloft to the sky. The few times he lowers it is for one of his familiars. He does not laugh, he does not smile. A frown furrows his brow; his features are constricted in a scowl. His eyes radiate a fierceness on all who look upon him. He surrounds himself with mystery, an aura of prestige and pretension because he won't lower his manner of speaking, won't relax the serried lines on his face.

'He won't raise his voice but will only whisper, since he does not want informants to report him. He builds a self-important wall around himself and reinforces it with self-delusion. Behind the ever-present sunglasses he sports, his eyes flick left and right, forever monitoring the slightest movement his audience makes.

'I saw him enter into the middle of a large group of advisors gathered around the minister once. He stood forcefully in front of him, his head aloft so that his nose almost touched that of the minister, as if he were one of the élite, intimidating the minister, thinking himself a distinguished personage. And when he speaks what should it be but to demand financial assistance? And when the minister orders a tidy sum of money to be brought for him, lo and behold, our friend starts arguing fiercely. He raises his voice to the minister, losing his temper and shouting him down. The minders intervene and forcefully make him submit in a humiliating manner. So off he goes, spluttering and coughing, his grimace deepening more and more, his whole body convulsing.

'The last time I saw him? In the café three hours ago. He was sitting in a dark blue, pin-striped suit. It was rather hideous, especially when one looked more closely and realised that it hadn't even been pressed. I remember now that he saw me heading for the café so he stopped, turned and headed for me, setting his course to barge into me. He struck me a forceful blow on the shoulder. He wanted to provoke me, to vent his spleen in a brawl with me but I ignored him and carried on as if he wasn't there.'

The bank manager looked at his watch and indicated to the critic to stop.

'Is that enough?'

'Yes. Go and see the clerk to get the rest of your fee.'

'Thanks.'

A few days later the bank manager asked for someone else to be found who could make a statement about Abdullatif Muhammad Ahmad. The emissary took little time over the matter.

'Abdullatif, interior decorator, is the only man who ever made a pass at me. He kissed me on the mouth while the street was teeming with people, as if he didn't care what any of them thought. I stared at him in silence, my cheeks burning with shame.

'My heart pounds in my chest whenever I see him and I feel a burning sensation, as if from a fiery furnace inside me. Every day I stand on the corner of Mataeem Street, begging from passers-by. He sits on his favourite bench, a piece of clean cardboard beneath him. When his mood is bright, he leers at me and pesters me with kisses. He teases and taunts me, uses nauseating language I have never heard anyone else utter before. I am seventeen years old. I hobble about on crutches and am seriously overweight. I suffered from polio as a young child and here I am today, a crippled, fat girl who nobody else wants. But I often imagine myself as his wife, and fantasise about our life together.

'Because I am obsessed with him, I have memorised his daily habits, his favourite food, the brand of cigarettes he smokes. I have learnt what pleases him and what he hates. I may even know him better than his mother does. His favourite food for breakfast is *fuul* with mince and he always eats it at a little restaurant hidden from view at the walled-off end of Mataeem Street. He has lunch at a nearby restaurant: a rich, creamy *salta*. I don't know what he eats for dinner.

My older brother takes me home by car at least an hour before sunset because once I was out late at night and was attacked by street youths who took my day's earnings and left me covered in bruises.

'Abdullatif is under fifty, of medium height, fair-skinned, with a trimmed beard and moustache, small sunken eyes, black hair with no flecks of grey, no . . . I don't think he dyes his hair. He wears pitch-black sunglasses, and the silence and arrogance which emanates from behind them strikes fear into the heart. He always wears a formal suit. I have never seen him dress casually in all the years I have known him. You will never see him in just a shirt, a sweater or the like. He prefers silver or green suits and gold or red ties. The only thing which spoils the sophisticated look is that his shoes don't match his suit, though his boots usually do. What attracted me to him most was the wonderfully coloured hats he always takes such care to wear, sourced from the finest milliner.

'He is an ordinary man, though he's a learned philosopher. I once heard him passing on some wisdom to some young boys: "If the world stopped revolving crazily on its axis, then mankind would stop chasing after their daily bread and relax."

'On the day war broke out between Lebanon and Israel, he turned up very late, his beard untrimmed, his face troubled and dark. He clutched the radio to his ear, with the aerial extended. He followed the war minute by minute, as if he were actually Lebanese himself and just living in Yemen. At that time he forgot all about me. He would spend the whole day listening to the news. He would pace up and down like a wolf trapped in a cage. But how I love the way he walks! It is like no other man's walk. He walks in short steps. There is a musicality about it, a dancing rhythm. His head moves in time with the rest of him as though he were walking not just with his feet but with his whole body. He walks like a proud lion.

'He once gave me a green leaf (I don't know which tree it came from) and asked me to look at it carefully and tell him what it reminded me of. I wracked my brains as best I could. I thought it over, yet still couldn't give him a reply. He left me mulling it over while he went to drink an Adani tea. He sipped it from time to time, and glanced at me from time to time too. It came into my head at last that I should say that the leaf was like the heart of humanity. I was relieved and

my face glowed with joy. I assumed this answer would endear me to
him. When he finished his tea, he stood and gave me an inquisitive
look. He guessed from my smile that I had found the answer and he
came over to me. A hand gesture indicated that he wanted my reply.
When he heard what I had to say, he raised his eyebrows, rubbed
his nose and replied that my answer was wrong. I asked: "What is
the right answer then?" He grabbed my hand and explained with his
forefinger: "This leaf looks like your cunt!" He walked off, guffaw-
ing from the depths of his soul. As for me, a tremor ran through my
whole body and I almost fainted from the shameful position he had
put me in. Later it became clear to me that he was right. Leaves do
resemble women's private parts, or perhaps the other way round, we
women make what we hide there resemble leaves.'

Just one week later the bank manager had a burning desire to know
more about Abdullatif Muhammad Ahmad. He contacted a journalist nicknamed 'Ranjala', who worked for a newspaper associated
with the opposition. He ordered him to stage an interview with an
obscure interior decorator. It was only days later when the interview
was published in the newspaper. It was a full-page article and in it
there was a picture of the interior decorator, looking at ease, his head
tilted to the right and his hand stretched out towards the photographer, as if seeking friendship. The text ran as follows:

Today we turn our spotlight on Abdullatif Mohammad Ahmad, one
of this wonderful country's greatest interior decorators. This sensitive
artist leads a disciplined life. You can set your watch by him, for he
always arrives in Mataeem Street at 7 a.m. precisely and takes his seat
near the Post Office to carry out his daily tasks. Examining him as
he sits on his raised bench, one gets the powerful impression of an
eagle perched unseen on a mountaintop, or of the ruler of a kingdom
beyond the knowledge of feeble humanity. He spends the day and part
of the night as if shackled to that venerable throne. It is as if it were
to him the centre of creation, a spiritual fulcrum preserved from the
absurd gyrations around it. It is fixed, still, ever present, never mixed
up in worldly conventions or the routine activities of ordinary people.

He asks the photographer and me for our press passes as soon as we approach him for an interview. Fortunately I have mine with me. He reads the details closely and returns it to me. He crosses his legs, stares ahead at a fixed point and conjures up a vivid past in words: a past which, though related to me in person, is difficult to believe.

'I am Abdullatif Muhammad Ahmad Bilbiid, born in 1958 in the Hadramawt District. I grew up an orphan in my grandfather's house. When I was ten, my uncle took me with him to Abu Dhabi, but after a few months he died and my aunt threw me out on the street. I was lucky enough to be adopted by a Lebanese Maronite family. I was treated as one of their own. I got to experience a real life at last. I got to have a truly rich upbringing, one that I could never have imagined. I caught up on my education, studied in French schools and learnt to draw, play piano, dance, speak French, English and Spanish. We used to spend the summer holidays in Beirut, but then, after the Civil War broke out there in '75, our vacation was in a different European country every year. My family's wealth allowed me to travel all over the world. I have crossed the Atlantic ten times and toured the American continent, North and South, country by country. I know Chile. I know the streets of Santiago like I know this café, because I lived there for two-and-a-half years under my Lebanese step-sister's roof. I tried to study Civil Engineering there but did not like it, so I left Santiago and headed for Paris to study interior design.

'I lived with my Lebanese family for seventeen years and tasted all the pleasures of the world, obtained all the luxuries I could imagine. Money poured into my hands out of bottomless coffers. I tasted every kind of wine the world had to offer. There's not a race, colour or nationality of women that I haven't had the pleasure of. I had twenty girlfriends in Chile alone. I still, to this day, keep the pictures of myself with these girls and, when I die, they will go with me to the grave. The Chilean women are the only ones who will remain in my heart for ever. When my adoptive father died, my family decided to emigrate once and for all to Europe, so I left them and moved into the field of contract brokering, where

I quickly made a name for myself in the market, earning a fortune
in the process.

'I have married twice. The first wife was French, a beauty queen
from Nice, but I only stayed with her for a year. The second,
who was Egyptian, I lived with for three years before divorcing. I
wasn't blessed with children with either of them. Fate landed me
in a tricky spot and I was sent to prison. Straight after release I was
deported from Abu Dhabi to my homeland. That was in the early
'90s. Relations were strained between the two countries because
of Saddam's invasion of Kuwait. In all my time in Abu Dhabi,
Yemen had never entered my head once, and returning there had
never occurred to me.

'I did not give in to despair but tried to rise above it. I put the
money I had made in the Emirates from my contract brokerage
to work and managed to win one of the biggest tenders being
advertised at that time by — Bank. My opponents wanted to wear
me down and, though I have about $800,000 in the bank, I could
not (and still to this day cannot) get access to it to withdraw it. My
morale fell even further with the civil war in 1994. That turned
me into a nervous wreck. I developed cerebral diatransmission
syndrome. It is a rare malignant condition about which science
knows barely anything. When I got the disease my nerve cells sent
their impulses out into space, taking every thought and capabil-
ity I had with them. They were captured in space by beings with
special devices. They used them to spy on me and prevent me
from achieving what I wanted. Then their evil signals attacked my
brain cells in waves, trying to destroy me and turn me into a criminal perpetrating bestial acts. They did this to me because I would
not become their follower, because I refused to carry out their
orders. They wanted to put an end to me by any means possible.
I have suffered from this disease for seventeen years. These beings
impeded any chance I had of earning a decent living and fought
against me wherever I went to find work. Even now, potential
customers are warned off, told that I am mentally ill. Despite all of
this, I am still in control of myself and my mental faculties.

'They are the dregs of creation, its rotting detritus. I challenge you to find an honourable one among them. And you can be sure that I am not, by any means, the only one in this land who has been deprived of the wealth he has earned and is entitled to. This is not a personal matter, but one for each and every one of those poor wretches who have lost money that's rightfully theirs. Isn't everyone choked by debt nowadays owed a share of the oil revenue? My problem is that I carry the burden of everyone's cares upon my shoulders. I cannot sleep for thinking of these things. They send their messages to my nerves all night long. I barely sleep one night in a week.

'Oppression, injustice, criminality were things I had heard about but was not familiar with. They were just words in dictionaries or films as far as I was concerned. But since I've returned I have found those things embedded in reality; I have felt them at every turn in this land. Is any slide more calamitous than this? This criminal scum has changed the country into a bottomless dustbin and a market where everything is for sale.'

This time the emissary of the bank went directly to Abdullatif. He found him in the café, sipping his grief. He picked him out on his own. He told him that the bank manager had read the newspaper interview and wanted to resolve the issue with his account. The interior decorator looked him up and down contemptuously and asked him to show his business card. The emissary opened his Samsonite case and took out a pink business card which served to confirm what he had said. The interior decorator spoke in a husky, menacing voice:

'So when will I get my money?'

'You will get it when you comply with one condition.'

'What condition?'

'We require you to carry out a crime. Just one. Then you can come to the bank and withdraw your $800,000.'

'What are you saying? Are you mad?'

The emissary took a black envelope from his Samsonite case and removed its contents.

'Look, Mr Abdullatif, here is a cheque for $800,000, payable to the bearer. If you comply with our single condition, you can present it and the money's yours. Here also is a list of seventeen types of crime selected by us. Your job is to choose one.'

The interior decorator took off his sunglasses, gazed intently at the list on the blue page and read it over to himself. The emissary saw the decorator's face turn the colour it would have done if someone had thrown hot oil over it. It flared a fierce red and his whole body trembled with seething anger. The emissary's stomach churned with fear as the decorator rose up like a giant and ripped the sheet of blue paper into pieces over his head. He began yelling madly, berating the bank, berating all banks everywhere. And suddenly, from all corners, a cacophony of whistles and shouts rose up and Mataeem Street turned in an instant into a spluttering, angry volcano of sound. The emissary hastily stumbled his way out of the scene in humiliation, almost falling head over heels in the process.

The bank manager did not ignore the humiliation his emissary had suffered, but nevertheless decided to take another tack. In time, a madman appeared at the café, taking the interior decorator unawares. He grabbed his cup and threw the hot drink in his face. They immediately fell like bantam cocks to fierce fighting. The police arrived in record time at the bank manager's behest. An officer poured a red liquid over the madman's head, making him look like he had lost consciousness. They handcuffed the interior decorator and took him to the police station. They took his mad adversary to the hospital in an ambulance. Not long afterwards, the interior decorator was referred for prosecution on charges of attempted murder, a charge which could lead to ten years in prison.

The interior decorator spent seventeen months in prison. He forgot what sunlight was. He forgot the happy times he had had before. He occupied a narrow cell crammed full of thugs, thieves and rapists. The experience changed him completely. Grey infested his hair, his back became bent, his beard grew and his body turned to skin and bone. The bank manager saw that the time was right to send his emissary into action.

One prison visiting day, the emissary arrived with a Samsonite case under his arm and reiterated the previous offer to Abdullatif in its entirety. This time the interior decorator did not erupt with anger. His expression did not change. He was as unmoved as a stone idol. The emissary grabbed hold of his pink tie and warned him:

'Look, we have burnt your file. That means you have two options. Either we can get you out of here with a simple phone call or we can lock you away till the end of your days because, in the eye of the law, you will be considered a criminal without a crime.'

A moment of silence passed as if they were there to mourn someone. Then the interior decorator awoke from his daze and said:

'One day the truth will come out.'

The emissary laughed so hard spit fell out of his mouth.

'The truth? How naive! My friend, the truth is worth what you're paid for it. We who pay the money have the right to own the truth you covet. You must understand that truth is in one's pocket. Your pocket is empty and mine is full, so the truth is not in yours but in mine!'

The interior decorator studied the short, slender fingers of the emissary for a while then spoke slowly:

'I want to know. What crime have I committed in your boss's eyes?'

'Your crime is that you haven't committed a crime at all!'

'So why does your boss insist on turning me into a criminal?'

'Because he dearly wants to give you what's rightfully yours . . . the $800,000 . . . but only if you prove you deserve it.'

'Deserve it? Do you call staining yourself with the blood of the innocent deserving it?!'

'My manager is a philosopher with a unique perspective. He has developed a new moral theory. You're one of the case studies he's working on.'

'Me?'

'Yes. In a nutshell, the theory is that man conducts himself in a certain criminal way, like a predator in a forest, in order to obtain his material and moral entitlements in society. And, because of his criminal record, he becomes, by definition, a good citizen!'

'So that means that the best citizen must be the worst criminal?'

'Precisely. '

'And if one rejects this theory, root and branch, can one remain innocent?'

'In these circumstances, one is not considered a good citizen. One would be classified necessarily as a criminal who has perpetrated the worst act of all: not having enough courage to commit a crime.'

'Your boss's morality is tortuous.'

'On the contrary, it's very, very straightforward. Once you accept it, you will see it just as I do.'

The interior decorator fell silent, pondering things deeply. The emissary was patient, not wanting to break the train of thought of the prisoner behind the metal grille who seemed to have parted from this life. The sun's rays were descending. The interior decorator stirred. He wrapped his arms around himself as if ashamed and spoke tremulously:

'Do you have a cigarette?'

The emissary took a packet from his pocket. He took one for himself and lit it. Then he took another, lit it and passed it through a hole in the metal grille. The decorator inhaled its smoke with profound pleasure. He groaned with the intensity of an orgasm. When he had finished it, he asked the emissary to give him the sheet of blue paper on which the list was written.

The interior decorator appeared in Mataeem Street the next day, clean-shaven and wearing a nice clean suit. People noticed that he had aged and had developed a stoop. They asked where he had been all these months but no one got a reply.

Winter came in with a bitter coldness. Many people avoided leaving the house before sunrise. The denizens of Mataeem Street passed on to each other news of the tragic death of a beggar girl, crippled since youth. She had been found in dawn's early light, lying face down on a stone terrace near the Post Office, a trickle of blood dripping from the corner of her mouth. The whisper went round that she had been poisoned.

Translated by John Peate

from the novel

Raven's Leg

Yahya Amqassim

Humoud Al-Khayr held an axe, a fleeting glint to its blade, as he sat upon a large piece of wood deep in the forest. He was naked and, in preparation for the circumcision procedure, he had placed his penis upon a smooth granite slab which shimmered before him like the still surface of a mountain pool. He had omitted to adhere to the first stage of the ritual, for he should have begun by inserting a lump of dry camel dung into his foreskin in order to push the glans as far back as possible and ensure that the axe blade made contact solely with the foreskin and nothing else, thereby protecting his penis from any potential error. However, he had made do with his index finger instead of the piece of dung, inserting it inside his foreskin and forcing the glans to the base of the shaft. Then, at the point where his fingernail met the head of his penis, he pressed the blade of the axe and, feeling reassured that he had achieved his desired aim, he removed his finger so that the foreskin spread out over the stone like a piece of old rag. He would have to cut it quickly, then complete the circumcision by detaching the skin from around his genitals and the insides of his thighs. In this way would he accomplish the traditional circumcision practice of his grandfathers.

While in this state of readiness he heard through the trees, far from his sight, the panting of a man and wondered what mischief he might be about. He was determined, however, that nothing would deter him from what he was about to do and no one would keep him from demonstrating his manhood and his ability to carry out this great deed, despite the punishment prescribed for any one who circumcised himself. Thus with his resolve suitably strengthened, he declared to himself: 'Let them kill me, yet not one of them shall deny my manhood as long as I am a son of Usayrah.'

He paid no attention to the breathing of the man as it receded from the place. No doubt he had been watching him since he entered the forest, and he reassured himself with the thought that it was an eye of his father's, or of his grandmother Sadiqiyyah, that eye that never left him. Then he repeated, 'Son of Usayrah,' as a challenge to whoever was listening, and who was not listening, and focused his thoughts on the task in hand, for even if the man bore evil intentions, that would not deflect him from his purpose, conceived days ago, for he was no less a man than anyone else in the valley of Al-Husayni.

'Son of Usayrah' was an expression which summed up all the glories of the tribes in the valley of Al-Husayni, and particularly in his village of Usayrah, the valley's principal settlement, whose name they would not invoke unless embarking on some momentous deed that could not be shirked. So when he cried out that he was a son of that village he kindled in the deepest recesses of his heart the flames of determination and ignited the fuse of fearlessness, and the blood rushed to the top of his head spurring on his zeal to bring the matter to an end. And the silence of the forest that afternoon did not disperse when he called out that phrase, nor the birds take flight through the thick branches, until his hand had raised the other stone and brought it down uncompromisingly on the head of the axe and the blade penetrated and made contact with the smooth slab, thus amputating his foreskin which jumped nimbly on to the ground, and the blood gushed forth from where the severed skin had been.

The axe fell alongside the bloodied stone and he rejoiced, filled with pride at what he had done. But he realised he had committed a dreadful error, for the blood gathered around him in a terrible way, the like of which he had not heard about before. He examined himself carefully and felt an excruciating pain, then discovered that he had nicked the glans on the right-hand side, thereby diminishing its rounded oval shape. The strange sight of it left him in a state of alarm and he refrained from completing the removal of the skin around his genitals and the insides of his thighs as he should have done if he were to perform the operation fully and correctly, in keeping with their custom in circumcision. He thought about his father, Sheikh Isa Al-Khayr, who would deal with the matter, no doubt about it, and he rummaged in the thickened dirt for the tiny missing piece of his glans then quickly inspected the routes through the forest for any road he could follow safe from lurking eyes ready to denounce him to the ear of the prince of Sabyaa', for his father's enemies were many and no doubt his circumcising himself would be an opportunity for them to lay some charge against his father with the prince, who had warned against anyone committing this deed and that the penalty for he who did would be severe.

Although he reached home undetected, the family knew that the treacherous eyes in the village could not be ignored. Immediately ascertaining the imminent danger, the father hastily hid his son from view and arranged with a number of his retinue medical treatment for the wound while the mother managed, with the assistance of the black slave girl Zahrah, to bury the severed part of the young man's penis.

At noon the sheikh mounted up and rode towards Sabyaa', where he made directly for the prince who received him with the magnanimity he deserved, even though he was somewhat taken aback by the sheikh's visit, for he had sent letters to the sheikh on more than one occasion requesting his presence to discuss various matters concerning the valley of Al Husayni, and had not received any response. All the sheikh had done with the handwritten invitations was to place them under his bed and order the prince's men at arms to go away bearing from him to their prince the single phrase: 'If he needs me my house is spacious enough.' And the sheikh never attended the prince's *majlis* unless he went down to Sabyaa' market on a Tuesday and the prince happened to hear about it and begrudgingly hurry to meet him and indulge the good sheikh's pride until he yielded to his powers of persuasion and agreed to pass by the prince's office for a cursory visit. The sheikh would never have gone to the prince's residence under duress, and nothing would compel him to do such a thing unless it was a most pressing matter. Perhaps the prince thought this to himself when the sheikh turned up.

So it was that the sheikh began to implement the most important step of his plan to extricate himself and his family from the eyes lurking around them and he invited the prince and his companions to attend the *shuhrah* of his son Humoud the following day, which would mark the beginning of the week's festivities leading up to his circumcision. And he impressed upon the prince in his invitation that he would be among the senior important guests who were invited by name to this great event. The prince apologised on the pretext of being busy and requested his chief adjutant to attend in his place, accompanied by some of his soldiers. The sheikh concealed his happiness at this acceptance by proxy but he did not reveal his feelings through any indiscreet reaction which might have given away his true feelings.

Having abandoned their homes, they stopped over in the foothills. They selected a place called Al-Qaayim, which means the high place, because it commanded a splendid view over the valleys on either side and was higher than the surrounding rocky land. Some huts made of straw and the branches of *samr* were set up by the women and children and the sheikh, and the remainder of the warriors did not arrive until each family had erected its shelter. A larger structure had been erected for the sheikh at the front, on the orders of the mother who had been the prime reason for them settling there after she reached an understanding with the notables of the area, who extended a welcome to her folk befitting those of influence and high standing. She had reassured them that the raiders had no place in her memory and that no book before had ever predicted a war such as this, and she had alerted the sheikhs of the tribes, and at their head their leader, her son, to the serious consequences of going out of their villages without heeding her intuition. Her orders had never been disobeyed before, but on this occasion she was overruled and it aggrieved her to differ with the men and her son, who insisted on going out of their valley.

That same night they caught up with their families, the mother met in her small hut with three women, her private assistants. No one thought it odd that she expelled everyone, including the ailing sheikh, from the vicinity of the hut when the screaming started. Nor did it occur to anyone to dare ask about the consternation etched on her face or the curses and profanities directed at whoever came too near her or the three women, even if it was to inquire after the reason why the woman in labour was screaming in such agony. Her slave girl Zahrah saw to it that no one approached to investigate the matter.

There were conflicting opinions about the name of the woman whose screams they could hear, as if she were asking them for help and none would come, just as later people reported that there was in fact more than one woman screaming, begging for assistance, and everyone began to surmise what they could, feebly attempting to find out the secret of that night.

In the morning there appeared on the face of the mother the strain of exertion that would not have afflicted her – in the estimation of her son the sheikh – if she had confided in him previously the causes of that exertion. It did not occur to him to approach one of the three women who had come out in appalled silence, for he would not get anything out of them as long as the mother was the one who had led the midwife team throughout the night as they ministered to two women giving birth at the same time – as he discovered later – and the sheikh preferred to remain silent until such time as she wished to talk. In any case, he was hardly in a position to interfere in such matters that could be resolved without him, especially as it was women's business.

That afternoon the mother asked them to perform the prayer for the dead over the two women and one child. Three funerals, the toll of the previous night's travail. One of the deceased women was the wife of Bishaybish, who was not there with them. The identity of the other woman was not known. The dead were prepared in the same hut, then, on the mother's order, one of the women was buried next to the quarters of Al-Sahili while the other one and the child were buried outside the camp. By the time night came Zahrah, the mother's slave girl, was slipping through the darkness towards their valley in the west, concealing among the belongings she carried with her the umbilical cord of the surviving little girl. Meanwhile, the grunting of Al-Bariq, Bishaybish's camel, as it mourned the loss of his master's wife, echoed around the camp, and they tied him to the upright of the mother's wooden bed, fearing that he might wander to the grave and rub out its markings, for the camel would not pull the mother's bed at night because he knew her. The mother had ordered Walad Bilal not to spend too long playing the dirge, as they were not in their own homes, so that the sound of the wailing flute would not afflict unnecessary distress on Bishaybish if he were to approach the camp, although she knew that at that hour he would be making for a cave to protect himself from the rainy night and would not catch up with them in Al-Qaayim until late the following morning.

That evening in the mother's shelter, as thunder rumbled in the sky, the sheikh continued in his state of deep depression, his torment exacerbated by the deaths and the prayer and the burial. Nothing could relieve him of this state except the mother who alone was capable of ministering to all his pains, and, sensing what lay behind his silence, she said to him suddenly: 'Your wives are dead but your cock is still alive.'

He smiled a smile sensed only by her, despite the presence of his retinue and those who had come to offer condolences for the wife of Bishaybish, who had still not appeared. It pleased them to see their sheikh's gloom receding and, in order that they might exploit the opportunity of the mother's cunning intervention by reminding him that his penis remained despite the deaths of all his wives, the last of whom, Umm Hamoud, had died two years previously, and in order not to be silent at such a moment, Subaya, the son of the youngest mother, commenting on what the old woman had said, announced: 'All that's left in your boy's cock is urine.' With these words Subaya increased the mirthful uproar about his brother Isa's member, hinting at its impotence, at which point Bin Shami, oblivious to their sadness, let out a roar of laughter. The mother, in her turn, replied to Subaya: 'I know my boy best, you simpleton. He's more of a man than the rest of you put together.'

And in another attempt to strike a chord, and perhaps encourage him to speak, she had defended him as the most manly of them all, but even so the sheikh did not join in but rather changed the subject to ask about the weapons and whether the women who had arrived the day before had brought the remaining rifles and ammunition.

The mother replied, confirming that everyone had arrived with all their weapons, and she sighed gently, recalling Bishaybish and wondering how he would receive the news of his wife's death. Then she added: 'They found a woman on the way. She was heavily pregnant, almost ready to give birth. She was in a terrible state. The camel riders must have caught her husband as he was escaping with her.'

Abruptly and with some alarm he asked his men: 'Who is her husband?'

The mother made light of it: 'We do not know her. It seems she is from Wadi Dhamad.'

He was silent for a moment, reassured, then he turned to her and asked: 'They told me that you delivered the children of two women, both of whom died together with a male child, but that one boy survived. Whose son is he?'

His brother Subaya corrected him: 'The surviving child was a girl, ya Isa.'

The mother was not inclined to answer the question. Instead, as if arousing their attention so that they would listen more carefully to what she was about to say, she took her stick and brandished it in the air in a gesture of admonishment, and, far from any attempt to answer his question, she said: 'You are approaching a time that no longer belongs to you. It is true that these northerners are not coming to make war with you as you believe they are, but they bring a different law with them. Our lives will change greatly. Look to your sons because after a time they will set off for the north and leave their towns and villages. They will follow a nation state and chase after paper money. They may even forget their families, their land and their life here altogether. The northern lands are not like they were before. There is a new nation there, a new law ruling brave and distant territories. Those who have passed through here are the soldiers of that nation. They will reach as far as Zubayd.'

A heavy burden had fallen upon them at the words of the mother and she stopped, reading in their silence a great apprehension about what she had said. Each one of them sat motionless and the throbbing of their hearts almost seized control of their *majlis*, dumbstruck at what they had heard. It had never occurred to them that matters would become so serious as to threaten them and their children and do away with everything of any value in their lives. They had never seriously considered an eventuality like this before, or that such a time would come upon them, for they were not accustomed to monumental events of this kind: the establishment of a nation in the north penetrating many lands and territories, its dominion extending as far as the city of Zubayd in Yemen. They could not comprehend that its hegemony would bring to naught the birthrights that derived from their own legitimate authority, and even more calamitous that its power would draw their sons to the north.

The sheikh cleared his throat and expelled a gob of saliva behind his seat in a gesture of rejection of these ideas the mother had mentioned, though he knew all too well her ability to reveal what was to the rest of them unknown. On this occasion she had unleashed an intolerable bitterness. How could they readily accept such insult, such havoc wreaked upon them by blind fate?

His voice quivered in her face as if he was about to ask her to talk about something more optimistic, for her words had singed the men's beards and slapped the women's faces, and the dreadful calamity had penetrated deep into their souls.

All they knew of the north was Mecca, to which they wound their way once in a lifetime to perform the Hajj. This arduous journey, which took many hard months, was the only one any of them undertook. How could they live through a time when their children would depart in that direction, some of them never to return?

Each of them was thinking about the same dilemma, that journey which would devour them without a fight, although the thought of it had never worried them before. They had an old adage they always repeated when discussing any matter relating to the travel of one of their sons, that saying which Al-Habbash had angrily shouted out at the end of the mother's speech: 'If your son sets off towards the north let him go, but if he sets off towards Yemen hold him back.' In so saying he had reminded them of the matter of their boys' travelling with or without their consent. If a son were to head north then his family should let him go, for he would encounter hunger and hardship and would be obliged to return to them. If he were to travel south, however, towards Yemen to be precise, then consent would be withheld for fear of his not returning, for Yemen was well known for its bounty and the good things there might prevent him from coming back to his village and his family, who would be deprived of his support in facing the trials of life. So, how were they to believe now that the north, with its scarcity and death, would take away their flesh and blood instead of Yemen? Al-Habbash had sown confusion in their hearts, turning calm acceptance at travel north into painful forbearance, when at last, with sorrow digging its claws into his heart, he asked the mother in amazement: 'Perhaps time will turn upside down, ya Sadigiyah?'

That same question was harboured in every heart that heard the mother's speech. The sheikh was like a rudderless boat in a stormy sea, and for many reasons, the most important being the safety and well-being of his people, and he paid little heed to the thoughts that concerned them, and that more than one raised, hoping for an unequivocal answer from the mother.

And in the midst of all the talking came the mother's long and well known sigh: 'Eeeeeeeeyhaa.' Silence fell once again and this presage of doom fell heavy upon their hearts, for the mother did not utter these sighs of hers unless a terrible foreboding overcame her. Then, commanding their undivided attention, she declared: 'There will be no more men. Only women will survive.'

Translated by Anthony Calderbank

Two Stories

Yassin Adnan

Small Talk in Shades of White

Look I'm getting annoyed now. If you carry on like this, I'm off. You want to know what you've done wrong? Why am I not surprised? For one thing, the way you're sitting and staring at me is winding me up. You're playing at being quiet and considerate, hoping that I take you for a civilised, intelligent man. Well, we're not in a mosque now. We're in a bar. And you're really getting on my nerves. Even that smile plastered across your lips so you come across all smart and reasonable. I find it really offensive. Do you really think you're that clever? And the other people here are shallow types who can only make small talk? No, darling, you're wrong. Shall I tell you what's going on in your head? You're playing at being clever, but you're not thinking clever. You've told yourself: 'This is just another slut. She looks drunk – brilliant. I'll only have to buy two beers and then I can invite her back to my place. She'll probably be tired and badly in need of *sleep*. Just sleep. When we get home, I won't ask her if she's had dinner. I'll take her straight to the bedroom. We'll turn off the light, and we'll sleep. Once I've had had my way with her, I'll turn my back. And then, as usual, I'll snore all the way to the morning.' Open your eyes, my friend. Seems like you've fallen asleep right here in the bar. Do you really think you've got it all worked out? God help you. Has it occurred to you, even as a minor possibility, that the woman sat next to you is not a slut? And that she's only drinking like this because of the pain

she feels, and that she badly needs a man of substance, who can have
a deep conversation and listen, really listen to her. Maybe that's why
she started talking to you. But even if I was out on the pull, what's
stopping me from thinking like you? You're just a filthy drunk. I
can down a few glasses at your expense and then give you the slip.
And let's suppose I did go back to your place with you. Who's to
say that I won't be the one to turn my back on you after sex? Why
can't I be the one to get what I want and then slam the door behind
me in the morning as I head out to get some more somewhere else,
while you're the one who stays behind to make the bed, wash the
sheets, and rub off the gunk that stuck on to you while you lay back
and closed your eyes in the hope of bringing back some of the heat
from the night's passion? Now who's the slut, you or me? Oh my
God, are you still smiling at me like I'm telling a joke? You really
are unbearable. Do you know what annoys me about men? It's that
lack of sensitivity which gives them a superhuman ability to look at
peace with themselves. You could sit there like you're not both-
ered, even if your insides were on fire. Take you, for example. You
look around you in the bar like it's a strange and foreign land. The
whores, the drunks, the shouting, the arguments – a madhouse. But
you forget that you're here, slap bang in the middle of the madhouse.
You've forgotten, haven't you? You think you're some kind of king
and these others are a troupe of actors performing in your honour. If
you're rubbing shoulders with them, it's only because you've come
down off your throne and stepped on to the stage. No, darling.
You've got it wrong. The basic difference between you and me is
that I actually consider myself part of this race of lowlifes. I know
that I am in a stinking bar. And when I leave at the end of the night,
I'm going to have to watch my step, because the likes of you feel no
shame in throwing up everywhere, hurling the beer that was fester-
ing in their guts out on to the counter or in the entrance, without
anyone blinking an eye. Sometimes they throw up into the laps of
their lady companions, forgetting that just a few moments ago they
were respectable gentlemen. I'm not claiming to be respectable. I'm
just a slut. But of course you're no better than me. You're as loose as
I am. You walked into this dump to fill up on cheap beer and take

a random woman home to your bed. Can you see how we're both the same when it comes to being worthless scum?

That's not to say that everyone here is a good-for-nothing. In this bar, I've met some real men. And they know what it means to be a man. Like that old fellow there – do you see him? – in the light brown overcoat, sitting by himself at the far end of the counter. No, that one there, behind Fateeha, the blonde. Ah, so you're not a real boozer – who here doesn't know him? His name is Saif Al-Mansouri, and he's worked since forever at the National Cooperative Bank. He's from Marrakesh, like you. He came to this city in the seventies and settled here for good. He's here every day, bless him. I've known him for years, and he's really sweet to me. Looks like he hasn't seen me. Mister Saif . . . Mister Saif . . . He didn't hear me. He once said to me that he prefers the noises of the bar to small talk. He can't stand talk, whether it's on the TV, from his wife or his kids. At least here he can lose himself in the noise and no one bothers him. Poor thing. If you knew how much he suffers. When he caught tuberculosis, everyone started avoiding him. He once said to me that even his wife kept her distance from him when they were in bed. Some of the really mean regulars gave him a nickname – Unsafe Al-Cansouri. The man's sick and the scumbags make fun of him. It's not the illness that he resents, it's people. Last Saturday, he told me that he had come to an understanding with the bugs that had built a home in his lungs, and then he said: 'But those turds would rather carry on talking about me behind my back. If I've got TB, it's my chest that's infected, it's me that's got to breathe with these lungs, not them, or their mothers. What can I do to look after my body at this age? I'm sixty-nine years old. I'm just dragging myself along, and I'm dragging all my years behind me as I splutter like an old train. I can tell you this, my love, there's nothing I'll regret more than dying while there's still one part of my body that's healthy. I'd rather break down gradually than burn out all of a sudden like a TV that's had a power surge.'

I can tell you, he really is a different sort of person. This one time, six years ago, he came out drinking with us at the Seven Dunes pub. He'd drunk a little too much, and I didn't want to leave him in the bar like that so I took him home with me. In those days, I used to

live with Samia from Rabat – do you know her? – and this other girl
who emigrated to Italy and got married there. The disease hadn't hit
him yet. I won't lie to you, we used to find him very attractive then.
Once inside, I took him to my room. I pushed him gently on to the
bed and lay down next to him.

Seriously, I never feel quite myself except when I take my clothes
off. I didn't hold back. I just had my underwear on. I embraced him
tightly against my chest. Did I really want him that night? I don't
know. But I hugged him close and rained kisses on his face. When
I began to unbutton his shirt, he whispered into my ears in a tired
voice: 'No Hajeeba. You are like a daughter to me . . .' My body
started shaking and I burst into tears. He had never cheated on his
wife. That's what he told me afterwards. And there was me, a slut.
I was just a slut. Crying was not going to help me at that moment.
I got out of bed and I began to get dressed, but he opened his eyes,
and looked at me:

'Stay as you are, Hajeeba,' he said to me, 'and come sleep next
to me. I will hold you like a father; put your head on my chest and
sleep. I love your white underwear. White is a noble colour, my pet.
So come and sleep in my arms, safe and sound.'

Since that night, I have always worn white underwear. White really
is a noble colour. Look at the people on religious holidays, what are
they wearing? White clothes. At the Friday prayer, worshippers wear
white robes. The dead are wrapped in white shrouds. At weddings,
they wear white. In mourning, it's white. As for you . . . Are you still
smiling?! What's that now you cheeky sod? You want to check the
colour of my bra for yourself? Then cough up the price of beer, you
cheapskate. Don't worry about dinner. I'll treat you to a light meal at
the Travellers' Diner. Tonight, I'll make you regret smiling like that.
I'll light a fire inside your body and I'll make every part of it scream.
Get up then. Oh, Mister Saif! Mister Saif . . . Enjoying your drink
. . .? How are things . . .? No . . . Sorry, dear . . . I have a friend for
tonight. I'm going now. Bye bye . . . Yes, tomorrow, of course . . . Of
course . . . Of course . . .

Ouarzazate, April 1998

Love and Firewood

No human being can cope with being alone, however resentful
or despairing of other people he may be. We are in constant
need of something to break the silence, even if it's the barking of a dog
in an empty space. I can tell you a few things about silence, loneliness
and cold. I have lived on my own in this secluded, freezing town at the
foot of the mountains for over fifteen years. All the plans I have made
here have ended in failure. I failed to marry Najwa, the daughter of
Mr Mashkour, the post-office manager. Her father refused to give his
daughter to a man he had never seen at the mosque, as if I were from
a different, unclean species that could never be brought into a holy
place. I failed in my scheme to run a bookshop, which I kept open for
ten months and did not sell a single book. I discovered that none of
the people in this town read and that only a madman would think of
selling them books. I also failed in the local elections, where I did not
gain a single vote, including my own. Seeing the election campaign
was enough to convince me that this was a dirty game which was not
worth playing. So I gave up on the dream for the sake of which I had
got into that mess in the first place: to plant some trees in the town's
one and only street without needing anyone's permission. I gave up
on this secret dream on the second day of the campaign, and I felt able
to boycott the elections with an easy conscience. All my schemes in
this town have ended up failing. The one thing I have made a success
of is hating them all. I have managed to hate the entire city and its
people, starting with Mehmad the grocer, who hardly ever has any
bread to sell me in the middle of the day and, rather than feeling
ashamed, insists on regaling me with stupid stories that never finish.
It's as if he actually means to infuriate me, because he chooses with
great care the topics I find most irksome. He's always got a new batch
of tedium to force on to me. It's one thing he never runs out of.

I always felt cold in this town. Amina suggested that I live in the
old part, as the mud houses there are warmer. I replied that, true
enough, I could not stand the cold, but I hated cockroaches even
more. Amina told me that the real cockroaches were inside my head

and that she could not understand how someone like me could look so normal and stable and yet hate the world so much.

But Amina, I don't hate the world! How can I explain it to you? I love God, His angels and messengers. On cold nights like these, I love banana-flavoured yoghurt and red wine. And I also love you, in the winter, when your body turns into soft firewood; and in the summer, when you wear your orange and sky-blue top and your short white skirt. And, to be honest, I love you when you're wearing other clothes too, but I don't say so. I'm so immersed in your love, Amina, and that's why I don't say anything. Love, my darling, is like a ritual – to be performed quietly. Of course, it's not that I love twenty-four hours a day. I'm not a machine. It's not fair or right when you ask me to do the impossible. It's impossible for me to love you morning and evening, and to keep saying it all the time, just like that, without alcohol or due occasion. The real problem with Amina is that she wants me to love her without offering anything in return. How about you, Amina? Do you love me at all?

'But I come to your place twice a week and sleep with you. I refuse to marry Muhsin the teacher because of you. What more do you want from me?'

What more can you do? Sometimes I feel that a woman really is completely different from a man. She becomes all stupid the moment you ask her to concentrate a little, and talking to her becomes the most tiresome ordeal. Amina, for example, does not understand a great many things, even though she has been coming to my flat for three years. I am a nice, simple person. All I ask is for a light supper, a glass of wine and a woman by my side to keep me warm and make me feel like a king. But Amina does not understand how to play the role of the king's consort. Even then, I love her. When we met for the first time at the newspaper stand next to my home, she was asking for a cookery magazine. I didn't think she was beautiful and nothing about her turned me on: her body was like filtered water, no taste or colour or smell, its particulars hidden under a grey robe; her hair, neither black nor fair, tied up in a stern-looking bun; and a lukewarm smile, like a nurse in the emergency ward. Nothing attractive about her at all, actually. But from force of habit, I began chatting to her about cookery in all its forms. We talked about couscous and pizza, about meat and plums and chicken tagine with lemon. Then she came up with me to my flat. And because I didn't have a TV at home, we had sex. That's how, from force of habit, Amina started coming to my flat and saying to me, 'I love you.' Because I am, by my nature, a kind, considerate fellow, I would say to her, 'And I love you.' Gradually, when we were in bed together, the genie started coming out of the bottle. It was astounding. Before I got to know this girl, the regular visitors to my bed had been pretty girls who wore bright-coloured panties. But with Amina, I found out that those chatty girls who made their way around the beds of the town's civil servants had very little real experience. Girls who have lots of sex and smoke cigarettes from other people's packets without sticking to a particular brand – they are not serious. That's why they fail to pick up any experience, regardless of the number of beds they jump in and out of. Amina was a girl who had never had any of this. Probably no one before me had chatted her up with talk of cookery and ingredients. No one before me had invited her back to his place for tea. But her body – natural, deprived, self-denying – worked wonders for me. The strange thing is that she never asked me to marry her. She didn't ask for anything. She just wanted to come over from time to time and sleep with me a while, and then lie down next to me, talking for hours about Muhsin the teacher, and her retired father, and her married sister in Marrakesh and her brother who was going to graduate as a dentist in two years' time. I didn't mind listening to these stories. But to ask me time after time to profess my love for her, without alcohol or due occasion, that I can't stand. It's true that this is a small town, and that the sexual endurance shown by Amina was not be found in the dainty, pretty young things that used to frequent my bed before that chance encounter at the newspaper stand. And it's true that the town is cold and that Amina is good firewood during winter, but I hate it when anyone demands that I profess or confess or declare anything at all. I once teased Amina and said: 'I'm not some criminal who needs to own up to a crime.' She didn't find that funny. I said: 'How about I murder you and then I can avow my love for you to the police?' She didn't find that funny either. The problem with Amina is that she is too serious. Now it's true that, when we're in bed, her seriousness and self-denial light up my being with fires of passion that make me forget the cold outside. But it's a man's right to share a joke with his sweetheart, by which I mean the woman who comes to his place from time to time and considers herself to be his sweetheart.

But Amina, tell me, why is it always my job to make the declarations? Why don't you find out for yourself how much I love you, just from the looks I give you, and the trembling in my voice on the phone when the weather is cold and you're far away? Why do I have to say everything?

In this town, you're expected to chatter away like a radio without doing anything or doing the exact opposite of what you say. Mehmad the grocer is always telling me what a smart businessman he is, but when the electricity in our area was down and I went to his shop for candles, he didn't have a single one. Mashkour the post-office manager, who gave me lessons in morality and virtue before throwing me out of his house, ended up marrying off his chaste pearl of a daughter, in an extravagant wedding, to Hameed Al-Nakoudi, owner of the Seven Dunes pub.

Amina. I'm not like them. I don't want anything from anyone. Even your body which keeps me warm, take it away to someone else's bed and leave me alone, with just my wine to help me battle the cold. I would rather be alone than submit to this foolishness. I refuse to allow anyone to extract confessions from me under duress. I don't want to confess, profess or declare anything. How about it? Just leave me. I beg you.

But Amina, who I used to think did not know how to play the role of the queen, the king's consort, gently placed my head against her chest and whispered, sobbing: 'My darling. Sleep in my arms and let me hold you.' She hugged me close, burying my head in her breasts, kissing me everywhere on my body, while she sighed and sobbed. I was stunned, and submitted myself utterly, not understanding quite what had happened. Amina completely lost herself in the part, as she rolled around on my chest, her tears gently raining down on my body. I could hear her crying now, overcome with feeling, as she buried her face in my thighs: 'Oh my darling. I didn't know that you loved me that much . . .'

Ouarzazate, 30 October 2003

Translated by Haroon Shirwani

Suicide 20, or *The Hakimi Maqama*

Youssef Rakha

Rashid Siyouti recounted what follows:

Imagine! You open the bonnet of your car after it breaks down on you in the middle of the street, and where the engine should be you find a corpse folded in the foetal position! That's not exactly what happened to me, but considering that this was my first visit to Cairo in three years, what happened was almost as strange.

Afterwards, when I found out what my lifelong friend Mustafa Nayif Shorbagi had been through, and what had made him leave Cairo a week before I arrived, things would fall into place. I was not to know Mustafa's story until after I resumed my normal life as a locum at Bethnal Green Hospital in East London, when I received an email with a huge PDF file attached, containing the manuscript in which Mustafa wrote about his separation from his wife and what followed. There was a single line in the message window wondering whether, after reading the attachment, I would think he had gone crazy.* That PDF would prove to me that I hadn't imagined that night on the way to Salah Salim Street, under the stress of my wedding plans, thinking too much about the greatest obstacle ahead. I live next to where I work in Bethnal Green, and since I moved there in 2005, about two years ago, I've been cohabiting with a Druze co-worker, with whom

---

* The attachment refers to *Kitab al-Tughra* or the *Book of the Sultan's Seal*, or *Marvels of History in the City of Mars*, an unpublished novel by the same author.

I am in love. I would have married her long ago, if not for the fact that her family would never let her marry a non-Druze. So when a ghost appeared to me in the flesh, saying that he was the nineteenth incarnation of God's Anointed Ruler, *Al-Hakim bi-Amr Allah*, whom the Druze worship, I wondered if it was a hallucination brought on by reading about that obscure religion and thinking about getting married, or the reason why I was forbidden to start a family with my girlfriend. For a few hours I panicked, afraid that, in having a relationship with this girl, I might be committing blasphemy.

Although the contents of the PDF in Mustafa's letter could not have crossed my mind during my time in Cairo, I remembered after my second phone call to his mother (the only person remaining there with a genuine connection to him) that what happened to him might resemble what I saw with my own eyes that night.

He who acknowledges that there is no god to worship in the sky, nor imam to worship on earth, save for our Lord Al-Hakim, may He be exalted, is one of the Monotheists.

(From *The Covenant of the Druze Faith* by Hamza bin Ali, known as *The Covenant of Induction into the Religion of the Ruler of the Age*)

That night I discovered that the imams of the line of Ubaydallah (the Fatimid dynasty) knew of a sixth and stranger disappearance. Ubaydallah Al-Hakim, their most famous representative, was an austere tyrant who forbade people from eating *mulukhiyya* stew and prohibited women from leaving the house, then committed a minor genocide in the first Muslim city in Egypt named after the country itself – *Misr* – by liquidating anyone who came near him. The disappearance of this inspired madman, as I discovered that night, was nothing but a suicide. This was followed by the appearance of the Druze faith, which claimed that he was the human embodiment of the One. 'If you're convinced that you're God,' – this is what the man who killed himself told me – 'this must necessarily lead to suicide. For how is God to live among the people, even if He is their Lord?' 'This suicide,' he explained to me, 'is repeated once every fifty years, dating from the first time it happened in 1021: the soul of Al-Hakim will have been incarnated in the body of an ordinary person with roots in Al-Mui'zz's Cairo. And after he commits suicide in his turn, he appears to his heir – precisely fifty years having passed since he killed himself – to inform him that he is next in line.' At the time, I remembered that up until they married, my mum and dad were born and lived their lives not far from the Mosque of Al-Hakim, the one with the minaret that resembles the trunk of an old tree, looking out over a wall that spreads out like a sheet. I remembered also that my grandfather used to claim to my father that he was a descendant of the sheikh of Borgwan Alley (that place named after the most famous of Al-Hakim's eunuchs, and one of his victims). My grandfather used to say, half jokingly, that our history in the neighbourhood goes back to the days of the Mamelukes. This was the way it went on my first trip, after an absence of three years, to my birthplace and my sweetest days, the subject now having fallen in love with a Druze woman. Now I had to imagine killing myself by the Sword of Al-Imam Al-Aziz Billah, the father of Al-Hakim, given that I was (woe is me!) Suicide Number 20.

Rashid Jalal Siyouti digressed, speaking in the voice of the ghost:
'He who dies alone does not know. He does not quiver in surprise, nor does the bright flash blind him.' (This is what Suicide Number 19 said to me on the way back, when my car stalled in the Qarafa parallel, as if it had lost power. It was a dark place, yet I pulled the handbrake and went out to open the bonnet. Suddenly, the light in the sky changed for an instant, as if the morning had dawned, only to vanish again. Meanwhile, the rocks from Muqattam Hills flashed above me as though fluorescent, while something like the palm of a hand pressed against my shoulder. I looked around me but there was no trace of him left. Eventually I returned to the driver's seat, trying desperately to start the car, when a neatly groomed young man appeared next to me in a retro-style, three-piece suit, holding prayer beads in one hand. He immediately started to speak.) 'He who dies without having control over his death will never know the fabulous rapture of departing this life.' Then:

Only he who kills himself is the Immortal, the Everlasting, and who else can ever have the joy of certainty? I speak to you from experience, believe me: you will not die like other people. You will kill yourself with your own hands at the decisive moment, and the decisive moment always includes others. I tell you this, despite the fact that I didn't make preparations for it, since I died in the presence of my father and sister and best friend, in the courtyard containing my mother's tomb, also behind Bab Al-Nasr, where Al-Mu'izz's Cairo was located a long time ago. Now, of course, there is nothing called time, yet there is no way to make you understand me except through that language of yours. My sister thought I was going to kill her with the Sword, while my father lay ill. Yet I was to call him too, so that he emerged one minute before my death. All those itinerant spirits around my soul, I tell you, witnessed me pass. By your measure, my age was twenty-four at the time, and if not for the fact that I – exalted be my name – was of divine lineage, I would not have realised the magnificence of disappearing early on, or learnt that all that happened, happened in order to lead up (in however illogical or murky a way that does not make it any less inevitable) to a single moment in the year 1958, the moment I plunged the Sword's tip into the spot my previous incarnation had precisely marked for me: under my left breast, about a thumbnail's length to the right. My arms were outstretched, as were my hands gripping the handle. It was as if my thin torso, in its black robe, had become a taut arc. And bracing my bare feet on the sandy ground, all at once, I held firm, I, the Perfect One, whose death comes by His own hand – and from that time onward, the One who carries the Sword of Al-Aziz Billah. Listen to my tale.

And mimicking the great *maqama* masters, Al-Hamadhani and Al-Hariri, Rashid returned to the beginning of his tale:

I came to Cairo, so to speak, for a vacation; in the company of my true friend Mustafa, I intended to walk from location to location. With him, that's what I agreed: to see what was left of the Islamic heritage in Cairo, its glory and deeds. It had been seven years for me in England, during which time I had severed the nerve of nostalgia.

That was a long time ago, when I agreed to meet with Darsh,★ and like a sultan to the throne returned, you should have seen what then occurred. I was appalled not to find him in anywhere, as if my city were bereft of any habitation. Our agreement, the bastard had erased; and because of the resulting shock, awesome sorrows I was made to face. Nostalgically, I imagined us among dusty and dirty alleyways, in Al-Mu'izz's Cairo, wandering from gate to gate. Suddenly, in my mind's eye, I said, 'Damn Mustafa – enough, I'll substitute his company with cigarettes and photography.' I took my father's car, heading out one night, when no sooner had I set out than I returned contrite. Were it to be revealed – what I saw in Bab Al-Futouh – it would give the Sphinx himself a fright. And if Mustafa has his own excuse for madness, I realised then that it was my turn to be mad. (You will not understand what happened to Mustafa until you have read the PDF and its fiction.) I say to you, as my limbs are struck with dread and apathy, without prior arrangement or scrutiny:

> He who suffers the spectre of death
> Is on the path of resurrection
> The purpose behind killing myself
> Is to quicken my crossing over

After the event, I spent only five days in Cairo; the shock and horror of the encounter shook me to the core. I fell into visits and family gatherings; at their tables I would stay, bottling up my suffering all the way. The whole time, nothing hidden or revealed could stop me from thinking about Mustafa and how he had disappeared. Since I found his mobile phone switched off the night of my arrival, there was no one but his mother to prevail upon; I called her at once, late one night, and in her voice there were shades of confusion and despair. Then I called her again, after the heir of the imam showed up, just three days before I was due to return to England. And so the thought has often returned to me: how, in April, Mustafa suddenly left, three weeks after he found his way to his mother's house. He

★ Darsh is a nickname for Mustafa.

hastened to divorce his wife as an expression of his indignation, and had gone back to live with his mother after their separation. After his departure, as she told me, he only called one time – to reassure her that he was safe and to confirm that he would not die. 'She senses that she has lost him for all eternity,' I thought, as she spoke to me, weary with agony. His suspicious disappearance was confirmed by this matter – and the fact that my emails to him remained unanswered, to the letter.

And then Rashid returned to what the Suicide said to him:

My name and my lineage will not matter. The important thing is that my corpse disappeared at the time of my death by the Sword of Al-Aziz. So that you know that the Sword will reach you too, and when you plunge it into its place, there will be no trace of you left. Eighteen suicides and I prove it to you. You can find out if you ask, since something that happens every fifty years does not attract a passing glance. You're afraid because you are not yet certain that you are Immortal, the Everlasting One, nor are you sure of everything that happens in that narrow room you think to be your life, including the likes of me, with your disbelief in my being here and your bewilderment at the sight of the mountain, in the light of your eyes. The light will not be reflected again until you die, when your divine vision begins to take over. Everything that happens takes place in order to lead up to one moment in the year 2008 …

The Suicide kept on in this way, talking to me – as terror shook my being then paralysed me. I was still in denial that he was right there next to me, so I didn't look at him as I insistently kept turning the ignition to start the car. The Suicide chuckled briefly – one short laugh – then stretched out his hand to indicate the spot in which to plunge my Sword. Right after the touch of his finger on my chest, I felt a tingle I had never experienced before in my whole life. There was pleasure in that touch – effortless, without instigation, endless, like an orgasm. 'You must take the studded gold handle in both your hands. You will

point the edge of the blade to your chest, under your right breast but a
thumbnail's length to the right. You must then bend over like a bow,
brace your feet on the ground – and then, all at once, thrust!'

As soon as he withdrew his hand, he began to sing:

I did not begin to understand until I thought I already understood,
then I saw things as if with the eyes of the Buddha:
that childish drawing of large forms, gazing out
from the facades of buildings,
which sees everything in everything.

Maybe my sister and my friend thought I was stunned at the sight
of them, since my posture with the Sword followed my discovery of the two of them precisely one night before, in the dark of
the courtyard. I had come in barefoot, the gas lamp in my hand,
only to find my sister's thighs propped up as if on something low,
underneath her hiked-up robe. It was impossible to see her top
half from afar: she was lying on her back on the floor, moaning
heatedly, as if sobbing. I recognised them, my sister's thighs.

And so continued the Suicide, after he ordered me – with a lukewarm smile – to start the engine. Now the car took off – down Salah
Salim Street, which seemed endless. I was driving very fast in order
to get out of this dark area, but however much I drove I never got a
centimetre further. When he finished speaking, without my knowing it, Salah Salim would go back to normal, and I would now know
for sure that I had escaped from the spot in which I met him. And
without my knowing, either, that he had disappeared.

I couldn't make out what was propping them up from underneath, until I drew closer and kneeled down. My friend was
slithering on his belly like a snake as his head was buried between
the two of them, his shoulders under her thighs. As I gasped, he
lifted her up and I saw my sister's shaved sex, swollen and red
in the light of the gas lamp, as my friend's saliva clung to the
stubble and leaked down around it. I screamed at them, 'Get

married! Go and get married!' and then turned around. They actually did get married without my father finding out what had happened, but they had to wait seven years after my unexpected suicide. Until they die, they will wonder if their buried secret was the reason for that wait.

Then, returning to the beginning of his story, Rashid said:
From the first day, I had decided to put off family matters that awaited me with each visit, so I would make excuses, saying that since I had not seen them for so long, I preferred to spend time alone with my mother and father, my sisters and brothers. In truth, I spent a week going from bar to bar in Zamalek, and from café to café downtown. I would use my father's Renault – parked most of the time – but only after the mechanic had inspected it, tried it out for a week and guaranteed that it was roadworthy, until I felt like going on my own to Bab Al-Futouh and what happened happened.

We live in Heliopolis, in a building built towards the end of the fifties, when Suicide Number 19 lived in Bab Al-Futouh, right next to my father, who turned seventy-five last year. Yes, that's what I thought of at first, until I remembered a story that was repeated in different forms on both sides of the family, without my knowing if it was true. My mother would deny it angrily every time the subject was raised, while my father would deny any knowledge of it with uncharacteristic curtness. My mother's brother, Uncle Fathi, was the only one of my parents' siblings whom I never saw even once. He died young; he is supposed to have died in a car accident, yet there is an aura of mystery surrounding his death, the kind of mystery that evokes a scandal or something frightening. There is nothing decisive to refute that he had taken his own life. My uncle had spied my mother and father together in an awkward position while they were still young and not committed in a relationship; meanwhile, my uncle and my father were friends and soulmates. There are those who say that he died in anguish after he learnt of his friend's betrayal and his little sister's wantonness. And there are those who say that he fought with my father, who killed him, and that the two families covered it up, since they were close to one another and keen to avoid scandal. I'm not entirely sure of the memory, but I thought I heard someone say that my Uncle Fathi was a blessed man, and that when he died his body evaporated and soared up into the sky. And so God had raised him up as he raised the prophet Jesus.* What confirmed my suspicion was that my maternal grandmother died when she was a young girl, and that her grave was on land my grandfather owned in Bab Al-Futouh. (During my trek, I wasn't able to reach my maternal grandmother's grave.) Honestly, I was afraid. And the fear grew in my heart to the point where I didn't dare to mention anything to my father or mother during my last five days in Cairo. We live in Heliopolis, I've said. One of the things I miss most in England is the feel of Salah Salim Street – which I have to traverse, even if just a part of it, on any trip I make from or to our house. You're truly on the body of a serpent that slithers on Cairo's entire back – from the north, where we live, to Roda Island in the south, parallel to Old Cairo. It's like a spine susceptible to dislocation. I parked quite far away, on the opposite side of the street, near Zizo's, the restaurant famous for its sausages. Then I crossed cautiously, taking bigger and bigger steps, and I didn't return for three hours. I was gazing at the ancient buildings as if I had lived in them in their glory days. I felt a violent familiarity for a place I only vaguely knew.

The leader rode one evening, on one of his night treks. He headed towards Muqattam Hills, then he was not seen after that, neither alive nor dead, his fate unknown, his body never found. Nor did any modern or contemporary story come to us – no decisive story about his death or his disappearance.

(From *Al-Hakim bi-Amr Allah and the Secrets of the Fatimid Call* by Muhammad Abdallah Anan, 1983)

Three months have passed now, and there is more joy in my relationship with my girlfriend than ever.

That night in Bab Al-Futouh I had thought about her for a long time as

---

* Orthodox Muslim belief holds that Jesus was never crucified, but was physically raised into the heavens by God's invisible hands.

my hand came into contact with the walls she has dreamed of seeing since she was a girl in Suwayda, Syria, and even after she came to Manchester with her family at the age of fifteen. (She had never visited Egypt, even though the story of Al-Hakim was of course present – specifically his end: he departed on his donkey, looking up at the stars in Muqattam Hills, and never came back. Later, they found no trace of him, except for the seven capes he wore; the buttons, caked with blood, could not be opened. They were simply dumped somewhere; some claim they were found in Helwan, wet.) Yet, until now, I still avoid talking to her about my last visit to Cairo. At first, it didn't occur to me that the emergence of the Suicide could be more important to me than our marriage, yet as time passed – after I finished reading Mustafa's PDF, to be precise – I became almost convinced that it truly was more important. What didn't please me – after recalling one or two memories of things that hadn't happened to me in the first place – was to find myself increasingly enthusiastic about the idea of killing myself, just as the Suicide had predicted. The day before yesterday – the second anniversary of our decision to live together without her family's knowledge – my girlfriend brought me an unexpected gift, which I also never expected would make me this happy. I was busy on the computer when she entered the flat, so I said hello without lifting my eyes from the screen, only to end up with a rectangular piece of metal sparkling before my eyes. She had snuck up behind me and locked my head between her two arms. And in her hands was what almost made me faint as I uttered its name: the Sword of Al-Aziz. Then she laid it on the table, saying that her father actually believed that it belonged to Al-Aziz Billah. She added that it couldn't possibly have been made over a thousand years ago, and it was in too good a condition to be the imam's. She had found it in her father's large safe and kept begging until he gave it to her. She hid it in the trunk of her car until the day of our anniversary. Slowly, I reached out and lifted it by its studded gold handle; it looked new, as if it had been crafted yesterday. I looked closer at the edge of the blade; it appeared sharper than anything made by human hands. I grew distracted for a bit. Bringing me back to reality, the angelic beauty of my girlfriend's face appeared, asking, 'Do you like it?'

Translated by Nader K. Uthman

Nine Poems

Zaki Baydoun

The Sky's Departure

One day everyone woke up feeling unsettled and strangely empty, as though the internal clock of their day-to-day thinking had gone wrong, as though an integral part of what it means to be human had gone missing. As usual when they're confused, they began to flock to their balconies for some breathing space, and here the horrifying thing that had happened became clear to them: the sky had departed ... yes, the sun, the moon, the planets, the stars and that infinite space that has room enough for all our imaginings and contemplations – all that had vanished and nothing remained except a terrifying void like a hellish window open on to the Absolute. Yes, it had escaped the scientists and the philosophers that the sky is a sensitive creature, and that she had grown annoyed with them violating her, ignoring her, and so she had upped sticks, disdaining all the laws of physics. The efforts of the municipality to calm things down by erecting a large blue tent failed.

It wasn't possible to ignore it all and get on with the daily grind as though nothing had happened because the sky just isn't the same . . . without a sky.

It was as though the punishment for the supreme sin that the men of religion had warned about had finally come, and people milled

around in the streets like a nest of deranged ants, unable to bear the
terrifying non-thought above their heads.

   This could not have gone on for ever ... but even so, the problem was not solved.

Death's Salesman

I'm Death's salesman. I present it strangely out of the fleeting
glances and strangled whispers on a marble platter.

I'm Death's salesman. More sincere than I sound, more modest
than I appear, I practise an idea which is like the drowsy silence in
the head of an elderly doorman.
Death alone does not lie, because Time is nothing but the inatten-
tion of a god who does not dare wake.

The Beginning

On the summit, no one hears anything but the silence . . . the
   sound of the beginning.
It is the mirrors of lethargy, the spirit of water, a hand made of dust,
   a glimpse of a mirage
or it is an intoxicated sun taking root in my eyes
my hands in the water
my face a chasm of the wind
the sun is stripped of its rapture on the brink of a dawn dissolved
or else it is my heart dissolving, a saccharine rapture in my mouth.
my thoughts taste of water
my blood apple juice
dredge my heart, darling; you may find dead gold there, and a smiling pain.
Today, nightfall is coming back to me in its entirety; even the sky
   has to transcend itself without ceasing to encompass the reach of
   my gaze.

My face, a lake of gales brushing against the face of the world. My face, a veil covering the other side, only to be pulled aside through the window of the eyes. My face, the mask of eternity, the silent scream which will cross the harshest and most frenzied of storms with the unstoppability of piercing rays of light.

On the summit, it is the silence alone that the world hears . . . the sound of the beginning.

The Emperor and the Oaken Door

The Great Emperor decided to journey to the edge of Existence and reach the ends of the Universe, so he readied his armies and set off trusting in God's blessing.

He passed over mountains, valleys, lands and ideas; he passed over heavens, earths, galaxies and black holes. He passed over everything, until it seemed he had passed beyond passing itself, when he finally arrived at a black wall, stretching away for a vast distance. He tried to blast a hole in the wall with his atomic bombs and hydrogen bombs, but he did not succeed; it seemed that the wall was stronger than anything else in the Universe, seeing as there was nothing else behind it. Therefore, our Great Emperor dispatched another expeditionary force to find the end of the wall. Years later, he was surprised to find that this 'end' was nothing but the beginning of yet another wall. Thus, as the long centuries passed, our emperor continued to be thwarted by the solid rock, reaching the end of one wall only to find another one starting.

But in the end – in the end of the end – to his great astonishment, he came to the last thing which he had expected to encounter in the course of his mighty imperial endeavours. He found himself confronted with a small door made of oak; taken aback, he stopped dead in front of it and his cosmic battalions came to a halt behind him. Gradually, the Great Emperor's confusion and uncertainty as to how to respond in the face of such a situation dispersed, when a spirit of gentleness enfolded him and he cast off his imperial gravitas, stepped forward and tapped softly on the door. Then he whispered: 'Who is there?' A deep voice answered, coming from somewhere beyond the silence: 'We are the fools who belong to eternity and for all eternity we will never leave this room.'

Betrayal

My eyes say most things in a language I don't understand; my eyes are mostly empty.

Many things passed by and went unspoken, even the tongue disregarding them, to be caught in the eyes.

Only the observer who cannot speak assumes the burden of the crime.

My eyes deceive me endlessly; I do not see what my eyes tell me . . . except through others' eyes.

Prayer

Whenever I walk, I try to imitate the horizon . . . because nothing is smaller than that moment.

The old creator is concocting his crime slowly. Blind window at which the idea of this world is immaturely thrown.

This is what the priests know well: eternity is a dish which it only does to prepare over a low flame.

Prayer and patience, the sustenance of believers.

Blessed be the sky, that vast blue bird endlessly taking wing, defiant horizon in which everywhere is lost.

Blessed be silence, diffident being, who always makes time to speak to others.

Blessed be the world, guileless man whom stupidity brings to the point where he makes himself his own prisoner.

Blessed be a faceless reality, the only hole in the margin of sleep-lessness, the wailing of restlessness, the howling of solitary time. It is not the wounded moon that troubles the night, but pain taking its ease.

Whenever I walk, I try to imitate the horizon, because the migrant moments are nothing but fate's accents in disguise, the horizon nothing but the edge of weary vision.

Cogito Myself

Finally, after twenty-two years of paying no heed, I've realised what I am: I'm a broken television . . . and my life is a search operation, dissatisfied with an undistorted channel.

An Indolent Wagon Pulled Along by Flowers

It's only a blind whisper in the mouth of a hurricane. I'm walking, my eyes a bridge for the phantoms of the sun, a heavy water in my heart. I'm walking, I'm flowing in the rivers of my head, flocks of swallows fleeing my horizon. I'm walking, I'm building warm villages for my ants; I'm gathering the teardrops of closed walls, walking like an indolent wagon pulled along by flowers.

The World Outside the Bathroom

One day, I'll go into the bathroom and shut the door firmly on myself, so as to imprison the whole world outside the bathroom.

Translated by Tristan Cranfield

Notes on the Text

***The Wounded Man*: Abdellah Taia**

17 *harira*: a traditional Moroccan soup usually eaten during Ramadan to break the fast.

18 *Arte* (Association Relative à la Télévision Européenne): a Franco-German TV network whose remit is to promote quality programming in areas of culture and the arts.

18 *The Wounded Man*: an important and controversial film written by Hervé Guibert and directed by Patrice Chéreau about a middle-aged man coming to terms with his homosexuality while in a relationship with a manipulative rent boy.

20 *faqih*: a scholar.

21 *mektoub*: fate.

21 *Laylat al-Qadr*: the anniversary of the night Muslims believe the first verses of the Quran were revealed to the Prophet Muhammad.

22 *habibi*: dear, darling.

Amazigh: Abderrahim Elkhassar

24   *Amazigh*: more commonly in English, 'Berber' – pertaining to various indigenous peoples of North Africa. 'Amazigh', and its variants, is the word the Berbers usually use to refer to themselves.

from the novel *The Twentieth Terrorist*: Abdullah Thabit

35   *Asiris*: people from the mountainous area of Asir, in the south west of Saudi Arabia.

37   *Samira Tawfiq, Umm Kulthum, Faiza Ahmad, Abdul Halim Hafiz, Saadun Jabir, Fairuz*: popular modern Arab singers – though Umm Kulthum died in 1975 and Abdul Halim Hafiz in 1977.

Frankenstein in Baghdad: Ahmed Saadawi

52   *baklaa*: beans.

Coexistence: Ala Hlehel

67   *Tell them to beware*: paraphrase of the last line of the poem 'Identity Card' ('Bitāqat Huwiyya'), one of the most celebrated verses of Mahmoud Darwish (1941–2008). Darwish is widely considered to be Palestine's national poetic voice.

67   *You I remembered*: the sixth-century Arabian poet Antara ibn Shaddad. The lines are taken from his best-known work, contained in the seven *Muallaqat* or *Suspended Poems*.

Three Poems: Bassim al Ansar

68   *Ishtar*: Babylonian goddess of love, sex and war identified with the planet Venus and abominated in the Old Testament for the practice of sacred prostitution at her cult centres.

Two Stories: Dima Wannous

76 *Hatem al-Tai*: sixth-century poet, known as a masterful horseman but most famous for his extreme generosity, which has become proverbial.

Mimouna: Faïza Guène

85 *hayek*: traditional costume comprising a piece of bright-coloured cloth which women wrap around themselves.

88 *Juha*: thirteenth-century Sufi figure and populist philosopher who lived in Anatolia, legendary for the satirical anecdotes and witty folk wisdom he dispensed. Middle Eastern, Central Asian and even Balkan countries have all adopted him as their own.

89 *jbel*: mountain or hill in Maghrebi Arabic.

89 *The Pledge*: unofficial English translation taken from the website of the Permanent Mission of Algeria to the UN (with minor amendments by this translator).

from the novel *Secret Pleasures*: Hamdy el Gazzar

103 *qasaid*s: ballads in classical Arabic.

103 *Sheikh Ali Mahmud*: (1878–1946) a major singer of religious music and celebrated Quran reciter.

103 *mawwals*: songs, often lovelorn and plaintive, characterised by word play.

103 *doors*: a responsorial musical form, popular in the early twentieth century.

103 *Nazim el-Ghazali*: (1921–63) an icon of Iraqi song, most active in the 1950s.

103 *taqatiq*: couplets sung by a soloist alternating with a choral refrain, popular in the early twentieth century.

103 *Sabah Fakhri*: (b. 1933) a leading exponent of Aleppine traditional vocal music who has also recorded Egyptian songs.

103 *goza*: a hand-held water pipe whose water compartment was traditionally made of a coconut (*goza*).

103 *Sheikh Rifaat*: Sheikh Muhammad Rifaat (d. 1950), a Quran reciter of legendary artistry.

105 *Nagat el-Saghira*: (b. 1939) a famous Egyptian songstress.

from the novel *The Last Hanging Poem*: Hussein al Abri

109 *The Last Hanging Poem*: the 'hanging poem/s' (*al-muallaqa/at*) are a series of classic pre-Islamic odes, said to have been hung on the Kaaba in Mecca. Al-Abri's original title is literally 'the last *muallaqa*'.

109 *mussar*: the Omani turban.

115 *dishdasha*: a long tunic, usually reaching the ankles.

Three Poems: Hussein Jelaad

122 *Abdel Halim*: Abdel Halim Hafiz, an Egyptian singer and film actor and one of the most famous and well-loved performers in the Arab world from the 1950s to the 1970s. His tragic death from bilharzia in 1977, a few days short of his forty-eighth birthday, is an integral part of his myth.

122 *Hijaz gold*: the Hijaz, a large region stretching down modern Saudi Arabia's west coast and inland, encompasses the Hijaz and Asir mountain ranges that are home to the *mahd al-dhahab*, or 'cradle of gold', anciently an important source of workable gold and silver sometimes identified with the biblical mines of King Solomon. It is still mined today.

122 *Sham*: loose geographical term denoting an area roughly equivalent to the Levant in its broadest sense, though it can more narrowly describe those countries that once belonged to 'Greater Syria' (i.e. Lebanon, Syria, Palestine and Jordan) or simply modern Syria itself.

122 *Thaniyaat al-Wadaa*: in the singular a name for Medina/Yathrib from the time of the Prophet and before, meaning Valley of Farewell, and in the plural (as here) a reference to any one of a number of locations from where travellers and traders would set out northwards on the ancient trade routes to Sham. These lines preceding this recall the words of welcome addressed to the Prophet by his young female supporters and recorded in the books of the Hadith: *A full moon rose over us from Thaniyaat al Wadaa.*

Layla's Belly: **Hyam Yared**

123 *Love is a punishment*: from Marguerite Yourcenar: *Fires*, trans. Dori Katz (Chicago: University of Chicago Press, 1994).

from the novel *The Threshold of Ashes*: **Mansour El Souwaim**

147 *rababah*: a musical instrument, Bedouin in origin and played with a horsehair bow. It has a quadrilateral sound box covered with skin and a single string made from horsehair, and is the essential melody instrument of the nomadic Bedouins. It is customarily played by the *shaer*, or poet-singer, to accompany heroic and love songs.

Haneef from Glasgow: **Mohammad Hassan Alwan**

162 *khimar*: a head and face veil.

Six Poems: **Najwan Darwish**

195 *Kol Ha Musica*: Hebrew for 'Voice of Music', an Israeli radio station for classical music.

195 *Qanun*: 'zither' in English, a Middle Eastern musical instrument similar to a harp.

from the novel *America*: Rabee Jaber

205 *Syrians*: in the First World War period and until 1918, 'Syrians' referred to inhabitants of the Ottoman-ruled Arab eastern Mediterranean (Levant), comprising roughly what is now Lebanon, Syria, Palestinian territories and Israel, as well as parts of south-eastern Turkey and western Iraq.

Guardians of the Air: Rosa Yassin Hassan

223 *sirwal*: voluminous trousers in the classical Ottoman style.

223 *fus'ha*: classical Arabic, the prestige dialect, the modern version of which is the *lingua franca* of the Arabic-speaking world.

224 *'Well, I know that'*: throughout this story, dialogue that originally appeared in English in the Arabic text has been italicised.

227 *Omar Hassan Ahmad Al-Bashir*: a colonel in the (northern) Sudanese army who, after a military coup, became (and still is at the time of publication) President of Sudan.

A Crime in Mataeem Street: Wajdi al Ahdal

242 *mataeem*: restaurants.

244 *Akhdam*: a black ethnic group in Yemen who are generally on the lowest rung of the social ladder, occupying positions such as street sweepers. They live quite separately from other Yemenis and have a status similar in many ways to the caste of the untouchables in India.

246 *fuul*: a very common breakfast dish across the Middle East and consists normally of mashed broad beans served with olive oil, chopped parsley, onions, garlic and lemon juice. It is not normally eaten with meat since the latter is too expensive for most Yemenis to eat every day.

246 *salta*: a spicy stew seasoned with fenugreek. It is a lunchtime favourite in Yemen and is considered to be the national dish.

247 *Adani tea*: tea made with milk and favoured in Aden, a major Yemeni port on the south coast.

248 *Ranjala*: this Arabic name is sometimes used as a nickname for someone of bowed or crippled gait. It can also have the metaphorical implication that someone stands bowlegged, as it were, from constantly having a foot in both camps.

249 North and South Yemen united in 1990, but a southern rebellion in April 1994 led to the declaration of a Democratic Republic of Yemen in the south, with Aden as its capital. A civil war raged from April of that year until the DRY was destroyed in early July by Sanaa government forces.

from the novel *Raven's Leg*: Yahya Amqassim

257 *majlis*: meeting place, session, a place where people come together to sit and discuss issues.

258 *shuhrah*: the ceremony marking the beginning of the circumcision activities.

258 *samr*: a tree whose branches are used for thatching and kindling.

Suicide 20, or The Hakimi Maqama: **Youssef Rakha**

272 The style of writing demonstrated in this piece is highly modernist, featuring frequent deviations in register and reference, as well as sudden shifts from standard, written Arabic to spoken, Egyptian colloquial. Further, the author invokes and imitates the *maqama*, a medieval literary genre featuring rhymed prose – a stylistic device employed in sections of this excerpt.

273 *Al-Hakim bi-Amr Allah*: Abu Ali Mansur Tariq al-Hakim (996–1021), the sixth Fatimid caliph, the sixteenth Ismaili imam and the creator of Tawhid ('monotheism'), the Druze name for their faith.

273 *imam*: Muslim spiritual leader.

273 *Al-Mu'izz*: Ma'dh Abu Tamim al-Mu'izz li-Dinallah (*c.* 930–975) was the first and most powerful of the Fatimid caliphs. His armies conquered Egypt and defeated the Abbasids; he founded Cairo and made it his capital in 972–973. He ruled over much of Morocco, Algeria and Tunisia, as well as Sicily.

275 *Bab Al-Nasr*: one of the major gates of ancient Cairo, built in the eleventh century.

279 *Bab Al-Futouh*: the north gate of ancient Cairo, built in the eleventh century.

279 *Heliopolis*: also called *masr al-gadida*, or 'New Egypt', a suburb of Cairo.

Notes on the Authors

Abdelaziz Errachidi was born in Zagora, south Morocco, in 1978. He is a writer and journalist. His novel, *Nomads on the Cliff*, was published by the Department of Culture, United Arab Emirates in 2006 and reissued by the House of Arab Publishers, Lebanon in 2008. His collections of short stories include *Alley of Death* (Group of Novel Research, Morocco, 2004), *Childhood of a Frog* (Union of Moroccan Writers, Morocco, 2005), and *Sands of Pain, House Faces* (Saudi Arabia, 2007). His volume of essays, *Foreigners at my Table*, was published by the Moroccan Ministry of Culture in 2008. He has received several prizes: the Union of Moroccan Writers' Prize for *Childhood of a Frog* in 2005; the Acharika Arabic Prize in the Emirates for *Nomads on the Cliff* and the Sakyat Essawi Prize for his short story, 'The Basket of Colours', in 2006; and a writing scholarship for *Almawred Takafi* in Egypt in 2007. He was also selected for an international residency at the Château de Lavigny, Switzerland, in 2008, and in Camac, France, for two months in 2009.

Abdelkader Benali was born in 1975 in the Netherlands, of Moroccan origins. Benali published his first novel *Bruiloft aan zee* (*Wedding by the Sea*) in 1996, for which he received the Geertjan Lubberhuizen Prize. His second novel, *De langverwachte* (*The Long-awaited*, 2002), was awarded the Libris Literature Prize. He has since published the novels *Laat het morgen mooi weer zijn* (*Let Tomorrow Be Fine*, 2005) and *Feldman en ik* (*Feldman and I*, 2006). He also writes plays and occasionally works in the field of journalism. In 2005, together with the historian Herman Obdeijn, he published *Marokko door Nederlandse ogen 1605–2005* (*Morocco Through Dutch Eyes 1605–2005*).

Abdellah Taia was born into a poor family in Rabat in 1973. He lived in the city of Salé until 1998 and now lives in Paris. Editions du Seuil has published five books written in French and inspired by his life; among them, *Le Rouge* *du Tarbouche* (2005), *L'armée du Salut* (2006) and *Une Mélancolie Arabe* (2008). His work has been translated into several languages. He was been shortlisted twice for the prestigious French Prix Renaudot. Abdellah Taia is the first Moroccan and Arab writer publicly to declare his homosexuality.

Abderrahim Elkhassar was born in Asfi, Morocco, in 1975. He has participated in many festivals in and outside Morocco. He has published three collections of poetry.

Abderrazak Boukebba was born in eastern Algeria in 1977. He earned a BA in literature in 1996 and worked as a consultant to the National Library and as the editor of a number of TV and radio shows. He is the recipient of the President Award in Algeria and has published a novel and three collections of poetry.

Abdullah Thabit was born in 1973 in the Saudi city of Abha. He holds a BA in Arabic language and literature from the University of King Khaled (KSA). He has published a novel and five books of poetry and short stories.

Adania Shibli, born in Palestine in 1974, has twice been awarded the Young Writer's Award by the A. M. Qattan Foundation, for her novels *Masaas* (*Touch*, al-Adab, 2002) and *Kulluna Ba'eed Bethat al Miqdar 'an al Hub* (*We Are All Equally Far from Love*, al-Adab, 2004). She has published short stories and essays in literary magazines, such as Ramallah's *Al-Karmel*, the Beirut literary periodicals *Al-Adaab* and *Zawaya*, and Alexandria's *Amkenah*. Shibli has a PhD in media and cultural studies from the University of East London.

Ahmad Saadawi was born in Baghdad, Iraq, in 1973. He is a novelist, poet, painter and journalist. He was a correspondent for the BBC for a number of years and currently supervises a show on the 'Al Hurra' satellite television station. He has published four books of poetry and two novels. His novel *Beautiful Country* won first prize in a literary competition held in the United Arab Emirates.

Ahmad Yamani is an Egyptian poet and translator who lives in Madrid. He was born in 1970 and holds a Diploma in Graduate Studies (DEA) from the Universidad Complutense de Madrid, where he is working on his PhD. Yamani has published four books of poetry to date.

Ala Hlehel, born in Palestine in 1974, is the author of a novel entitled *Al-Sirk* (*The Circus*), a collection of short stories entitled *Stories in Time of Need* and a play. Two-time winner of the Al-Qattan Young Writer Award, his script, *The Inheritance*, was awarded second prize in the School of Screenwriting (Tel

Aviv) Competition. He has written numerous short stories, plays for theatre and scripts for film and television. In 2003 he took part in the annual international playwrights' residency at the Royal Court Theatre in London.

Bassim al Ansar was born in Iraq in 1970. He holds a BA in business from Al-Mustansiriya University in Baghdad. He has been publishing his poetry since the early 1990s, and in 1997 published a play in verse called *The Man of the Willows*. In 2007 he published his first book of poetry under the title *The Hymns of the Son of Adam*. Al Ansar has been living in Denmark since 1998.

Dima Wannous was born in Damascus, Syria, in 1982. Her first short-story collection was published in 2007 to critical acclaim. In 2008 she published her first novel, *A Chair*. She presents a cultural television show on a satellite network.

Faïza Guène was born in France in 1985 to Algerian parents. She wrote her first novel, *Kiffe kiffe demain (Just Like Tomorrow)*, when she was seventeen years old. It was a huge success in France, selling over 360,000 copies, and has been translated around the world. She is also the author of *Du rêve pour les oufs* (2006) and *Les gens du Balto* (2008).

Hala Kawtharani was born in Beirut in 1977. She studied political sciences and Arabic literature at the American University of Beirut. She publishes a weekly short story in the Beiruti magazine *Laha*. She has published two novels.

Hamdy el Gazzar was born on 1 October 1970 in Giza, Egypt. He gained a graduate degree in Philosophy from the University of Cairo in 1992. He has published many short stories and two novels, of which *Black Magic* was awarded the Sawiris Foundation Prize for Egyptian Literature in 2006 and published in English by AUC Press in Cairo in 2007.

Hussein al Abri was born in 1972 in Oman. He has published three novels and a collection of short stories since 2000. He lives in Muscat and works as a hospital doctor.

Hussein Jelaad was born in Jordan in 1970. He has published two books of poetry, *Eternal Crucifixion of the Prominent* (1999) and *As Prophets Lose* (2007). He is currently working as a journalist at Al Jazeera, writing about political and cultural affairs. He has contributed to *Al-Arab Al-Yawm* and the Arabic daily *Al-Ra'i*, as well as working as a freelancer for *An-Nahar*, published in Lebanon. Jelaad is the Jordanian Ambassador to the Poets of the World Movement, a literary organisation based in Chile with a membership of thousands of poets worldwide. He is also a member of the Administrative Body of the Jordanian Writers League (2004–2006).

Hyam Yared was born in 1975 in Beirut. She has published two books of poetry with Dar An Nahar and two novels, *L'Armoire des Ombres* and *Sous la Tonnelle*. Her books have received several awards, including the France–Liban Prize.

Islam Samhan was born in Jordan in 1982, from Palestinian origins. His collection of poetry, *Light-hearted*, was published in Oman in 2008.

Joumana Haddad was born in Lebanon in 1970. She is head of the cultural pages of the prestigious *An Nahar* newspaper, as well as the administrator of the IPAF literary prize (the 'Arab Booker') and editor-in-chief of *Jasad* magazine, a controversial Arabic magazine specialising in literature and arts relating to the body. Her books include *Time for a Dream* (1995), *Invitation to a Secret Feast* (1998), *I Did Not Sin Enough* (2003), *Lilith's Return* (2004), *Conversations with International Writers*, (2006), *Death Will Come and It Will Have Your Eyes* and *Anthology of 150 Poets who Committed Suicide* (2007).

Kamel Riahi was born in the village of al Manafikh, Tunisia, in 1974. He has published two collections of short stories and a novel, *Al-Mishrat* (*The Scalpel*). He teaches in Algeria.

Mansour El Souwaim was born in the south of Darfur in 1970. He has published two novels and two collections of short stories. His novel *Dhakirat Shirrir* won the Tayeb Salih Award for Creative Writing. A collection of his short stories was published in Arabic and French in 2004.

Mansoura Ez Eldin was born in Egypt in 1976. Her collection *Dhaw'a Muhtaz* (*Shaken Light*) was published in Cairo in 2001. Her successful debut novel, *Maryam's Maze*, was published by Merit in 2004, with the English edition published by AUC Press in Cairo. She has worked in Egyptian television, and presently runs the book review section of the renowned Egyptian literary magazine *Akhbar al-Adab* (*Literature News*).

Mohammad Hassan Alwan was born in Saudi Arabia in 1979 and has published two novels and a collection of short stories.

Mohammad Salah al Azab was born in Egypt in 1981. His first novel, *A Long Cellar with a Low Ceiling That Makes You Crouch*, was published in 2003. That same year, his short story collection, *Blue in a Sad Way*, was published by the Higher Council for Culture in Cairo. His second novel, *Repeated Stopping*, was published in 2007, followed by *The Italian's Bed* in 2008. He has won seven literary awards, including the Suad Al-Sabah Award for Fiction in 1999 and the Higher Council for Culture's Short Story Award in 2004. He also won the Higher Council for Culture's Award for Fiction in 2004.

Nagat Ali was born in Cairo, Egypt, in 1975. She earned an MA cum laude for her thesis 'Irony in the Short Stories of Yusef Idris'. She has published three books of poetry and is currently working on her PhD dissertation on 'The Narrator in the Novels of Naguib Mahfouz'.

Najwa Binshatwan was born in Libya in 1970 and has published a novel, *Madmun Burtuqali* (2007), and two collections of short stories, *Tifl Al-Waw* (2006) and *Qisas Laysat Lil-Rijal* (2004).

Najwan Darwish was born in Palestine in 1978. His first book, *He Was Knocking at the Last Door*, was published in 2000, and since then his poetry has appeared in several anthologies. He is the editor of a new cultural magazine which publishes the work of the emerging generation of Arab writers.

Nazem El Sayed was born in Lebanon in 1975. He has published four collections of poetry and his work has been included in several anthologies.

Rabee Jaber was born in 1972 in Beirut. He is the editor of the weekly cultural supplement of the daily newspaper *Al-Hayat*. He has published sixteen novels since 1992. Jaber is considered one of the most talented novelists of his generation.

Randa Jarrar was born in Egypt in 1978. She is an award-winning short-story writer, novelist and translator. Her first novel, the critically acclaimed *A Map of Home*, was published in six languages and won the Hopwood Award, the Gosling Prize and the Arab American Book Award. She is currently working on a new novel and a collection of short stories. She has been living in the US since 1991.

Rosa Yassin Hassan was born in Damascus, Syria, in 1974. She completed her degree in architecture in 1998. Her first book of short stories was published in 2000. Her first novel, *Ebony*, which has been translated into German, was published in 2004 and won the Hanna Mina Prize for Fiction. Her second novel, *Negative*, features female political prisoners in Syria. Her third novel, *The Guardians of the Air*, was published in 2009.

Samar Yezbek was born in the city of Jabla, Syria, in 1970. She has published two books of poetry and three novels. She also writes screenplays for television films. Her *Low Skies* won first prize for a television screenplay in a UN competition.

Samer Abou Hawwash was born in 1972 in the southern Lebanese city of Sidon. Abou Hawwash has published several poetical works and two novels, *Valentine's Day* and *Al Saada or Silsilat Infijarat Hazat Al Asima* (*Happiness or A Series of Explosions Rocked the Capital*). He translates poetry and prose and has contributed to many Arabic cultural supplements. He has been living and working in the United Arab Emirates since 2004.

Wajdi al Ahdal, born in Yemen in 1973, is the author of *Quarantine Philosopher*, which was nominated for the Arab Literary Prize in 2008.

Yahya Amqassim was born in Saudi Arabia in 1971. He has published two books, *The Crow Leg* (2008) and *Stories from Saudi Arabia* (2004).

Yassin Adnan, a Moroccan writer born in 1970, is the author of three books of poems: *Mannequins* (2000), *Rasif al-qiyama* (*Resurrection Pavement*, 2003) and *La akad ara* (*I Can Hardly See*, 2007). He has also published two collections of short stories, *Man yusaddiq al-rasa'il?* and *Tuffah al-zill*, as well as *Marakish: asrar mu'lana* (2008), a literary text which attempts to outline the history of his home town in prose and poetry. He is the recipient of the Moufdi Zakaria Prize (Algeria, 1991), the Union of Writers in Morocco Poetry Prize (1998) and the Buland al-Haydari Prize for Young Poets (Asilah, 2003).

Youssef Rakha is a writer and photographer. Born in Cairo in 1976, he earned a BA in English and philosophy from Hull University. He has been working as a reporter, copy-editor and cultural editor at *Al-Ahram Weekly*, the Cairo-based English-language newspaper, since 1988. He took a sabbatical to work as a features writer at Abu Dhabi-based daily *The National* in 2008–2009. His reportage, travel writing, photography, fiction and poetry – written originally in both Arabic and English – have appeared in numerous publications in Cairo, Beirut, London, Berlin, Italy and the US, as well as online. Rakha has exhibited his photos at the Goethe Institute, Cairo, and has published four books in Arabic: a collection of short stories, *Azhar Al-Shams* (Dar Sharqiyat, 1999), a photo travelogue, *Beirut shi mahal* (Kitab Amkenah, 2006) and two books of travel writing with the Beirut-based Dar Riyad El Rayyes. His poems are soon to appear in a book entitled *Kull Amakinina*. He is currently working on his first novel.

Zaki Baydoun was born in Tyre, Lebanon, in 1981. He is a poet and a painter. He has published two books of poetry and has exhibited in a number of shows in Lebanon. He earned an MA in philosophy from the Université de St Denis in Paris. His thesis was on 'Kant's Concept of Tripartite'.

Notes on the Translators

Asmaa Abdallah has translated news and opinion articles for Arabic newspapers including *Al-Hayat* and *Al-Masry Al-Youm*, as well as producing English reports for the International Crisis Group. She is also a regular contributor to *Enigma*, an Egyptian English language lifestyle magazine. Abdallah is currently preparing her MA in English and comparative literature at the American University in Cairo.

Rowan al Faqih is a filmmaker who was born in Jerusalem and is currently living and working in Ramallah. She holds a Master's degree in urban planning and is one of the founders of the Palestinian Filmmakers' Collective and producer of the film collection *Palestine, Summer 2006*. Her first film, *Summer of '85*, was selected at various film festivals, including Oberhausen, Locarno and Docusur.

Roger Allen is a literary translator, the author of many books and Professor of Arabic and Comparative Literature in the Department of Near Eastern Languages and Civilization at the University of Pennsylvania. Last year he was honoured by Egypt's Supreme Council for Culture for his translations of Arabic literature. He has translated many works of the late Nobel laureate Naguib Mahfouz, as well as novels by Jabra Ibrahim Jabra and Abdelrahman Munif. He is editor of the series *The Cambridge History of Arabic Literature* and series editor for the *Dictionary of Literary Biography Arabic Literature Project*, and he has edited a number of journals, including the *Journal of Arabic Literature* and *Literature East & West*. He is currently a contributing editor to *Banipal* magazine.

Sinan Antoon is a poet, novelist and filmmaker. He was born in Baghdad in 1967 and moved to the US after the 1991 Gulf War, where he earned a doctorate in Arabic literature in 2006. He is currently an assistant professor at New York University, where he teaches Arabic literature and culture. His books include *The Baghdad Blues* and *I'jaam: An Iraqi Rhapsody*, a novel which has been translated from the Arabic into five languages.

Sarah Ardizzone won the Scott Moncrieff Prize in 2007 for her translation of Faïza Guène's first novel, *Just Like Tomorrow*, and an English PEN recommendation for her work on the same author's *Dreams from the Endz* in 2008. Sarah is also twice winner of the Marsh Award for Children's Literature in Translation, with *Toby Alone* by Timothée de Fombelle in 2009 and *Eye of the Wolf* by Daniel Pennac in 2005.

Marilyn Booth is the Iraq Professor of Arabic Studies at the University of Edinburgh. In addition to her research publications on Arabic literature, gender politics in Egypt, autobiography and translation studies, she has been a prolific translator of contemporary Arabic fiction, including *Disciples of Passion* and *The Tiller of Waters* by Hoda Barakat.

Anthony Calderbank has translated a number of novels and short stories from Arabic into English by authors including Naguib Mahfouz, Sonallah Ibrahim, Miral Al-Tahawy, Yousef Al-Mohaimeed and Hassan Haggag Oddoul. He has also translated excerpts from Fawaz Haddad, Ali Al-Muqri and others. He has lived in the Middle East for many years and is currently based in Riyadh, Saudi Arabia, where he is Deputy Director of the British Council.

Peter Clark has been translating novels, histories, short stories, plays and poetry from Arabic since 1980. He has written books about Marmaduke Pickthall and Wilfred Thesiger, and obituaries of Arab writers for the *Guardian*. He is a cultural and tourism consultant, a contributing editor of *Banipal* magazine and a trustee of the International Prize for Arabic Fiction. He has worked for the British Council in seven Arab countries.

Tristan Cranfield is a freelance translator of Arabic and French based in London. He acquired an honours degree in European and Middle Eastern languages in 2007, having studied at St John's College, Oxford and at l'Institut Français d'Etudes Arabes de Damas in Syria.

Humphrey Davies has translated Arabic novels, short stories, literary non-fiction, biographies and historiography by writers including, in addition to Hamdy el Gazzar, Bahaa Taher, Khaled al-Berry, Elias Khoury, Alaa Al Aswany, Muhammad Mustagab, Yusuf al-Shirbini, Gamal al-Ghitani and Ahmed Alaydi. His translation of Khoury's *Gate of the Sun* was awarded the *Banipal* Prize, and that of Al Aswany's bestselling *The Yacoubian Building* was voted Best Translation of 2007 by the Society of Authors.

Lubna Fahoum has a Bachelor's degree in English literature from Jordan University as well as a Masters in Arabic from SOAS, University of London.

She has recently completed the translation of a poem by Adonis soon to be published in the Lebanon.

Alexa Firat has translated works by the Syrian short-story writer Ibrahim Samuel and the Egyptian writer Naim Baz.

Ghenwa Hayek is Lebanese and currently lives in the US, where she is completing her dissertation in comparative literature at Brown University. She has translated several short stories, which have appeared in *Banipal* magazine.

Kristen Hope is a Beirut-based translator, researcher and activist.

Fady Joudah is a poet, translator and physician. His first poetry collection was the winner of the Yale Series for Younger Poets in 2007. He is also the translator of Mahmoud Darwish's *The Butterfly's Burden* and *If I Were Another*.

Susan Massotty, winner of the 2007 Vondel Translation Prize, has also translated *The Diary of Anne Frank*, *My Father's Notebook* by Kader Abdolah, *All Souls Day* by Cees Nooteboom, *Wedding by the Sea* by Abdelkader Benali and *The Kreutzer Sonata* by Margriet de Moor. She lives and works in The Netherlands.

Robin Moger is the translator of *A Dog with No Tail* by Hamdi Abu Golayyel, winner of the 2008 Naguib Mahfouz Medal for Literature.

Suneela Mubayi is doing graduate work in Arabic literature at New York University. She has translated poems and stories by young and upcoming Arab writers which have been published in *Banipal* magazine and online.

John Peate is a doctoral candidate in translation studies at the University of Salford. He teaches translation studies and Arabic at the same university and is also a freelance translator. He has BAs in both English and Arabic from the University of Leeds, an MA in translation studies from the School of Oriental and African Studies in London, and has also studied Arabic extensively in Fez, Cairo and Damascus.

Anne Shaker is a freelance translator; this is her first literary translation. Previously she has translated Arabic news articles for publication in English.

Haroon Shirwani is Head of Arabic at Eton College. He studied Arabic, French and history at Oxford and London universities. Each year he produces *A Taste of Texts* – a selection from Arabic literature, with his translations – for use by students and teachers.

Nader K. Uthman is a scholar and translator of modern Arabic literature. He has taught in various areas of inquiry – including Arabic language and comparative literature – at the University at Albany, Emory University, Columbia University, the United Nations and the *New York Times*. As of 2010, he is Clinical Assistant Professor of Arabic at New York University. Uthman lives in New York.

Frank Wynne has won three major prizes for his translations: the 2002 IMPAC for *Atomised* by Michel Houellebecq, the 2005 *Independent* Foreign Fiction Prize for *Windows on the World* by Frédéric Beigbeder, and the 2008 Scott Moncrieff Prize for *Holiday in a Coma* by the same author. Most recently he has translated *An Unfinished Business* (*Le village de l'Allemand*) by Boualem Sansal.

Nariman Youssef is a PhD candidate at the Centre for the Advanced Study of the Arab World (CASAW), University of Manchester. She has an MA in cultural and critical studies and an MSc in translation studies.